G000122397

1,000,000 Books

are available to read at

---◆---

www.ForgottenBooks.com

---◆---

Read online
Download PDF
Purchase in print

ISBN 978-1-332-40451-3
PIBN 10422573

This book is a reproduction of an important historical work. Forgotten Books uses
state-of-the-art technology to digitally reconstruct the work, preserving the original format
whilst repairing imperfections present in the aged copy. In rare cases, an imperfection in
the original, such as a blemish or missing page, may be replicated in our edition. We do,
however, repair the vast majority of imperfections successfully; any imperfections that
remain are intentionally left to preserve the state of such historical works.

Forgotten Books is a registered trademark of FB &c Ltd.
Copyright © 2018 FB &c Ltd.
FB &c Ltd, Dalton House, 60 Windsor Avenue, London, SW19 2RR.
Company number 08720141. Registered in England and Wales.

For support please visit www.forgottenbooks.com

1 MONTH OF
FREE
READING

at

www.ForgottenBooks.com

By purchasing this book you are eligible for one month membership to ForgottenBooks.com, giving you unlimited access to our entire collection of over 1,000,000 titles via our web site and mobile apps.

To claim your free month visit:

www.forgottenbooks.com/free422573

* Offer is valid for 45 days from date of purchase. Terms and conditions apply.

English
Français
Deutsche
Italiano
Español
Português

www.forgottenbooks.com

Mythology Photography **Fiction**
Fishing Christianity **Art** Cooking
Essays Buddhism Freemasonry
Medicine **Biology** Music **Ancient
Egypt** Evolution Carpentry Physics
Dance Geology **Mathematics** Fitness
Shakespeare **Folklore** Yoga Marketing
Confidence Immortality Biographies
Poetry **Psychology** Witchcraft
Electronics Chemistry History **Law**
Accounting **Philosophy** Anthropology
Alchemy Drama Quantum Mechanics
Atheism Sexual Health **Ancient History**
Entrepreneurship Languages Sport
Paleontology Needlework Islam
Metaphysics Investment Archaeology
Parenting Statistics Criminology
Motivational

"OUR CONSTITUTION."

AN EPITOME

OF OUR CHIEF LAWS AND SYSTEM OF GOVERNMENT.

WITH

AN INTRODUCTORY ESSAY.

BY

ALEX. CHARLES EWALD, F.S.A.,

(OF HER MAJESTY'S RECORD OFFICE,)

AUTHOR OF "A REFERENCE BOOK OF ENGLISH HISTORY;" EDITOR OF "THE
CIVIL SERVICE GUIDE," ETC. ETC.

. . . "Esto
Liberque ac sapiens."
PERSIUS.

LONDON:

FREDERICK WARNE AND CO.,
BEDFORD STREET, COVENT GARDEN.
1867.

JN
114
E8

LONDON :
BRADBURY, EVANS, AND CO., PRINTERS, WHITEFRIARS.

LIBRARY
APR 26 1966
UNIVERSITY OF TORONTO

1070025

PREFACE.

THIS little volume is intended to occupy an intermediate position between technical works on English Law and the various kinds of Students' Manuals on the same subject. The author has endeavoured to avoid on the one hand those wearisome repetitions and legal peculiarities of expression which often render works on our laws confusing to the general public, and at the same time to avoid that superficial class of information which is too often the fault of an epitome or a vade mecum.

"Our Constitution," the author trusts may prove a useful book of reference, not only for county magistrates, members of Parliament, and those to whom English Law is familiar, but also to the general public, who, without wishing to dive into abstruse points of law and pages of irrelevant matter, may obtain in a brief and concise form that kind of legal information which bears upon the transactions of every-day life. In this work the author has however entirely confined himself to *English* laws and customs.

The author here begs to express his grateful thanks

to Messrs. LONGMANS & Co., for their kind permission to use and condense, where occasion required, various articles from "Tomlin's Popular Law Dictionary." As Mr. Tomlin's work has not been revised for some years, it has been necessary, in some cases, to extend his information to the present time.

The other works which the author has been indebted to in the compilation of this volume will be found in the List of Authorities. Those works in the list which appear printed in italics have been freely used.

THE TEMPLE,
June, 1867.

LIST OF AUTHORITIES.

Ancient Laws and Institutes of England and Wales.
Blackstone's Commentaries.
Blount's Law Glossary.
Bond's Handy Book for Verifying Dates.
Burn's Ecclesiastical Law.
Calendars of State Papers.
Campbell's Lives of the Chancellors.
Chambers' Dictionary.
Chitty's General Practice.
Chitty's Archbold's Common Law Practice.
Chronicles of England.
Clarendon's History of the Rebellion.
Coke upon Littleton.
De Lolme on the Constitution.
Dod's Parliamentary Companion.
Du Cange Glossarium.
Encyclopædia Britannica.
    ,,   Metropolitana.
Fortescue de Laudibus legum Angliæ.
Foss's Judges of England.
Froude's History of England.
Guizot's History of Charles I.
    ,,   ,, of Civilisation.
Hallam's Constitutional History.
    ,,   Middle Ages.
Haydn's Dictionary of Dates.
Hook's Lives of the Archbishops of Canterbury.
Hume's History of England.
Jacob's Law Dictionary.
Kerr's Commentaries.
Knight's English Cyclopædia.
    ,,   History of England.

Locke on Government.
Le Neve's Fasti Ecclesiæ Anglicanæ by Hardy.
Lingard's History of England.
Lush's Common Law Practice.
Macintosh's History of England.
Maddox's Exchequer.
Mahon's (Lord) History of England.
May's Imperial Parliament.
    ,,   Parliamentary Practice.
McCulloch's Commercial Dictionary.
Mosheim's Ecclesiastical History.
Nicolas's Chronology of History.
Rees's Encyclopædia.
Reeves' History of the English Law.
Reports of the Deputy Keeper of Public Records.
Russell's (Earl) English Government and Constitution.
Smith's Handbook of Chancery Practice.
Smith's Mercantile Law.
Smith's (Dr.) Student's Hume.
Spelman's Glossary.
Story on Contracts.
Story's Equity Jurisprudence.
Statutes of the Realm.
Stephens' Commentaries.
Thomas's Handbook to the Public Records.
Tomlin's Law Dictionary.
Townsend's Manual of Dates.
Turner's Anglo Saxons.
Wharton's Law Lexicon.
Wood's Institutes.
Woodfall's Landlord and Tenant.

AN ESSAY

ON THE

RISE AND PROGRESS OF THE ENGLISH CONSTITUTION.

By the term Constitution, as applied to our national system of polity, we understand, first, the three estates of the realm, namely, the King, the Lords, and the Commons ; and secondly, the fundamental laws, ordinances, and customs by which these estates are severally and collectively bound and governed, and by which their peculiar and distinctive rights, privileges, functions, and prerogatives are duly set forth and determined. No single document, however, exists in which the principles of the Constitution are fully embodied and defined—a circumstance which has sometimes given rise to the popular but erroneous impression that we have no "constitution" in the proper sense of the term ; or that, if we have, its principles are so vague, and its provisions so incongruous and disjointed, that they virtually elude our grasp in endeavouring to apprehend them.

The Constitution, as it is presented to us in the pages of history, is made up of detached fragments, having no very obvious properties of cohesion or unity ; and as it is a structure which has been raised by successive generations, extending over a period of several centuries, it may lack in a measure that

B

unity of design which, under different circumstances, it might have possessed. We can scarcely say with certainty when our Constitution may be said to have commenced, but it probably had its origin in the common law or common custom of the realm, based upon immemorial usage. Its first faint outlines may be traced in some measure to the time of our Anglo-Saxon ancestors, amongst whose ancient laws and institutions we find the prototype of what subsequently became moulded into shape as the "English Constitution" properly so called. The progress of the Constitution, from its cradle downwards, has undoubtedly been fitful rather than regular in its pace. There have been periods of retrogression in its history, when the principles on which it is based were virtually ignored; but then at certain epochs, after long intervals of inactivity, it would seem to have gathered up its strength and to have made secure and rapid strides onward towards the goal of its destiny. Throughout all the vicissitudes, however, to which it has been exposed, the fundamental principles of the English Constitution have never been entirely subverted. On the contrary, one of its most distinctive features has been its elasticity and its power of adapting itself to the progressive requirements of civilisation without prejudice to its component parts, whether separately or collectively considered. It has undergone various modifications from its commencement to the present time, and is perhaps rather practically efficient than logically perfect in its essential characteristics; for it is the work of statesmen rather than of speculative theorists. In short, the English Constitution is the result of the cumulative labours of all the eminent statesmen, jurists, and legislators whom our country has produced for the last six hundred years. Having made these prefatory remarks, let us briefly advert to the Anglo-Saxon form of government which had been in existence, in a more or less modified form, for several centuries before the Conquest.

In theory the Anglo-Saxon form of government was that of a limited elective monarchy; but, in practice, hereditary monarchy was the rule rather than the exception. The King and his Council conjointly were invested with the sole legislative and judicial power. Over this Council, which was called the Wittenagemote, the King himself presided in person. It was composed in early times of " Freemen" and " Warriors," and at a later period of Bishops, Abbots, Earls, Thanes, or landed proprietors, and of the principal men of note in the kingdom; and seems, we are told, to have resembled what our modern Parliament would be if Lords and Commons assembled together and debated in one House. Moreover, it is said that with regard to laymen the holding five thousand acres of land under the Crown was a necessary qualification for a seat in this assembly : Bishops and Abbots, however, were members of it by virtue of their office and as chiefs of the clerical order. The King, of himself, had no power to make laws, nor were any of his acts deemed valid or legal without the assent and confirmation of his Council. Subordinate to the Chief Court or Council were numerous County Courts, in which sat the lesser Thanes or smaller proprietors of land, whose office it was to administer justice in their respective districts, and to transact all affairs of a merely local character. From these minor courts the Council received appeals and gave final judgment, while it also confirmed grants made by the Crown, and adjudicated upon all matters of public or national importance. It is now somewhat difficult to determine with precision how far the King's prerogatives extended, or by what bounds they were limited ; but from the fact that he could make no laws without the concurrence of his Council, we must infer that his authority was far from being absolute, and that, although there existed in those times no such thing as popular representation in the modern sense of the term, yet there was such a check imposed upon the arbitrary will of the Sovereign, as in some measure afforded a guarantee for the rights and liberties of the subject, and for the due administration of justice.

History informs us that the Norman Conquest produced a complete change and revolution in the affairs of this kingdom. We are told that the ancient fabric of Saxon legislation was almost wholly overthrown by the Conqueror. His government at the outset was mild, but he soon found pretexts for seizing the conquered territory by degrees into his own hands, and distributed the greater portion of it amongst his Norman followers, as the reward of their past services, and as a means of permanently securing their future support for himself and his successors. He also arrogated to himself legislative as well as judicial power, and trampled under foot those laws and customs which he found in existence, and which at the outset policy had taught him to respect. The vanquished Anglo-Saxons of every rank became the mere passive objects of the Conqueror's caprice: subject to the influence of a military despotism, they had no rights but such as their absolute ruler chose to accord them. Taxes, too, were arbitrarily imposed, and were levied by corrupt judges, who not uncommonly made traffic of the justice which they should have dealt impartially to all; so that between judicial cupidity and arbitrary power the rights and liberties of the people were systematically crushed, if they did not become utterly extinguished. Accordingly we cannot wonder that the people, prostrate and paralysed under the influence of the Conqueror's *régime*, lost all power of active or effectual resistance. Their attempts to throw off the victor's yoke had been attended with such signal defeat and with retribution so severe and unrelenting, that their spirits at length were broken, and their energies exhausted. The old Saxon English found themselves strangers in their own land, their homes plundered, their lands confiscated and given over as booty to their new master and his adherents; themselves stripped of their honours, offices, and dignities; their customs proscribed, their laws abolished, and the high places which they once held in the State now filled by their victorious enemies. The Normans became lords of the soil, while the Saxons were almost reduced to the condition of serfs. We are told that such of the English as held offices of trust or honour were deprived of them without form or ceremony; that Bishops and Abbots of English birth were successively deposed; and that for a hundred years after the Conquest none of the English of Saxon race were raised to any dignity in the Church or State. The English nobles, too, were forced to seek refuge in foreign lands, until the name of an Englishman at length became a byword, and the English language a mark of inferiority for those who used it as their mother tongue.

But the tide of affairs was eventually destined to turn. It was not the native English alone who suffered oppression at the hands of the Conqueror and his successors; the haughty Barons themselves, who had won for William of Normandy his crown, were in their turn made to feel the weight of that power which they had created, and which their former leader now wielded with absolute sway. The King established a court called the "Aula Regis," which was held in his own palace, and over which he presided in person. This court followed the King from place to place; it heard and gave final judgment upon all appeals from the courts of the Barons, and the Barons themselves were liable to be cited before this tribunal, as well to answer any charge which the King might bring against them as to compose any feuds that might arise amongst themselves.

It was but a natural result of the constitution of this court —which for the most part was composed of the creatures and favourites of the King—that the Barons were held in a certain degree of awe and submission. Their haughty minds, however, could ill brook the restraints thus imposed upon them, and accordingly a spirit of opposition and of active resistance to the iron

rule of the Conqueror was the eventual result.   The Great
Barons who were the immediate tenants of the Crown possessed
then, as well as in subsequent times, considerable power in the
State.   Their number exceeded six hundred.   Within their
several spheres they exercised the authority of petty sovereigns; the King they regarded more as a chief than as
master; and as many, if not all of them, held seats in the
Great Council, they possessed considerable influence in the
direction of public affairs.   In many respects, indeed, they
were as independent as the King himself : like him they owed
their fortunes to their own swords, and, although they were
bound in time of war to render military service for their lands,
yet this service offered a field for personal distinction in the
career of arms most grateful to the warlike spirit of the age.
The isolated position of the Barons, however, their personal
feuds and rivalries, and the want of frequent intercourse
amongst themselves, enabled the King to oppress them individually, from time to time, with impunity.   Such were the
relationships in which the King and the Barons stood towards
each other about the end of the Conqueror's reign, and, indeed,
during the century that followed.

Previously to the establishment of the House of Commons,
the Great Council of the kingdom—which was sometimes
called "Curia de More," "Curia Regis," "Commune Concilium," or "Commune Concilium Regni"—was composed of
Lords Spiritual and Temporal, namely, of Barons, who were
summoned by virtue of their tenure, as holding *in capite* of
the King, and of Bishops and Heads of Religious Houses,
whose tenure was in chief of the Crown; but it is probable
that ecclesiastical dignitaries were called to this Council as well
on account of their clerical character as by reason of their
tenure.

Considerable difference of opinion has at all times existed
among jurists and antiquaries as to the peculiar nature and

extent of the privileges conferred by particular modes of tenure, and as to the right by which Barons were summoned to the Great Council of the nation. We are probably justified, however, in assuming that before the time of Edward I. the *chief* Barons were convoked by writs issued immediately by the Crown, and that the *lesser* Barons were called by general notice from the sheriffs. When assembled, they all sat in one common hall or chamber, but it is by no means easy to determine what their respective functions were, or whether they debated and voted together on terms of perfect equality. Some high authorities maintain that this assembly formed as real and complete a Parliament as has ever been held in England, while others consider it to have been merely a Privy Council, entirely dependent on the King, by whom it was called together two or three times a year to deliberate upon the affairs of the kingdom.

The King, conjointly with this assembly, or rather perhaps with the advice and assistance of this body as his counsellors, exercised the legislative function; but to what extent he had the right of independent action, or how far his prerogatives were carried, are points which do not appear to have been accurately determined. Neither do we know with certainty whether the Great Council had or had not the right of initiating measures or of framing laws, subject, as in modern times, to the sanction and approval of the King. Indeed Guizot tells us that "it is in vain to seek the limits of these assemblies, for at that time" (by which he means the period antecedent to Edward I.) "no power was fixed or determined." It seems to be certain, however, that the Great Council deliberated upon all questions whatever of a public nature: upon ecclesiastical matters; upon questions of peace and war; upon extraordinary taxes; upon the succession to the Crown; upon the administration of justice and the domestic affairs of the King; in a word, upon the interests of the kingdom at large, both in its internal and external relationships. But it is equally certain that the King arbitrarily imposed taxes and aids, levied import and export duties on merchandise, and inflicted penalties and exacted fines, without in any way consulting his Great Council. It is evident too, from the Patent Rolls, that in various transactions of this kind the King was in the constant habit of making corrupt bargains with his subjects, and of converting his "favours," and even "justice" itself, into marketable commodities. Virtually therefore the King, in early times, exercised a species of absolute and irresponsible power; although we can scarcely suppose that when he assembled his Council for the consideration of public affairs he acted in direct opposition to its resolutions. Sometimes, indeed, the Great Council seemed to exercise the chief power not only in the legislature, but even in the general administration; yet, on the other hand, we find the royal prerogatives exercised in a manner as absolute and arbitrary as if no assembly existed, and as if these prerogatives knew neither limit nor control.

Accordingly the Barons, after having been exposed for more than a century to the vexatious oppressions of the Conqueror and his successors, at length resolved to unite in their own defence and take active measures for resisting the arbitrary encroachments of the King, and for obtaining from him certain specific acknowledgments which should define their own rights and privileges and those of the people at large, and which should at the same time set a limit to the royal prerogatives. Hence it is to the Barons—with whom are included the Bishops and Abbots—that we are indebted for the establishment of those great fundamental principles on which the superstructure of our constitutional rights and privileges was afterwards raised.

The struggles between the King and his Barons had been revived from time to time with increasing fierceness, until they were at length destined to come to a crisis in the reign of King John. This reign forms the most important and memorable era in our constitutional history, for it gave birth to the Great Charter of our national liberties. The Great Charter was not, however, the first that had been granted : five previous charters had been given since the Conquest ; one by the Conqueror, one by Henry I., two by Stephen, and one by Henry II. But these were vague, general, and limited in their provisions, and chiefly affected the interests and privileges of the Barons or of the Church : few, if any, concessions were made to the great mass of the people, and even these were faithless and delusive. Of the five charters in question the most important was that granted by Henry I., and it was upon this charter, which had grown virtually obsolete (so little were its provisions observed), that the Barons at length took their stand for redress.

The proceedings more immediately connected with the granting of the Great Charter are recounted at length by Blackstone in his " Introduction to Magna Carta ;" but his narrative is too long to be given here in detail. Guizot, however, in his essay on the " Origin of the Representative System in England," has given so clear and concise an epitome of Blackstone's " Introduction," that it will probably be as well to give the entire passage from the original :—

" In August, 1213, the Barons and the superior clergy are assembled in London, whither the King has summoned them in order to obtain subsidies. The Archbishop of Canterbury, Stephen Langton, induces the Barons to hold a secret meeting, and, on the 25th August, produces in the midst of this assembly the Charter of Henry I., which he has just discovered. The reading of it is heard with acclamations. The Barons make an appointment with a view to take measures for constraining the King to renew this guarantee of their rights. They meet again on the 20th Nov. 1214, at St. Edmondsbury, and, with Stephen Langton still as their president, they come one after another to the altar to take a solemn oath to cause the Charter of Henry I. to be put in force.

"On the 6th of January, 1215, the confederates, armed, present themselves in London, and demand (*requièrent*) of the King the renewal of this charter as well as of the laws of Edward the Confessor. John knew nothing of this coalition, and was quite unprepared. He asks for time, and is allowed till Easter. Meanwhile he endeavours to profit by this delay. He grants to the clergy a special charter, and despatches William Mauclerc to Rome to seek assistance from the Pope against the Barons. Without waiting for the Pope's reply, he takes up the cross on the 2nd of February, and makes a vow to set out for the Holy Land, hoping thereby to cover his despotism under the privilege of the Crusaders.

"Neither the Barons nor the clergy, however, allow themselves to be intimidated. They also send to Rome one of the most zealous of their number, Eustace de Vesey, in order to maintain the lawfulness of their enterprise ; and without waiting his return (as soon as the delay agreed upon is expired), they meet at Stamford, in the county of Lincoln, on the 19th of April, 1215, followed by upwards of two thousand knights. The King sends to know their pretensions. They ask for the Charter of Henry I., and forward to the King articles, which in explaining this charter extend its provisions. 'Why,' exclaimed the King in a rage, 'do not the Barons also ask me for my kingdom ? I will never grant them liberties which would reduce me to slavery.' All negotiation is immediately at an end. On the 5th May following the Barons, having assembled at Wallingford with their troops, solemnly renounce their oaths of allegiance ; Robert Fitz-Walter is named Marshal of the Army of God and of the holy Church ; and war is declared."

"Letters arrive from the Pope to the King, the Barons, and the clergy—but they are of no avail. On the 24th May the Barons take possession of London, with the consent of the citizens. John retires to Odiham. Alone and fugitive, he again attempts to negotiate ; he offers the mediation of the Pope, which is rejected, for it is necessary that despotism should confess itself vanquished: the public proclamation of his defeat is indispensable to the victory of liberty.

" At length a conference is opened on the plains of Runnymede, between Windsor and Staines. The King signs the preliminary articles proposed by the Barons, and on the 15th June, 1215, the Great Charter itself is granted."

" The Great Charter," says Hallam, " is the keystone of English liberty." It is, in fact, the bulwark and fountain-head of all the rights and privileges which we inherit from our ancestors : it is in a manner the groundwork and basis of our civilisation ; for civilisation properly commences only when personal rights and the rights of property are duly recognised, guaranteed, and upheld. Without these there would be no progress, and society would relapse into the primitive condition of savage life, where every rude warrior must fight single-handed with his fellow-man for the means of existence, and where the law of might is right is daily exemplified in its full force.

The benefits conferred by Magna Charta were derived rather, perhaps, from the confirmation of franchises embodied in previous charters—but which had never been acted upon—than from any new rights or liberties which it granted. People were no longer in terror for their personal safety or their possessions. A new soul was infused into the English people, and once more was revived that spirit of sturdy independence which had formerly characterised the Anglo-Saxon race, but which for the space of a century and a half had been bowed down by oppression and crushed beneath the yoke of a harsh and exterminating despotism.

Without reciting the provisions of the Charter at length, we will enumerate some special points and indicate generally its

bearing and principal features. After confirming the immunities and franchises pertaining to the clergy, it elucidates defi-
nitively the obscurities and ambiguities which existed in the
feudal laws, while it determines the import of those laws with
precision ; it fixes the amount, hitherto arbitrary, of the fine or
relief due to the Crown of an heir when he came into possession
of his estates ; it takes precautions for securing their just revenues to the widows and children of the King's vassals, and for
the marriage of his feudal wards ; while it provides ample remedies for those abuses which creep into the feudal relationships,
to the prejudice of the vassal. The twelfth article of the Charter
ordains that no scutage or aid shall be imposed on the kingdom
but by the Common Council of the kingdom, unless to redeem
the King, to make his eldest son a knight, or to marry his
eldest daughter ; and that in the latter cases only a reasonable
aid shall be imposed. The fourteenth article runs in the following terms :—"For the holding the Common Council of the
kingdom for the purpose of levying any aid other than in the
three cases specified, or for levying a scutage, we will cause to
be convoked the archbishops, bishops, and abbots, the earls and
great barons, individually and by letter from ourself ; and we
will cause to be convoked in a body by our sheriffs all those who
hold of us directly. The said convocation shall be holden on a
certain fixed day—namely, at the interval of forty days at least,
and at a certain place to be determined ; and in the letters of
summons we will explain the cause of the convocation ; and the
convocation being thus called, the matter shall be treated of on
the day appointed, with the advice of those who shall be present, even if all those who shall have been convoked should not
be present."

Again, all the liberties enjoyed by the King's vassals are
declared common to the vassals of the lords. By the seventeenth
article it is determined that in future the Court of Common
Pleas shall not follow the King in his movements from place to

place, but shall be held in a fixed locality—namely, at Westminster. In Article XVIII. the King promises that he himself, or in the event of his being absent from the kingdom, his grand justiciar, will send two judges into each county four times every year, who, with four knights chosen by such county, shall hold assize on the day and in the place where the County Court shall meet.

It is further ordained that no freeman shall be arrested or imprisoned or dispossessed or outlawed or exiled or attainted in any manner, save by virtue of a lawful judgment of his peers and in accordance with the laws of the realm; that right and justice shall not be sold or delayed or denied to any man; that all merchants and traders shall have full and free liberty of coming into or of leaving the kingdom, of residing in any particular locality, and of travelling by land or water, to buy and to sell without any oppressive tax, according to the ancient laws of custom. Furthermore, the King promises to appoint none but judges of ability and integrity,—to forbid them to condemn any man without having heard the witnesses; to reinstate every man disseized without legal judgment; to make amends for the wrongs committed under Henry II. and Richard, and to restrain the vexations of every kind exercised towards the merchants, traders, citizens, and rural inhabitants. He guarantees to the city of London, as well as to all other cities, boroughs, towns, and seaports the enjoyment of their ancient customs and liberties; and he engages to send away forthwith all foreign troops and mercenaries, with their arms and horses, who are now in the kingdom to the great detriment of all his subjects.

It would seem, however, that King John had secretly no intention of observing the Charter any longer than he could help, for he soon communicated with the Pope, requesting his aid and intervention with a view to annul the Charter once more. The Pope accordingly replied on the 7th of September,

1215, in these terms :—" We reprove and absolutely condemn such a treaty ; we forbid the King to pay any regard to it, and we forbid the Barons as well as their accomplices, under pain of anathema, to require its observance. We declare the said Charter to be radically null and void, as well as all its obligations and consequences." But Archbishop Langton refused to promulgate the decree of Rome, whereupon fresh disturbances again ensued. The King, with the aid of foreign mercenaries, took up arms agains the Barons, while the Barons on their side called in the assistance of French troops, and invited a French Prince to accept the English crown ; but the timely death of the King brought matters to a final issue and terminated the civil wars.

During the following reign of Henry III. the Great Charter was renewed five times ;—on some occasions the ceremony took place at the close of a great national council—sometimes after violent civil wars. In 1227, Henry having attained his majority, was induced probably by some of his ministers, who for the most part were foreigners, and who paid but little regard to English laws, to revoke not only the Great Charter, but also the Charter of the Forests which he himself had granted, on the ground that he had yielded them at a time when he had no free command of his person or of his seal. But the Barons peremptorily demanded a reconfirmation ; and whenever these charters were violated the Barons sought to obtain further concessions from the King in addition to those already existing in the charters which had been infringed. In 1253, sentence of excommunication was solemnly denounced against whomsoever should violate the royal charters : at the end of the ceremony the prelates threw down their smoking torches and uttered a terrible anathema against all who should incur the sentence ; and the King promised " so help him God, he would not violate any of these things, as he was a true man, a Christian, a Knight, and a crowned and anointed King !" Not content with this promise, however, the Barons subsequently constrained the King to ordain that twice in each year, at the festivals of Easter and Michaelmas, the two charters should be read in the County Court House in the presence of all the people ; that the Sheriffs, Judges, and Seneschals of the King, and of his Lords, should swear to observe the same, and that the citizens should be dispensed from obeying any magistrate who had not satisfied this obligation.

Our next inquiries will be directed to the origin of the Representative System—which may perhaps be termed the Complement of the Great Charter, and without which the provisions of the latter could never have been carried out in practice. We have already seen by what strenuous and unwearied exertions the Barons succeeded in laying the foundations of the English Constitution. But the fabric still remains to be erected,—and centuries have to elapse before the structure will be complete. As yet the Third Estate of the realm—the corner-stone of the building—has not been laid. Power and authority are still exclusively in the hands of a privileged class; and the great body of the People have no voice in the councils of the nation, or in the direction of public affairs. They are governed it may be by just and equitable laws, but in making those laws they have had no share. The taxes and imposts to which they are subjected are levied without their consent. A grievance is felt and it is expedient to find a remedy—which is eventually discovered in the Commons Representatives, who in theory at least are the organs of the popular voice.

At what period then, and under what circumstances, was the Commons' House of Representatives first called into existence ? This question, strange to say, is involved in a little obscurity ; for although the Commons may represent in a measure the collective wisdom of the nation, yet, unlike the famous god-

dess, they did not spring at a single bound full-formed and
many-gifted from the brain of their great parent—the English
people. On the contrary, their birth and origin were very
obscure. Indeed the Deputies who were first returned to Parliament were scarcely "representatives" in any sense of the
term, for they possessed no legislative powers or authority whatever at the outset. Those Deputies who were called together
from time to time by Henry III., were limited in their functions to "inquiring into grievances and delivering their inquisition into Parliament," in which character they seem to have
acted the part of Commissioners, rather than of popular representatives. We cannot, therefore, regard such functionaries as
members of the legislative body, for they lacked the dignity and
essential attributes of Deputies properly so called. This subject has indeed given rise to various learned disquisitions—into
the merits of which we cannot here enter. Nor will it be necessary for our purpose to make any special note of the famous
"Provisions of Oxford," or of the irregular proceedings connected with the insurrection of Simon de Montfort. Passing
on, however, to the reign of Edward I., we shall probably be
right in fixing the origin of the Representative System in the
22nd year of that King.

The main object for which Deputies were first summoned was
to grant supplies. The King required a subsidy, and he accordingly issued Writs to the several towns, counties, and boroughs
throughout the kingdom, directing his sheriffs to return from
each two Deputies, "cum plenâ potestate pro se et totâ communitate predicta ad consulendum et consentiendum pro se et
communitate illa his quæ *comites, barones et proceres* prædicti
concorditer ordinaverint in præmissis." In the 28th of Edward I., the Knights or Deputies are directed to be sent " cum
plenâ potestate *audiendi et faciendi* quæ ibidem ordinari con-
tigerint pro communi commodo," which shows how rapidly their
powers increased. So far as we can learn these Deputies were

elected in all cases by the freeholders exclusively, and they were summoned to Parliament once or twice in each year for the purposes above named : sometimes by the King's direction the same members were again returned, and sometimes new members were chosen. At first, we are told, they occupied the lower end of the chamber in which the Barons and other magnates sat, but they did not mingle or vote in common with the Peers. They assisted as spectators, without any voice in the deliberations, but with the right of assenting to, though it would seem not of dissenting from, what had been done by the Lords of Parliament. Perhaps indeed the chief, if not the sole function of the early Deputies, was to consent to the taxes that had been imposed upon their constituents. And therefore we cannot wonder that the worthy burgesses and freeholders of those days did not at first fully appreciate the advantages of the representative system. So far from hailing it as a boon or privilege, we find that some boroughs considered it a burden, and that the electors neglected and even refused to send Deputies to Parliament, on the ground of their own poverty and consequent inability to defray the expenses of their representatives. And here it may be proper to observe that in early times, and even down to a comparatively modern period, the members of the Lower House received pay for their services—on a scale more or less liberal according to circumstances : in more recent times the honour and dignity attached to this office have been considered an adequate recompense for the duties which pertain to it.

In the reign of Edward I. was passed the famous statute, ever memorable in our constitutional annals, which enacted that, " No tax should be levied without the joint consent of the Lords and Commons "—a statute of so much importance that to it is chiefly owing the great influence which the House of Commons acquired in subsequent times.

Ever since the reign of Edward II., the Lords and

c

Commons have occupied separate chambers; the precise date, however, of their separation has not been determined by historical writers. But from that period downwards the power and influence of the Lower House of Parliament have continued to increase, until it may fairly be said now to have become predominant in all State affairs. This must be undoubtedly attributed to financial considerations in the first place, and secondly to the growth of a wealthy and enlightened middle class, who by their intelligence, commercial enterprise and industry have been the chief means of raising this country—so far, at least, as its vast material and pecuniary resources are concerned—to that degree of preëminence which it now holds amongst the kingdoms and empires of the whole civilised world. To the Commons belonged, moreover, the exclusive right of initiating all money bills, of granting subsidies, both ordinary and extraordinary, and of imposing taxes. Hence it was, as we have said, that they acquired so much influence almost from the outset, and that they soon grew weary of the barren privilege of taxing themselves and their constituents. No doubt they felt a noble ambition stirring within them, and urging them on to higher deeds than any they had yet achieved in a senatorial point of view. Mute and inglorious had been their functions during the reign of the First Edward,—for we are told that they "had not even the right of remonstrating" against any law; but so much did a sense of their own dignity and importance, and of their fitness for better things, grow upon them in the space of a few years, that under Edward II. they granted the King the twenty-fifth penny of their goods, "upon condition that the King should take advice and grant redress upon certain matters wherein they were aggrieved." Amongst other grievances, they complained of not being governed according to the Articles of the Great Charter, and then proceeded to give a catalogue of their troubles, which the King promised to remedy.

During the reign of Edward III. three essential principles of the Constitution were established on a firm footing,
namely, "*the illegality of raising money without the consent
of Parliament, the necessity for the concurrence of the Lords
and Commons in any alteration of the law, and the right of
the Commons to inquire into public abuses and to impeach the
ministers of the Crown.*" These measures are indeed the great
safeguard of the Constitution, and their importance cannot be
overrated. Such rapid strides seem almost incredible; but it
was during this and the two subsequent reigns that the great
and distinguishing features of our Constitution, as it approached
its more complete and mature form, were chiefly consolidated.

Subsequently to the Parliament of 14 Edward III., a certain
number of Prelates, Barons, and Counsellors, together with twelve
Knights and six Burgesses, were appointed to sit from day to day,
in order to convert petitions granted into statutes; and the laws
were declared to be made by the King, at the request of the
Commons, and by the assent of the Lords and Prelates. In
the fifteenth year of the same reign petitions were presented,
praying that commissioners be assigned to examine the
accounts of those who had received public moneys; that the
Judges and Ministers be sworn to obey the Great Charter and
other laws, and that they be appointed *in Parliament*. The
King, though unwillingly, complied with this request, but the
latter clause was soon after repealed—the Chancellor, Treasurer,
and Judges having entered a protest against it.

Owing to the minority of Richard II., on his accession
to the throne the Commons acquired additional powers and
privileges; for the King was compelled to consent that during
his minority the Chancellor, Treasurer, Judges, and other chief
officers of State should be appointed in Parliament. Upon
attaining his majority the Commons petitioned the King, "to
ordain in Parliament certain chief officers of his household and

other lords of his council, with power to reform those abuses by
which the crown was so much blemished, the laws violated, and
the revenues dilapidated." This petition was granted, and a
Commission, consisting of fourteen persons of "the highest
eminence for rank and general estimation, was established, and
heavy penalties imposed upon any one who publicly or privately
should oppose what they might advise." This Commission,
which in modern times would have a most unconstitutional
character, but which had been rendered necessary from the
various abuses that appear to have prevailed in the executive at
that time, lasted but a twelvemonth : and if we refer to it here,
it is only to show the expedients to which the Commons were
forced to have recourse in order to purge the abuses that had
crept into the administration of public affairs.   Although
towards the latter part of this reign the Parliament would
seem to have been too forgetful of its duties, and of its dignity,
and too submissively compliant with the wishes of the King,
who, it is said, had become as truly absolute as his ambition
could desire, yet we find that it was during this reign—that of
Richard II.—that the Commons acquired the important right
of *appropriating the public revenues to special purposes, and of
inquiring into the mode of their expenditure.*

During the reign of Henry IV. constitutional principles acquired new developments, and measures were taken for restraining the royal prerogatives, which had been unduly exercised in
the previous reign.   A request, however, made by the Commons,
that an answer should be given to their petitions before making
their grant of subsidy, was refused on the ground that it was a
practice unknown to the King's ancestors, and contrary to the
good customs and usages of ancient times.   Notwithstanding
this refusal, the Commons renewed their complaints in the
eighth year of the same reign, and presented thirty-one Articles,
none of which the King ventured to refuse, although encroaching upon his prerogatives.   Amongst other important

matters, the King was to name sixteen Counsellors by whose advice he was *solely* to be guided, and none of whom should be dismissed unless guilty of misdemeanour. He was likewise to assign two days in each week to receive petitions—it being both "honourable and necessary that his lieges who desire to petition him should be heard." The Council and Officers of State were sworn to observe the common and statute law, and were not, without the consent of the Judges, to determine any cause cognisable at Common Law. These, with some other provisions, furnished additional guarantees for the liberty of the subject, and formed new links in the chain of constitutional development —links which received increase of strength from the way in which the doctrine of ministerial responsibility was at the same time laid down. It was in the reign of Henry IV., too, that the Commons obtained the privilege of freedom from arrest during the Session ; as it was likewise in the same reign (9 Hen. IV.) that the famous maxims were established, " *That the Commons possess an exclusive right of originating all Money Bills,*" and that " *the King ought not to take cognisance of any matter pending in Parliament.*"

The brief but memorable reign of Henry V., which shed an unfading lustre on English history, and to which we must ever look back with pride as the most brilliant period in our annals, was not productive of any peculiar results in a constitutional point of view. The national mind was too much engrossed by military affairs, and by the contemplation of those glorious exploits which our arms had achieved on the Continent. It may, however, be mentioned, that owing to the great expenses incurred by Henry V. in the French wars, and the more readily to obtain supplies, he submitted his accounts to Parliament— " A circumstance which contributed in no slight degree to establish a regular correspondence between redress and supply, which for several centuries proved the balance-spring of the Constitution."

We have now arrived at the period of the civil wars between the rival houses of York and Lancaster, when for more than half a century the kingdom became a prey to intestine strife, and when the best and bravest of England's sons, pitted against each other in a bitter contest, were swept as by a plague from off the face of the land. Here we cannot fail to perceive that the Parliaments betrayed a want of firmness and dignity ill-suited to the circumstances in which they were placed,— now veering and shifting according as either party became dominant—siding with the strong and abandoning the weak, while they did and undid by turns, and became " all things to all men." Owing to this vacillation, the Commons continued henceforward to lose much of their moral weight and influence in the direction of public affairs ; they acquired a lower tone and character, and became altogether more subservient to the Crown, which found in them the ready and pliant instruments of its will—more especially during the period of the Tudor dynasty. Hence, by degrees, the Constitution suffered from the inroads of arbitrary power—of which the establishment of the Court of Star Chamber, in the reign of Henry VII., furnishes a striking example. This Court was certainly of the most unconstitutional character, as it was in no wise subject to the rules of procedure of the ordinary courts of law —civil or criminal. It was a species of Privy Council—resembling, perhaps, in some measure the " Aula Regis " of the Norman period—which, while virtually ignoring the Statute and Common Law of the realm, arrogated to itself the functions and authority of a regularly constituted Court, and decided, if not upon the lives, at least upon the liberty and property of individuals, and this without the aid or intercession of a jury. In fact the officers of this Court themselves performed the functions of judge, jury, and prosecutor without appeal to any higher authority. Thus it became a scourge in the hands of the Sovereign to chastise and overawe his rebellious or disaffected subjects as occasion might require,—as it also became a source of immense profit and revenue to the Crown, owing to the enormous and ruinous fines which it imposed upon those who had the misfortune to fall into its hands. These fines, too, were imposed for what would now be considered venial offences and misdemeanours. And here it may be observed that it was not merely causes of great importance involving the dignity of the Crown, or the interests of the State, which were tried in the Court of Star Chamber, but even petty offences, cognisable at Common Law, were frequently prosecuted before this tribunal. The immense mass of records extant pertaining to this Court, from the time of its first foundation to its abolition in 1641, furnish the best evidence of the vast extent of its jurisdiction, and of the despotic nature of its authority. The iniquities, however, which were perpetrated by this Court can never be ascertained to the full extent in the absence of its decrees, which have either been lost or destroyed, and which would have thrown a flood of light upon the arbitrary and unconstitutional practices both of the Tudor and Stuart dynasties. This much at least is certain, that for a century and a half the essential and fundamental principles of constitutional liberty were violated systematically, and with impunity, and in this violation the craven and servile Parliaments of those days shamefully acquiesced.

We now approach that great movement of revolution which took place in England in the sixteenth century, and which is emphatically called the Reformation—the causes or effects of which it will not be necessary to enter into any more than may be needful for ascertaining its immediate consequences in a constitutional point of view. And here it may not be improper to allude to a popular error which has been taught by many modern writers—more especially by the exponents of certain theological schools—namely, that the Reformation was the com-

mencement of an era of " liberty " such as had not been known
at any previous period. This is certainly untrue in every sense ;
and those who maintain such views generally ignore altogether
the history of this country antecedent to the Reformation, and
speak as if "liberty" and " Christianity," twin-born, had
sprung up simultaneously in the middle of the sixteenth century, and had never before been known or heard of. Those,
however, who have studied the history of the sixteenth century
calmly and dispassionately, must be aware that so far from the
Reformation having given any additional liberty to the subject,
as one of its immediate effects, it rather deprived him of much
of that freedom, in a constitutional point of view, which he
formerly possessed ; for it placed an enormous increase of power
in the hands of the Crown by making the King supreme
Head of the Church as well as of the State—irresponsible
power, too, be it remembered ; for the King professed to receive
his authority from Heaven alone—thus uniting in his own person
all the functions and prerogatives of a temporal sovereign
together with the *quasi* infallible attributes—in nowise limited
by external circumstances—of a sovereign Pontiff. Henry VIII.,
therefore, and his immediate successors, held all but unlimited
and absolute sway over the destinies of their subjects, and
exacted from them a degree of abject submission which had not
been paid to any monarch since the days of William the Conqueror. All the old nobility who, in times of peril, would
have presented a barrier against the encroachments of arbitrary
power, had been swept away during the civil wars. The entire
constitution of the Upper House of Parliament had been
changed, owing to the elimination of the great majority of the
dignified ecclesiastics and heads of religious houses, who had had
seats therein before the dissolution and the rupture with Rome.
Those who elected to remain behind, and who took the oaths of
supremacy, were for the most part servile instruments in the
hands of the King—who secured their services and their ready

acquiescence by means of the Church and Abbey lands which he had distributed largely amongst his supporters in both Houses of Parliament. Men thus bribed could have no independence, and were powerless to defend the Constitution and the liberties of the nation.

It will probably be alleged that if the Constitution suffered at the period of the Reformation from the arbitrary assumption of power by the Crown, yet that at least the people gained "religious liberty" and "freedom of conscience." Nothing of the sort. It was from no love of religious liberty that the King shook off the Papal authority and declared himself Pope, or Head, of the Church of England. The King's motives were wholly selfish and personal; and had Clement VII. not refused to grant a divorce between Henry and Katherine of Arragon, (through fear of offending the Court of Spain,) the English monarch would never have separated from the Roman See. True, indeed, the people were relieved in a measure from the thraldom and the superstition of the old Church, but they were not at liberty to embrace the doctrines of the Reformation properly so called, as taught in Germany, where the movement had originated. On the contrary, they were compelled by law to accept a new creed and new forms of worship, as laid down by the King and his Parliament. From this creed they dared not swerve, at the peril of their lives, liberties, and fortunes. Permission, indeed, was granted to read the Scriptures in the vulgar tongue; but this was certainly no very great boon at a period when reading was no ordinary accomplishment. Moreover, it was a mere mockery to give men the Bible without allowing them to interpret or expound it according to the dictates of their conscience. Such "liberty," therefore, only served as a snare and a stumbling-block. From all this we naturally infer that whatever advantages or benefits were eventually destined to accrue from the Reformation, yet that the revolution produced by that great movement in the polity of this kingdom was at the outset highly detrimental to the Constitution and to the liberty of the subject. So utterly base and demoralized were the Parliaments of Henry VIII. that they suffered the King's proclamations in many instances not only to have the force of law, but even to supersede the statute and common law of the land; and so reckless were they of their own dignity and of the interests of the Constitution that, had their Master desired to dispense with Parliaments altogether, they would have abdicated their own functions, and would have acquiesced in his wishes. We may therefore safely assert that in this reign the royal prerogatives were exercised with scarcely any limit or control. So much so, that a species of despotism took root in the soil, and was not eventually eradicated until the kingdom had passed through the sanguinary ordeal of Revolution and Civil War.

During the remainder of the sixteenth century, under Edward VI., Mary, and Elizabeth, the Constitution continued to suffer from the rude shock which it had experienced under Henry VIII. Nay, it was even doomed to renewed assaults from each of the Tudors in succession. They all of them ruled with a high hand. They still found "The Council" (as the Star Chamber was sometimes called) and the Parliaments ready to do their bidding, and execute their behests. Even with our modern latitudinarian views upon many theological questions, we can scarcely conceive how it was that statesmen and Parliaments were found in those days with principles so lax, and with consciences so elastic, as to concur in alternately establishing, overthrowing, and re-establishing a national religion, to suit the predilections or the caprice of the Sovereign for the time being. At all events, we can have but little respect for the motives by which such men were swayed in their tortuous and vacillating career. No wonder, then, if the Parliaments lost that prestige which they possessed under the Edwards and the Henrys of former days; no wonder that Queen Elizabeth should snub and browbeat her most loyal and submissive Commons by telling them that they were "ignorant beasts," who had neither right, power, nor capacity to meddle with State matters—political or ecclesiastical. Tamely dutiful in their generation, they only vied with each other in exalting the Royal dignity, and in magnifying the kingly office and prerogatives. Upon this subject, indeed, the most extravagant notions were entertained during the reigns of Elizabeth and James I. The Church, the Universities, the Bench and the Bar seemed to outdo each other in paying fulsome homage to the sovereign power and the royal office, for which they claimed a divine origin. Their King was at once a Prince, a Priest, and a Prophet; and doubtless James I. realised this idea to the full extent both to himself and to others—for he was looked upon as a very "Solomon." What marvel then if, puffed up with this inordinate flattery, the King at length looked upon his royal office and person with something more than mortal self-complacency, and in his more exalted moods whispered to himself, in imitation of an old Roman Emperor, "Verily, I am becoming a god." In ancient times heroes and warriors ranked, after death, with the lesser deities; at a later period, hermits and anchorites were raised in due season by the faithful to a somewhat similar dignity; but it was reserved for the sixteenth century to decree in a manner the apotheosis of kings while still in the flesh.

Under James I. all loyal subjects were supposed to hold the doctrine, "That monarchy and lineal succession are of divine institution, and are consequently sacred and inviolable; that the persons as well as the authority of kings are ordained by God; that the King is the sole fountain of power, and that all liberties and privileges of the people are but so many concessions or extortions from the Crown; that the King is not bound to the people by his coronation oath—but only before God, to whom he is accountable." The language of this

monarch was that of an absolute Sovereign.   In calling together
his first Parliament he tells the electors and the electees what
they must severally do, at the peril of incurring the King's
displeasure, besides severe penalties if they do not comply
with his proclamation.   In one of his speeches to Parliament
he says, " As it is blasphemy to dispute what God may do, so
it is sedition in subjects to dispute what the king may do in
the height of his power."   On another occasion he reads them
a similar lecture, and tells them that " Parliaments are at his
disposal, to convoke, assemble, and dissolve them, and that
according as he may find their fruits good or bad, so shall they
continue or cease to be."   Symptoms of a reaction, however, in
the tone and attitude of Parliament (more especially of the
House of Commons) were becoming visible by degrees.   This
reaction had even set in before the end of Elizabeth's reign,
but did not exhibit itself in any marked degree until some
years after the accession of James I.   It was chiefly owing to
the increase of the Puritan element in the Lower House ; and
we may even conjecture that the Commons were growing
ashamed of the subserviency and abasement of their order
under the Tudor dynasty.   Indeed, James does not forget to
remind his Parliaments of their submissive and even servile
demeanour to his immediate predecessors.   Yet, despite his
haughty and domineering temper, his dictatorial speeches and
messages to both Houses of Parliament, his dogmatic proclamations, his learning and his logic, he was unable to repress
that spirit of constitutional freedom which was growing up in
the House of Commons, and which broke forth with such
overwhelming violence under his son and successor, Charles I.

From what we have said in the foregoing pages, it will be
evident that Charles I. had learnt the art of government in a
very bad school. The lessons of his father, and the example of

the whole Tudor dynasty, were but little calculated to prepare him for the evil times in which his lot was cast. His reign was emphatically the period of transition from the effete ideas of government, and the right divine of kings, to the more rational views of monarchical rule which have prevailed in modern times. Had Charles I. held the reins of power with the same firm and unyielding hand as Elizabeth, or had his Parliament met him in a more submissive tone, he would never have lost his Crown or his head. But the refractory state of a stiff-necked House of Commons made him obstinate and equivocal by turns, until his subjects lost all confidence in that royal word which he had so often solemnly pledged, and so often found means to evade. Again, the "popular" or Puritan party, whose policy was both aggressive and unyielding, had now acquired considerable weight and influence, both in Parliament and in the country. Their numbers, too, were in every way formidable; and as they felt their growing strength, so their demands for what they deemed constitutional redress became more urgent and exacting. And these Puritan reformers for the most part were men of narrow minds, slender acquirements, and strong prejudices. Their views of government were mainly drawn from two sources :—from the biblical history of the Jews, and from the history of the ancient Republics of Greece and Rome. Thus all political objects at which they looked were more or less distorted by the medium through which they were seen. Many of those Puritan leaders, moreover, were Republicans upon principle at a period when the Commonwealth was never dreamt of; so that in dealing with a King who had inherited the most extravagant notions of royal prerogative, they were always at issue and never satisfied. They were what we should call at the present day "impractical men"—mere men of theory—whose political principles were warped and tainted by their half-Jewish, half-Christian views of theology and Church government. But then they were men of

austere lives and character, who had taken as their model the
Jewish worthies of the Old Testament.   They were moved, too,
by a spirit of religious enthusiasm which had animated and
supported them in the midst of trial and persecution; and
above all, they were men of an earnest though bigoted purpose.
Such were the opponents whom Charles I. had to encounter at
the commencement of, and throughout, his reign.

At the outset of his career, Charles followed closely in the
wake of his predecessors; nay, excited by the conduct of his
Commons, he attempted to carry the royal prerogative to
greater lengths than even the Tudors had done, for he contemplated nothing less than dispensing with Parliaments altogether
and usurping their functions himself.   Not that he was by
nature more arbitrary or self-willed than Henry or Elizabeth,
but that he was *driven to extremities by the desperate state of his
pecuniary circumstances.*   The Church lands and other collateral
sources of profit had supplied the necessities of Henry VIII. and
of his immediate successors; but that fountain was now dried up,
and there were no lands (unless in Ireland) to be confiscated
under some plausible pretext.   What was Charles to do in this
emergency?   He had a war to maintain with Spain—a very
unpopular war, which brought neither glory nor profit to the
nation—and funds must be provided at any cost.   The Parliaments would not grant the supplies which the King required.
He dissolved them in rapid succession, but each new election
only served to strengthen the determined opposition of the
Commons.   He tried what he could do without them by virtue
of his royal prerogative; he imposed certain duties, under the
name of tonnage and poundage, on wine and other articles of
imported merchandise; the proceeds whereof not sufficing for
his wants, he caused Letters of Privy Seal to be addressed to the
wealthier classes of his subjects generally, for the purpose of
raising forced loans or "benevolences," and further levied a
tax upon sea-port towns for the support of the fleet.   All

these measures could not fail to be unpopular, and to embroil
the King with his subjects and with his Parliaments. In fact,
the history of Charles I., from the commencement of his reign
to the outbreak of the civil war, extending over a period of
sixteen years, is one continued series of conflicts with his Parliaments and with his subjects; all, be it remembered, more or
less intimately connected with the undue exercise of his prerogatives in the matter of taxation to which he was forced to
resort from the illiberal policy of his Commons. Had Charles
(who was by nature a man of kind and amiable disposition and
domestic habits) possessed ample resources at his command, all
his difficulties would have been obviated. In fact, had the
Commons met Charles I. in the conciliating spirit with which
he met them, and granted him subsidies suitable to the emer-
gencies in which he was placed, there would have been no
necessity for his unconstitutional acts of arbitrary taxation, and
in all probability a civil war had been avoided. The first great
constitutional measure which Charles was constrained to grant is
known as the famous Petition of Rights, to which he gave an
unwilling, if not an equivocal, sanction, in his third Parliament,
and the provisions of which he afterwards not only evaded but
virtually ignored. The Petition of Rights complains of the
violation of the Great Charter, and of divers other constitutional rights and liberties of the subject—both as to person and
property ; and prays that in future no loans, taxes, or subsidies
be levied but by the consent of Parliament, that no one be
cited to justice, nor obliged to take an oath, nor arrested for
having refused compliance with such demands.

The King, however, still pursued what he considered his
rightful course, and the Star Chamber was at hand to aid him
in executing his schemes for raising money, and to chastise all
those who showed themselves refractory. As we have already
had occasion to observe in a former part of this essay, the Star
Chamber took cognisance of divers kinds of offences ; and it was

now used by the King as a kind of high-pressure engine for extorting money—the heavy pecuniary fines and penalties which it imposed being a considerable source of profit to the Crown. However, its enormities continued unabated until 1641, when it was finally abolished.   At the same time, also, the Court of Wards and Liveries, which had likewise been an instrument of oppressive exaction and feudal revenue, may be said in a great measure to have ceased its operations, although it lingered on until the next reign.   In the 16th of Charles I. it was enacted, " That if the King neglected to call a Parliament for three years, the Peers might assemble and issue writs for electing one ; and that in case the Peers neglected to do so, the constituents might meet and elect one themselves." This statute, however, as Blackstone observes, was " detrimental and injurious to the royal prerogative," and was repealed in the following reign.

Throughout the period of the Civil Wars, and indeed up to the time of the Restoration, the Constitution was in the most abnormal and unsettled condition.   In fact, from the year 1642, the " Constitution," properly so called, of 'King, Lords and Commons,' was virtually at an end.   From this time forward the only real power in the State was the Parliament, or rather the House of Commons, for the House of Peers had already become a mere shadow.   A semblance of constitutional forms was, however, still maintained.   The administration and the judicial business of the kingdom was still carried on in the King's name, and even the grave farce was enacted of levying war against the person of the man Charles—in the name of Charles the Sovereign.   We know the result, which it is much easier to account for than to palliate or excuse.   Charles Stuart was made the scape-goat on whose head were laid, and in whose person were expiated, all the sins, misdeeds and enormities, of his royal predecessors for more than a hundred years.

Charles doubtless had his faults, both as a sovereign and as a man ; for his manners, though correct, were austere ; his truth sometimes questionable; and his love of power, derived from the tuition of his father, very great. But had he found his first Parliament less encroaching, it is probable that his rule would have been more gentle, and better in accordance with the growing spirit of freedom; as it was, his prejudices came so early into collision with those of his people, that a reconciliation at any future period was rendered next to impossible. With respect to the faction which persecuted him even to the death, but one opinion can now be formed. They were no friends to public liberty; for never, under the most arbitrary monarch, were the people of England subject to a more rigid tyranny; neither did they compose the majority of the nation, which, at least latterly, had recovered its reverence for the person of the King. Even of the Commissioners appointed to sit in judgment on him, scarcely one half could be induced to attend at his trial; and many of those who concurred in his condemnation, subscribed the sentence with feelings of shame and remorse. But it is ever so in revolutions. A few violent men take the lead; their noise and their activity seem to multiply their numbers: and the great body of the people, either indolent or pusillanimous, are led in triumph at the chariot wheels of a paltry faction.

We need not follow the Commonwealth beyond observing that the remnant of the Long Parliament, which scarcely numbered one hundred members, converted the kingdom for a brief period into a Republic, or what was tantamount to one. It abolished the House of Lords and the Established Church, as well as the monarchy, and declared the supreme power vested in itself. It appointed a Council of State, consisting of forty-one members, which it invested with full executive power and authority to administer the affairs of the nation. This Executive Council was to hold office for the year, and was only responsible to Parliament for its acts. It must be said in favour of this Council that it set to work with considerable vigour to reform abuses and to amend the laws; and when we take into consideration the inexperience of its members in the conduct of public affairs, and their narrow-minded fanaticism, we are only surprised that their administration was marked by so much judgment and discretion. At length Cromwell, having violently dissolved the Long Parliament, seized the reins of power himself, for which he had long been intriguing, and established a species of military despotism on the ruins of the Commonwealth. If this usurpation of his can be justified at all it is only on the ground of expediency, and from the circumstance that impending anarchy seemed to require a military Dictator at the head of affairs. Cromwell was evidently the best man at that time to rule over those bigoted spirits who had plunged their country into its then unhappy condition. He restored order at home, and made the name of England feared all over the continent of Europe. Under him the government of the nation was reconstituted upon a system very nearly resembling that of a limited monarchy. The Lord Protector, as chief of the Executive, exercised all but regal power. He commanded the army and navy, and, subject to the approval of Parliament, appointed all the high officers and functionaries of State, made peace and war, concluded treaties with foreign Powers, and exercised with few limitations the authority of a Sovereign Prince. He was assisted by a Council of State, or ministry, responsible to Parliament, and in whom was vested at first the right of nominating a new Protector when the office should become vacant, though eventually this right was conferred upon Cromwell himself. This Council was composed of civil and military elements, in which the latter was predominant, and the members could not exceed twenty-one in number.

The legislative body, which now consisted of 460 members for the three kingdoms, had been remodelled by Cromwell, and several reforms were introduced into the representative system, of which we may presume, however, that numbers were not the basis; for whereas England alone had 400 members, Ireland

and Scotland had but sixty members between them. At a somewhat later period an "Upper House" was formed, consisting of sixty-one members, of which the Protector had the nomination, but it exercised no power or influence whatever on the State, and was merely "magni nominis umbra."

But we need not follow the destinies of the Commonwealth any farther. The nation had long since grown tired of it, and had it not been for the army and the powerful chief who commanded it, the Commonwealth could not have lasted a twelvemonth, for it never had a place in the hearts of the English people. Accordingly the Restoration was hailed with delight by all, soon after death had snatched the vigorous but despotic Protector from the helm of government.

As soon as Charles II. was recalled from exile by the unanimous voice of the nation, the whole fabric of constitutional polity raised by the Commonwealth was swept away, and even pains were taken to remove every trace of its existence. The old Constitution of the kingdom was restored in its integrity. The Church and the House of Lords resumed their ancient status, and matters went on once more as they had been wont to do for centuries, while the memory of the Commonwealth and of the "Regicides" was justly execrated by every staunch royalist. In a constitutional point of view, the reign of Charles II. is famous for the substitution of indirect for direct taxation, for the final extinction of the feudal system, and for the passing of the Habeas Corpus Act. No previously existing law seemed to have been sufficiently explicit for guarding against the arbitrary detention of the subject in prison; for although in the 16th of Charles I. a statute was passed ordaining that "If any person be committed to prison by the King, or by any member of his Privy Council, he shall without delay have granted to him a writ of Habeas Corpus; whereupon the judge shall determine the legality of such imprisonment within three days," yet we are told this statute was evaded in a variety of ways, under various pretexts, and that it had often been found necessary to have a second and even a third writ issued before the person accused was brought to trial. At length, in the 31st of Charles II., was passed the famous Habeas Corpus Act, which Blackstone calls the "Second Magna Carta, and stable bulwark of our liberties." It enacts that " any officer neglecting to make due returns, or not delivering to the prisoner or to his agent, within six hours after demand, a statement of the circumstances under which the accused is detained, shall for the first offence forfeit *one hundred* and for the second *two hundred pounds* to the person aggrieved; that any person committed for treason or felony shall, if he require it, in the first week of the next Term or on the first day of the next Session, be indicted in that Term or Session, or else be admitted to bail,—unless it can be proved upon oath that the King's witnesses cannot be produced at that time; and that if not indicted and tried in the *second* Term, he shall be discharged of his imprisonment for such imputed offence;" and moreover, "That any of the twelve Judges or the Lord Chancellor who shall deny a Writ of Habeas Corpus on sight of the warrant, or on oath that the same is refused, shall forfeit severally to the party aggrieved five hundred pounds."

It is impossible to exaggerate the importance of this statute, which thus guarantees in the most distinct terms the immunity of the subject from illegal imprisonment. Taken in connection with trial by jury, it offers the most complete security that human laws can afford against the arbitrary infliction of punishment by the Sovereign. Still it must be said that more depends upon the mild and equitable administration of the laws than upon the written provisions thereof; for we know that a corrupt judge and a partial jury can render nugatory the most humane laws and institutions that society has ever devised. Of the truth of this assertion the most signal illustrations were afforded during the reign of James II., to which we must now briefly advert. Unfortunately, James had but little regard for his word. The lessons which he should have learnt from his father's fate were wholly lost upon him. Almost from the day on which he ascended the throne he set himself systematically to the subversion of the Constitution. His first efforts were directed against the Established Church, which he had promised by his coronation oath to maintain in its full integrity. To this course he was doubtless impelled by the Jesuitical faction by whom he was surrounded. He suffered himself to be blindfolded and hurried along to his ruin by men whose views were warped and distorted by the illusory medium through which they regarded political objects. In short, he was a priest-ridden devotee, who had always one leading idea present to his mind, and that was the speedy restoration of the Roman Catholic religion in this kingdom. Had he proceeded more slowly and more cautiously in his design he might have succeeded to a certain extent ; for the example of the Sovereign and "fashion" would in process of time have enabled the higher classes first, and the multitude afterwards, to discover truths in Romanism which might otherwise have eluded their inquiries.

No prince, indeed, could have desired more loyal or more devoted subjects than James II. possessed on his accession to the throne. All classes seemed to vie with each other in paying him homage ; they even connived at his premature attempts for the restoration of Roman Catholicism, and at all times manifested the utmost forbearance towards him. Still he went on in his mad career, heedless of the murmurs which he provoked. Not only did he intrude upon the rights and liberties of the universities in the most arbitrary and nnwar-rantable manner, and compel the Bishops and clergy to obey unlawful proclamations, but actually succeeded in appointing officers of his own creed to posts of importance in the army and navy, and in the civil departments of the public service. Nay, some of his Cabinet Ministers openly professed the Romish faith. All this was carried out contrary to the express laws of the realm; but the King thought he could over-rule those laws by virtue of his royal prerogative, and so he went on, actuated by the blind impulses of religious zeal, recklessly trampling down the landmarks of the Constitution as he proceeded.

While James was thus violating and undermining the Constitution of the realm both in Church and State, he was secretly entering into treaties and stipulations with France, whereby he not only compromised his own dignity as a Sovereign, but imperilled the safety and independence of his kingdom. In fact, he became the vassal of Louis XIV., who was privy to, and encouraged, his ultimate designs of subverting the English Church, and who promised him troops and subsidies in the event of his subjects rising up against him. At length he had driven matters to such an extremity that those who had been his most zealous supporters abandoned him, and were the foremost to invite the Prince of Orange to land in England in defence of the Protestant religion.

The flight of James II. was the most fortunate event that could have happened under the circumstances, for had he remained and contested his ground with the Prince of Orange, a civil war must have been the inevitable result. William, however, quite aware of the delicate position in which he stood, showed great prudence and discretion in all his acts. He proceeded cautiously at first, feeling his way as he went, and waiting to know the wishes of those by whom he had been invited. He was not kept long in suspense. A Convention Parliament was held forthwith, in which, after prolonged discussion, it was resolved that James II., by abandoning his kingdom, had virtually abdicated the throne, which must, therefore, be considered vacant; whereupon the Crown was offered to the Prince of Orange, and a declaration of the inherent and indefeasible rights of the nation was at the same time presented for his acceptance. In short, a formal compact was concluded between the Parliament as the representatives of the people, on the one hand, and the Prince of Orange on the other. The Prince, after promising to uphold the Constitution and to maintain the rights of the people, was raised to the throne.

In this famous Declaration, or Bill of Rights, is embodied the grand and final development of the English Constitution, which, since the Revolution of 1688, has suffered no fundamental or essential change in its theory or in its distinctive principles and characteristics—although, in a practical point of view, its component parts have become considerably modified in their reciprocal influence upon each other, while both the spirit of the Constitution, and its subordinate forms, have been gradually adapting themselves to the progressive requirements of civilisation.

The most important changes that have influenced our legal polity since the passing of the Bill of Rights are : the Acts of Toleration and Settlement, the Acts for uniting England and Scotland and England and Ireland, the Reform Bill, the Repeal of the Test and Corporation Acts, and the Catholic Emancipation Act ; all of which will be found under their respective headings in the ensuing pages. The result of these Acts has been to assert our liberties in clearer and more emphatic terms, to regulate the succession of the Crown by Parliament as the exigencies of religious and civil freedom required, to maintain the superiority of the laws above the Crown by pronouncing the dispensing power to be illegal, to restrain the royal pardon from obstructing parliamentary impeachments, to make Judges completely independent of the Sovereign and his successors, &c., &c. As regards the administration of private justice, the chief

alterations of importance are : the solemn recognition of the
law of nations with regard to the rights of ambassadors, the
regulation of trials by jury and the admission of witnesses for
prisoners upon oath, the allowing a counsel for the defence of a
prisoner instead of his having to defend himself, the translation
of all legal proceedings into the English language, and lastly
the great system of marine jurisprudence.*

"The events of the last hundred years have changed the face
of Europe ; and although our own country has not sustained
those disastrous shocks which have been felt from time to time
by most of the continental nations, it has not remained a
stranger to the general progressive tendency which has been
discernible more or less over the whole civilised world.   On the
contrary, the state of continuous healthy progress which seems
to be peculiar to our own institutions has, perhaps, carried us
further in the direction of political and social freedom than any
other nation in the world.

"Our civil liberties have been further secured by that amendment of the law of libel which vests in the jury the right in
such cases of deciding as well upon the law as upon the fact ;
and by the statutory recognition of the privilege of Parliament
to publish whatever it pleases.   The boundaries of religious
liberty have been extended by the repeal of the Test and Corporation Acts ; whilst the Catholic Emancipation Act has
relieved those who adhere to the Church of Rome from the civil
disabilities to which they were previously subject.   The admission of the Jews into Parliament is another feature of the liberal
tendency of the age.   Comprehensive measures have also been
adopted for the better management of the cathedral revenues,
and for the subdivision of large and populous parishes, the formation of new parochial districts, and the extension of the
Church and its institutions.   The National Church has greatly

* Blackstone's Commentaries by Kerr, vol. iv. p. 503, *et seq*.

increased its strength from the commutation of tithes and from those statutes which have been passed for the abolition of pluralities and for compelling the residence of the beneficed clergy. The education of the poorer classes for the last few years has been under the supervision of a committee of the Privy Council specially constituted for the distribution of the large sums of money voted annually by Parliament for that purpose.   Attention has also been directed to the municipal corporations, which have been remodelled and purged from numerous abuses.

" The statutes respecting the law of marriage have been amended in such a manner that every individual is now enabled to enter into this solemn contract in the mode which he considers necessary and proper.

"The abolition of colonial slavery, accomplished at a very great pecuniary sacrifice, is an event in our history never to be forgotten.   The spirit of philanthropy which dictated this measure is a very prominent feature of our age, and has displayed itself in a variety of other enactments, particularly those modifying the severity of the laws relating to unfortunate traders and debtors, securing the proper care and treatment of lunatics, amending the discipline of prisons, and providing reformatory institutions, not only for criminals who seek an opportunity of regaining their lost position, but for those unfortunate children who are born, as it were, into crime, and have rarely, if ever, been taught to distinguish between good and evil.   The laws for the relief of the poor have been remodelled, and some steps taken, falteringly, it is true, but in the right direction, towards a more equitable adjustment of the heavy taxation which is imposed for their support ; the numerous charities which are to be found in every part of the kingdom have been placed under the regulation and control of a body of commissioners, whose sole duty it is to see that the funds of these institutions are properly applied ; the laws relating to game, always a fertile source of crime, have been so far modified that we may anticipate an early

repeal of all penal enactments on the subject; and several statutes have been passed, having for their object the improvement
of the sanatory condition of populous places, and the preservation of the public health.

"The interests of trade, commerce, and manufactures have
been unceasingly studied and promoted since the restoration of
peace in 1815. This is not the place, however, in which to
attempt any enumeration of the various statutes which have
been from time to time passed for regulating these matters, the
legislation relating to which has been often affected and controlled by financial necessities, or by the conflicting views of
political economists. It may be enough to allude to the various
statutes throwing open the trade to the East Indies and removing many of the duties previously levied under the unpopular
names of customs and excise, to the consolidation of the laws
relating to the mercantile marine and to the repeal of the Navigation Acts; all tending towards establishing a system of commerce free from all restraints, other than those which the
collection of the public revenue and the machinery required for
that purpose render indispensable. The law with regard to
bankruptcy has been further consolidated and amended; real
property has been subjected to the payment of debts; the rights
of authors and inventors have been extended and secured; and
the formation of joint-stock companies has been simplified and
cheapened, the most ample regulations being made, at the same
time, for the guidance of these bodies. The operations of the
mercantile classes have been facilitated by several statutes
having reference exclusively to commercial affairs; and protected
to some extent by other enactments which have made breaches
of trust, committed by bankers, factors, trustees, agents, and
servants generally, severely punishable.

"In regard to landed property and its transmission, the most
important improvements have taken place. The alteration of
the law of descent, the limitation of the time within which

actions for the recovery of real estate may be brought, the shortening of the time of prescription or legal memory, the abolition of those complex modes of assurance, fines, and recoveries, the modification of the wife's claim of dower, the annihilation of satisfied terms,—these, among other things, have tended greatly to facilitate the transfer of property, have got rid of endless doubts and difficulties which perpetually arose upon titles, and have materially shortened conveyances. A great improvement has also been introduced into the law of wills, and there is less danger now than formerly of the wishes of a testator being frustrated. An attempt has been made to get rid of copyhold tenures, and repeated efforts, hitherto without effect, however, to introduce a system of registration of the titles to real estates.

" The administration of private justice has been greatly simplified by the numerous alterations which have been made in the procedure of the Superior Courts of Law and Equity. The abolition of real actions, and of the many fictions which formerly encumbered suits at law, was an important and beneficial change ; but not so advantageous to the suitor as more recent improvements in the practice of the Courts at Westminster. Even these alterations have been less beneficial to the great mass of the community, however, than the establishment of the new County Courts, a measure warmly recommended by Sir William Blackstone, and to some extent a return to the ancient Saxon system, restored if not established by King Alfred, for securing the administration of justice at every man's door. The old rules of law excluding the evidence of the parties to the suit, and prohibiting persons who are considered disqualified either by reason of interest or by crime from being witnesses, have been rescinded, and all practical difficulties in eliciting the truth removed.

" The proceedings of the Courts of Equity have been simplified and shortened, and the trial of contested facts by a jury introduced, at the same time that these Courts have been enabled to

assess and award damages, instead of remanding the suitor for
such redress to a Court of Law. The increase in the number of
Judges has prevented the possibility of delay in the hearing of
causes there pending ; and there seems to be no reason why, in
ordinary cases, the obtaining of justice in the Court of Chancery
should not be a speedy and not ruinously expensive process.

" The cognisance of matrimonial and testamentary causes has
been taken from the Ecclesiastical Courts, and conferred on lay
tribunals, which have been provided, at the same time, with a
simple and intelligible procedure. The law of England has also
recognised at last the right of divorce for adultery ; and put
that remedy, which was previously only attainable by a private
Act of Parliament, within the reach of all who are likely to
demand it.

" The criminal law has been, as to many of its branches,
amended and consolidated ; and the severity of punishments at
the same time much softened, and adapted more carefully than
formerly to the nature and magnitude of the offence. The barbarous sufferings prescribed for those attainted of treason no
longer stain the statute-book, and the punishment of innocent
parties for ancestral guilt, which often resulted from the doctrine of corruption of blood, can no longer happen ; while the
offences involving capital punishment, which the convict only
escaped by claiming the benefit of clergy, have been gradually
reduced in number, until the extreme penalty of the law has
become in practice confined to the frightful crime of murder.
The trial by battel, and the mode of proceeding by appeal, have
been formally abolished ; the law relating to principal and
accessory has been divested of its niceties, and the forms of the
proceedings in the Criminal Courts so far simplified and improved, that offenders who have now the advantage of being
defended by counsel rarely escape punishment on purely technical objections."

Having discussed at some length the principal events connected with the rise and progress of the Constitution, let us now enter more fully into an examination of the whole structure as it is presented to our view in its more complete form.

In a former part of this essay we defined the word "Constitution" to mean not only the Three Estates of the Realm—the King, Lords, and Commons—but also "the fundamental laws, ordinances, and customs by which these Estates are severally and collectively bound and governed, and by which their peculiar and distinctive rights, privileges, functions, and prerogatives are duly set forth and determined." We have now, therefore, to consider more at large the attributes pertaining to each of these Estates or Powers respectively :—

1st. The King is the Chief Magistrate in the realm, and the source of all judicial power. From him must emanate all authority exercised by Judges and other public functionaries throughout the empire. To him, as Head of the Executive, belongs the sole and exclusive right of putting the laws in force. He sits upon his throne by hereditary right ; yet by the Act of Settlement his profession of the Roman Catholic faith would entitle the next heir to the crown, being a Protestant, to succeed to the sovereignty. The King of himself has no power to make new laws, or to dispense with those which already exist ; but as he forms an integral and component part of the Legislature, his consent is necessary before any statute passed in Parliament can become valid or have the force of law. His royal prerogative, however, enables him, if so advised by his Privy Council, upon whom the responsibility in that case would fall, to withhold his sanction from any parliamentary act that he might think inexpedient,—whether as detrimental to the public welfare, or as encroaching upon his own prerogatives. This right of veto which the sovereign possesses affords a guarantee both to himself and to his subjects at large that the kingly office and authority will not be invaded by the other branches of the Legislature.

The King is also Head of the Church in all causes, both ecclesiastical and temporal. He appoints the Archbishops and Bishops to their several sees. He exercises supreme control over all matters pertaining to church polity, and without his authority no ecclesiastical act, ordinance, or decree can have any legal effect.

As the King is the "Fountain of Honour," so it is he alone who can confer titles of honour and dignity, and without his special permission his subjects have no right in this country to assume titles received from any foreign prince or potentate. The King, moreover, commands the army and navy, raises troops, equips fleets, receives ambassadors from foreign Courts, declares war and peace, and makes treaties and contracts alliances with foreign States—as to him seems best, with the advice of his Privy Council. It is the exclusive right and privilege of the Sovereign to assemble and dissolve Parliament; and, as "by a fiction of the law," he is supposed to be the universal proprietor of the kingdom, so all criminal prosecutions are conducted in his name.

Being the "Fountain of Justice," the *"King can do no wrong"*—such at least is the presumption and the language of the law. For, as he has no peer in his own realm, and as he cannot, therefore, be judged by any competent tribunal, nor by those who, being his representatives or deputies, exercise their authority and jurisdiction by virtue of his commission, he is held blameless by the Constitution, while the Ministers of the Crown are held responsible for all acts of the Government, and are liable to be cited before the House of Peers for any maladministration or abuse of power.

Having thus enumerated some of the principal functions and powers of the Executive, we have next to inquire what guarantee the nation possesses that those powers will not be abused. This we shall discover by considering the relationships which exist between the Crown and the two Houses of Parliament. The Commons, as we have already seen, possess the exclusive right of introducing Money Bills in their own department—of imposing taxes, and of granting supplies for the various purposes of government, subject to the consent and approbation of the Upper House of legislature. And as the King has no power, himself, to levy aids or subsidies, he is wholly dependent on the nation for the means of upholding his own dignity—of supporting his household—of maintaining his Army, Navy, and Civil Service, and of keeping in motion the entire machinery of the State; so that the matter at length assumes the form of a business-like transaction between the ruler and the subject, in which the mutual interests of each are concerned, and in which both parties are bound to observe their respective engagements with good faith. A certain sum is annually voted for certain specific purposes—for the expenditure of which sum the Government is obliged to furnish an account; and as Parliament possesses not only the right of limiting the supplies which it grants, but of withholding them altogether if it should think fit, the nation possess the best possible guarantee that the government of the country will be properly conducted, and that the authority of the Executive will not be abused. At the time of the Revolution a rule was established which has ever since been adhered to, that all the expenses of the army, navy, and ordnance should be annually brought under the review of the House of Commons, and that every sum voted, for whatever purpose, should be applied to the particular service specified in the vote. From that period downwards the Commons have been the great power in the State; and we have the authority of Hallam for stating that, "since the Revolution they have virtually possessed the power of appointing and removing Ministers, of declaring war, and concluding peace."

Not only is the King Head of the Executive and Chief Magistrate in the realm, but he also forms one of the component parts of the Legislature. He is supposed to preside over the House of Lords, and in former times actually did so in person, but is now represented by the Lord Chancellor—Keeper of the Great Seal—who acts as Speaker of the Upper House.

The House of Lords is the most ancient and dignified Court in the kingdom, and is the highest Court of Appeal, beyond which no cause can be carried. It exercises both legislative and judicial functions ; but in its judicial capacity its authority is delegated for the most part to those of its members who, having been elevated from the Bar to the Upper House, are conversant with the law bearing upon those questions that come before them from time to time, and are therefore the most competent to decide. Yet, when any question touching the dignity or privileges of the House itself is raised, the whole of the Peers take part in the deliberations, and give their decision, which is final. The members of the House of Peers are legislators by hereditary right. By the same right they are the Counsellors of the Crown, "and may be called together by the King to impart their advice, either in time of Parliament, or when there is no Parliament in being." In consequence, however, of the great importance acquired by the Commons in modern times this custom has fallen into disuse. Still, to a Peer of the realm belongs the privilege, if he should think fit to exercise it, of demanding an audience of the Sovereign, to lay before him " such matters as he may deem of importance for the public weal."

The House of Lords has likewise the right of initiating in their Chamber any Bills,—save Money Bills, which, as we have elsewhere seen, must originate with the Lower House. The Lords have, moreover, a negative voice on the acts of the Commons, which, though it gives them the power of frustrating really useful measures which may be obnoxious to themselves, yet affords a guarantee to the State against the encroachments of the Lower House of Parliament. The number of Peers of the Realm is not fixed or limited, and has varied considerably from time to time, owing to divers causes. During the Tudor and Stuart dynasties there were much fewer Peers than there had previously been, or than we have at the present day. Indeed, the great majority of existing peerages are of comparatively modern creation. The Crown possesses the exclusive prerogative of adding to their number whenever it may see fit to do so; but the Peers themselves are very jealous of having their numbers augmented from the ranks of the commoners, and in the reign of George I. they introduced a Bill to limit their body to those then existing, but the Bill was rejected by the Lower House.

The principal council belonging to the King is the Privy Council, which is chosen by the King himself, who regulates the number of his Privy Councillors, which, however, is not limited. From the Privy Council is chosen the Cabinet Council, or Administration, consisting of the great Ministers of State at the head of the several public Departments, who conduct the government of the country while the party to which they belong hold the reins of power.

Privy Councillors are removable at the King's discretion, and no person born out of the dominion of the English Crown, unless the son of English parents, can hold the office of a Privy Councillor. The duties of a Privy Councillor, as defined by Blackstone, are seven in number, " 1st. To advise the King according to the best of his knowledge and discretion. 2nd. To advise for the King's honour and the good of the public—without partiality, through affection, love, reward, doubt, or dread. 3rd. To keep the King's counsel secret. 4th. To avoid corruption. 5th. To help and strengthen the execution of what shall be there resolved. 6th. To withstand all persons who would attempt the contrary. 7th. To observe, keep, and do all that a good and true Councillor ought to do to his sovereign Lord."

Let us now briefly glance at the Commons. What we have already stated in the sketch of our Constitutional history will afford some idea of the great influence, power, and importance pertaining to the House of Commons. Unlike the Lords, however, the Commons do not hold their seats by any hereditary right, but are merely elected for a limited period. Before the Revolution there was no time determined for the summoning or duration of Parliaments. It would seem to have been optional with the King to call a Parliament whenever he pleased, as he was entirely governed by his own discretion, combined with his personal exigencies and the " form and pressure " of the times. At all events, great irregularity prevailed upon this point, for we sometimes find that the same members continued to sit for several Sessions consecutively—as, for instance, in the Long Parliament,—while at other times new members were elected for each Session. However, in the reign of William and Mary it was enacted that a new Parliament should be called every three years ; but it was found by experience that frequent elections were productive of great inconvenience and expense, as well to the electors as to their representatives, and that the excitement created by the tumultuous meeting of popular assemblies at such brief intervals was calculated to provoke fruitless clamour and discontent rather than to give weight and stability to the Legislature ; and we find, accordingly, that the law of triennial Parliaments was repealed under George I., and the term extended to seven years. We may add, however, that in practice it is seldom found that Parliaments hold out so long without a dissolution.

The Commons cannot assemble without the authority of the Crown. They are accordingly summoned by the Queen's writ, issued forty days before their meeting by the Privy Council. The Sovereign meets her Parliament either in person or by proxy, and lays before it a brief statement of the circumstances of the nation, the position in which she stands in her relationships with foreign States, and the business which her Government proposes to transact during the current Session. This statement, or "Speech," of the Sovereign is delivered in the Upper House, to which the members of the Lower House are summoned to hear, after which they return to their own chamber, and are straightway at liberty to proceed with the business of the Session, having first, however, taken the oath of allegiance and supremacy.

The House of Commons is presided over by the Speaker, who is chosen from amongst the members themselves, and who holds his office till the dissolution of the Parliament in which he was elected. He is supposed to be selected for those qualities which chiefly command the deference and respect of the members of the House : namely, his personal dignity, his acquaintance with the rules, forms, and modes of procedure of the House, his urbanity, and the grave suavity of his manners. He is precluded from taking part in the deliberations of the House unless when sitting in Committee. We have elsewhere observed that perfect freedom of debate belongs to both Houses of Parliament ; but it must not be understood by this that members are at liberty to propose measures derogatory to the dignity of the Crown, or in any way disloyal—only that no court of justice, nor even the Sovereign himself, can take cognisance of any matters debated within the walls of Parliament. Each Chamber enjoys a species of absolute control and authority in respect of the conduct of its own members, without being responsible to any higher power.

Having thus referred to the Three Estates of the realm, let us now say a few words respecting what now claims to be a species of "Fourth Estate," or power of the realm, namely, the Press. That this is a *power*, and a very vast one too, cannot for a moment be denied. In former times and in the early ages of Constitutional history, it had no existence whatever, and in point of fact it was not until after the Revolution of 1688 that the newspaper press of the kingdom began to make its influence felt in the guidance and formation of public opinion. Even during the eighteenth century it had not reached that point of development and preëminence when it could fairly be called a "power" in the State. It is the present century almost entirely that has witnessed the establishment of the Press in the rank of an "Estate." True, it has no recognised constitutional existence, as an integral portion of the Legislature. It does not muster rank and file in a division. But surely it has a voice, and a very potent one too, in all the debates and deliberations in both Houses of Parliament. It does not go into the lobby *in propriâ personâ,* but who can deny that it influences and frequently determines the vote of many a man upon questions of the gravest importance? It holds its debates daily in public, and sits the whole year round. It has no "vacation"—no "recess." Its eye never slumbers, and its voice is never mute. It speaks to millions thunder-tongued. Amongst its vast auditory are kings, princes, priests, and senators, yet it does not address them with hushed accents or bated breath. It does not tickle their ears with the honeyed poison of flattery; but it tells them truths which in bygone times would never have reached them,—wholesome truths in high places which preserve the body politic from corruption and decay. But not this only. The Fourth Estate has it eyes cast abroad in all the corners of the earth in search of knowledge; its emissaries explore the utmost recesses of civilised and savage life, and accumulate, for the benefit of the present and of the future, the vast treasures of experience and information which are amassed and redistributed day by day in the interests of human progress and enlightenment. In a word, there are none so low that the teaching of the Press does not in some way reach and affect them, and none so high as to be raised above the lessons of instruction and wisdom which it conveys.

In this Essay we have briefly sketched the Rise and Progress of the English Constitution, from the commencement of our legal polity to the present time. " Of a Constitution so wisely contrived, so strongly raised, and so highly finished, it is hard to speak with that praise which is justly and severely its due :—the thorough and attentive contemplation of it will furnish its best panegyric." To assist this " attentive contemplation," we have arranged the information contained in the following pages in an alphabetical form, so that it may more readily catch the eye, and thus avoid the trouble of research. This information we have endeavoured to render as briefly as is consistent with accuracy, merely relating all what directly bears upon the subject without the tedious repetitions of legal technicalities, in the hope that thus condensed it will be more serviceable to the student and general reader, for whom this work is only intended.

" OUR CONSTITUTION."

Abjuration Oath.—The last Act to which the royal assent was given by William III. on his deathbed, March 2, 1702, required all persons in office, members of the universities above eighteen, members of the legal profession and school-masters, Peers and Members of Parliament, to take the oath abjuring the claims of the Stuarts. The oath was altered in the reign of Queen Anne, and put into a new form by 6 Geo. III. c. 53 (1766). It was changed for Roman Catholics by 31 Geo. III. c. 32 (1791), and in 1829 by the Roman Catholic Relief Act. By the statute 21 & 22 Vict. c. 48 (July 23rd, 1858), one oath was substituted for the three oaths of Abjuration, Allegiance, and Supremacy.

Abjuration of the Realm, was an engagement, on oath, to quit the realm, and never return to it without the king's license. The ancient common law of England allowed a person who had committed any felony, except treason and sacrilege, to make such an oath before the coroner within forty days after taking sanctuary, under the penalty of death by hanging if he broke it, unless he was a clerk ; in which case he was allowed benefit of clergy. Abjuration underwent several modifications in the reign of Henry VIII., and was abolished as a privilege, together with that of sanctuary, in 1624. By 35 Eliz. c. 1, Roman Catholics and Protestant dissenters convicted of having refused to attend the service of the

Church of England, might be required to abjure the realm. From this Act, which was passed in 1593, Protestant dissenters were exempted in 1689, but Popish recusants not until 1791.

Abeyance.—When the inheritance to which a party claims to be entitled is not in the possession of any one, it is said to be in abeyance. Titles of honour and dignities are said to be in abeyance when it is uncertain who shall enjoy them ; as when a nobleman, holding his dignity descendible to his heirs general, dies, leaving daughters, the Queen by her prerogative may grant the dignity to which of the daughters she pleases, or on the male issue of one of such daughters. During the time the title to the dignity is thus in suspension, it is said to be in abeyance. A parsonage remaining void, is also said to be in abeyance. In a more loose sense, this term is used to denote that a judgment is pending relative to a matter or right undetermined, and of which no one has the immediate enjoyment, the right being in a state of suspension.

Abuttals, or Boundaries.—The buttings or boundings of lands, East, West, North, or South, with respect to the places by which they are limited and bounded. The sides or the breadth of lands are more properly described as adjacent or bordering, and the ends in length abutting or bounding. Boundaries are of several sorts, such as hedges, ditches, and inclosure of walls, land-marks in common fields, trees and boundary stones in parishes, brooks, rivers, highways, in manors or lordships, &c.

It is the duty of a tenant to preserve as he found them, distinct, the boundaries of his landlord, and of landlords of adjoining property ; and if he suffer them to become confused, he may be bound to substitute land of his own of equal value, to be ascertained by commissioners.

Where freehold and copyhold land is intermixed, it is prudent to obtain and mark, from time to time, the boundaries of the different parts of the estate, which should be done in the presence of the steward or bailiff of the manor, or at least he should have notice to attend.

Accedas ad Curiam.—The title of a writ which removes a plaint from an inferior Court, the issuing of which is a preliminary to trying a question of right upon a distress of goods by the proceeding called Replevin.

Accessory, before the fact, is defined to be a person who, being absent at the time of the felony committed, yet procures or abets another to commit a felony. After the fact—is a person who, knowing a felony to have been committed by another, receives or assists the felon ; but a bare knowledge of the felony will not make him accessory, even if he agree for money not to give evidence against the felon. All who are aiding and abetting when a felony is committed, and as such being accessories, are styled principals in the second degree, in contradistinction to principals in the first degree, who are the persons actually committing the felony. However, it is to be recollected that, in the highest and lowest offences, high treason and misdemeanour, all are principals, and must be indicted as such. In murder also, all aiders, abettors, and accessories before the fact, are treated as principals in the first degree.

It is therefore only in felonies below treason that there can be accessories. The accessory before the fact of any felony is deemed guilty of felony, and punished accordingly. He may be tried before the conviction of the principal, but the best and most usual way is to try the principal and accessory together.

Accountant-General.—An officer in the Court of Chancery, being one of the Masters in Chancery appointed to receive all money paid into that Court : his duty is to convey all money to the Bank, which he does by investing the same in stock. All stock ordered to be paid into Court is transferred in his name. The Accountant-General's salary is paid out of the interest arising from the Suitors' Fund. To forge his handwriting is punished by penal servitude for life.

Act of Attainder, *see* ATTAINDER.

Act of Bankruptcy, *see* BANKRUPTCY.

Act of Oblivion, *see* OBLIVION.

Act of Settlement, *see* SETTLEMENT.

Act of Supremacy, *see* SUPREMACY.

Act of Toleration, *see* TOLERATION.

Act of Uniformity, *see* UNIFORMITY.

Action is the remedy to be pursued for a wrong done, or is the right of suing by law for what is due to any one. Actions are divided into two classes — criminal and civil. Criminal actions are proceedings by indictment or inquisition against another so as to obtain judgment of death, penal servitude or imprisonment; or by information in the Queen's Bench, to have judgment by fine or imprisonment, or both, against another for misconduct, breaches of the peace, &c. Actions brought for some penalty or punishment under particular statutes when the party proceeded against is liable to corporal or pecuniary punishment, are called penal.

Civil actions are divided into real, personal and mixed. Real actions are those which concern real property only: personal actions, those which relate to contracts both sealed and unsealed, and offences or trespasses; and mixed actions, those which lie as well for the recovery of the thing as for damages for the wrong sustained. In all cases of actions there must be a person able to sue and a person suable, and every one must bring his action in the form assigned by law. The causes for which actions can be sustained are infinite in their varieties, but there is no wrong to which a form of action is not applicable. We briefly mention the chief causes for which actions are generally instituted :—

Actions upon promises or mutual contracts not under seal.

Actions to recover money in respect of deeds or contracts under seal.

Actions to recover fixed sums of money.

Actions to recover a certain thing detained.

Actions to recover damages for forcible wrongs done to the person or property of another.

Actions in the case of words or writings affecting a person's reputation.

Actions to recover land or any interest therein.

Actions to recover a widow's dower.

Actions to recover an advowson or right of presentation to a cure or benefice.

Actions in the case of damages from fraud or misrepresentation, &c., &c.

In all actions of trespass, battery, &c., the death of either party determines the suit.

Real actions survive. Every one, before the commencement of an action, should be assured that the cause of action has actually accrued. "It is expedient, in actions to be brought against sheriffs and others for seizing disputed property, to inform them distinctly of the right claimed therein, and it is absolutely necessary that in actions against justices of the peace or magistrates, commissioners of bankruptcy, revenue officers, and many other public functionaries, for acts done by them in the execution of their office, a written notice of action should be duly served at least a month previous to the issuing of the writ, in order to give them an opportunity of tendering amends before action, and which action must be brought within the time limited by the various statutes for that purpose, generally six calendar, and against customs and excise officers within three lunar, months."

Act of Parliament, is a statute, law or edict made by the Queen, with the advice and consent of the Lords spiritual and temporal, and the Commons in Parliament assembled. Acts of Parliament form the *eges scriptæ*, or the written laws of the kingdom ; they cannot be altered, suspended or repealed, but by the same authority of Parliament which created them.

Statutes are either public or private, general or special. A public or general Act is a universal rule applied to the whole community, which the Courts must notice judicially. But special or private Acts are rather exceptions than rules, since they only operate upon particular persons and private concerns, and the Courts are not bound to take notice of them if they are not formally pleaded, unless an express clause is inserted in them that they should be deemed public Acts. All the Acts of a Session together make properly but one statute, and therefore when two Sessions have been held in one year it is usual to mention statute 1 or 2. Acts of Parliament bind all persons within the territory to which they extend, but not the Crown unless it be specially mentioned. They do not extend to the Isle of Man or to the Channel Islands, unless expressly mentioned.

As to the Colonies, if acquired by occupancy, all Acts of Parliament passed previously to their acquisition, so far as they are suitable, extend to them upon their acquisition ; but it is otherwise if they have been acquired by treaty or conquest. Colonies of both kinds are not, however, affected by Acts of Parliament passed since their acquisition unless express mention of them be made. So also an Act of Parliament does not apply to India unless expressly mentioned.

Act of Settlement, *see* SETTLEMENT.

Adjournment.—An adjournment of Parliament is a continuance of the Session from one day to another. It differs from prorogation, the former being done by the Houses themselves, whilst the latter is an act of royal authority. Either House may interrupt or postpone any debate, or altogether adjourn its sittings. The adjournment of one House is no adjournment of the other. The Lords frequently adjourn " during pleasure ; " the Commons on the contrary always adjourn to a time specified. All unfinished proceedings during an adjournment remain in *statu quo*.

Admiralty, Board of.—This office is the representative

of the Lord High Admiral of England, and is now put into commission. The Commissioners are generally members of the House of Commons, and are composed of naval officers and civilians, all of whom are styled Lords of the Admiralty, and who, together with the First Secretary, quit office on a change of Government. The other officers have permanent appointments. These Lords Commissioners exercise their supervision over all naval matters, and exclusively control the expenditure of the sums annually voted by Parliament for the naval service. Hours—11 to 5 at Whitehall ; 10 to 4 at Somerset House.

Admiralty, High Court of.—A civil Court, erected in 1357, for the trial of causes relating to maritime affairs. It possesses one Judge, who is usually an eminent Doctor of Civil Law. In 1857 it was ordered that the Judge of the Probate Court should be also Judge of the Admiralty Court. The Admiralty has jurisdiction upon the high seas—that is, upon all parts of the sea which are not within and do not form a part of any country. As to offences committed on the coasts, it has exclusive jurisdiction over those committed beyond the low-water mark, and between that and the high-water mark. It has also jurisdiction of offences done on the water when the tide is in, and the Courts of Common Law of offences committed upon the strand when the tide is out. "The Court of Admiralty* has general power to determine all matters arising upon the seas, which, had they arisen *here*, would have been cognisable by law ; therefore, seamen's wages, batteries, collision of ships, suits for obtaining possession of a ship, restitution of goods illegally taken on the high seas, questions of possession or right between the part owners of ships, suits for pilotage, on bottomry and respondentia bonds, for officers' and seamen's wages, and for salvage, and relating to

* These matters are tried in the Instance Court of the Admiralty—the Prize Court judges cases of captures and seizures of ships and goods taken during war.

wreck, are properly brought in this Court; but, on the other hand, generally speaking, the Court of Admiralty has no jurisdiction over contracts under seal, or deeds (except bonds or instruments which hypothecate or mortgage the ship for money advanced on its credit, and for its use), or agreements which have no relation to maritime affairs, although executed and signed on shipboard, as a bond, note, or engagement to pay money in London or elsewhere in England."

The criminal jurisdiction of the Admiralty Court was abolished in 1844. It now sits at *Westminster* instead of at Doctors' Commons. From its decisions an appeal lies to the Privy Council.

Advocate, Lord, is the principal public prosecutor in Scotland. He occupies the same position as Attorney-General in England. This office existed in 1479, but it was not till 1540 that it became a great office of State. The Lord Advocate is virtually Secretary of State for Scotland.

Advocate, Queen's.—An officer appointed by letters patent to advise and act as counsel for the Crown in questions of civil, canon, and international law. He claims precedence of the whole bar.

Advowson.—The perpetual right of presentation to an ecclesiastical benefice or cure, corresponding to the right of patronage in the canon law. All advowsons formerly belonged to some manor, whose lord, having endowed the church with a house and glebe, obtained the right to present a parson thereto; but in process of time the manor and advowson became separated; and now comparatively few advowsons remain annexed to the manors, which are generally co-extensive with the parish. Thus the distinction of an advowson *appendant* and an advowson *in gross* was created; the former being the advowson as originally annexed to the manor, and the latter in its separated and disunited state. The first disunion of the advowson from the manor was in favour of ecclesiastical corporations, and subscquently of colleges, the annexation to which is styled an *appropriation*, as the acquisition of an advowson by a lay person, *i.e.*, not in holy orders, is termed an *impropriation*. The right of presentation may be, and very often is, parted with for one turn only; but such an assignment *must* be made during the life of the present incumbent, and before a vacancy in the church, else the presentation would be void, as an encouragement of simony.

The separation of the advowson from the manor may be effected by the patron, at the present day, by conveying the manor with a reservation of the advowson, by conveying the advowson without the manor, or by presenting to an incumbent as an advowson in gross, that is, treating it or naming it as already separated.

An advowson can only pass by will or deed, and if appendant to the manor as part of the inheritance, or it may be granted for one or more turns within a limited time.

Advowsons are either vested in ordinary persons, or in a bishop, college, corporation, or in the Queen, or in any person founding a new chapel by the Queen's license; and when the patron, not being the Queen or an ecclesiastical or collegiate corporation, presents his parson to the bishop of the diocese for institution, it is termed a *presentative* advowson. When the advowson is lodged in the bishop, who presents by reason of the patron not presenting in six months, it is termed a *collative* advowson; and when the Queen or other person does, by a donation in writing, put the parson in possession, by that single act, of a chapel, prebend, or church, for the most part founded by the Queen, or by a subject with the royal licence, and exempt from ecclesiastical visitation, it is termed a *donative* advowson.

All persons who have ability to purchase or grant, can likewise present to vacant benefices; but a dean and chapter cannot present the dean, nor may a patron who is a clergyman present himself, though, if the bishop admit him on his solicitation, the institution shall be good. A parson about to be admitted makes oath that he has not made *any* corrupt or simoniacal contract.

Ad quod damnum.—A writ addressed to the sheriff of a county to inquire by a jury whether a grant intended to be made by the sovereign will be to his damage or that of others. This writ is also employed for the turning of ancient highways, which cannot be lawfully done without the royal license obtained by this writ on the jury finding that such a change will not be detrimental to the public.

Age—in law, signifies those special times which enable persons of both sexes to do certain acts which before, through want of years and judgment, they were prohibited from. For instance, a male at twelve years of age can take the oath of allegiance to the sovereign; at fourteen he may consent to marriage, and choose his guardian for several purposes; and at twenty-one he may alien his lands, goods, and chattels. As regards a woman: at twelve she may consent to marriage; at fourteen she is at years of discretion, and may choose a guardian; and at twenty-one she may alien her property. Fourteen is the age by law to be a witness; but those of tenderer years who understand the nature of an oath are now admitted to give evidence. Persons under twenty-one are legally styled "infants under the age of twenty-one years." No one can be a Member of Parliament under the age of twenty-one. No man can be ordained priest till twenty-four, nor be a bishop till thirty years of age. He cannot be sworn on any jury or inquest till twenty-one; nor can he practise as an attorney or public notary till that age. In criminal law the discretion of infants varies according to the nature of the offence; but no infant can be guilty of felony or punishable for a capital offence under seven. At fourteen they are presumed capable of contracting guilt. Between the ages of seven and fourteen their capacity for doing evil is measured by the strength of the culprit's understanding, the law putting the most merciful construction on his or her acts.

Alderman.—Originally a dignity of the highest rank, both hereditary and official, and nearly synonymous with that of king. At the present day he is an associate of the civil magistrate of a city or town corporate.

Aliens are those born in a foreign state or country not under the dominion of Great Britain. Those who are children of fathers, natural born subjects, and their children, even though their mothers were aliens, are considered Englishmen. The children of a British mother by an alien have now the same privileges as natural born subjects. An alien desirous of domiciliating himself in England, must obtain letters of denization, which are letters patent, to make him a British subject, or by naturalization. A denizen is, however, but in a middle state between a foreigner and an Englishman, whilst naturalization places an alien in the same situation as if he had been born an Englishman. The statute 7 and 8 Vict., c. 66, provides a simple and inexpensive mode by which aliens may obtain all the privileges of natural born subjects, except those of sitting in the Legislature, or being of the Privy Council, from the Secretary of State for Home Affairs.

Alimony is the allowance made to a wife out of her husband's estate for her support, either during a matrimonial suit or at its termination, when she proves herself entitled to a separate maintenance and the fact of a marriage is established. But she is not entitled to it if she elope with an adulterer, or leave her husband without just cause. Alimony is within the exclusive jurisdiction of the Court for Divorce and Matrimonial Causes.

Ambassador.—A diplomatic minister sent by one sovereign power to another to treat on affairs of State. He is either ordinary or extraordinary. Ordinary if he resides in the place where he is sent, the protection of commerce being his greatest

care ; or extraordinary if employed upon special matters, as con-
gratulations, overtures of marriage, &c. The person of an ambassador is protected from civil arrest.

Amortization.—An alienation of lands in mortmain to
any corporation, guild, or fraternity, and their successors, that
is to say, to some community that never is to cease. It cannot
be done without license from the Crown.

Animals, Cruelty to.—*See* CRUELTY.

Appeal.—Signifies the removal of a cause from one court to
another that is superior, for ultimate decision ; and this may,
in effect, be done by stating sufficient matters of erroneous
judgment in order to have it reversed, which are strictly termed
proceedings " in error ;" or by appealing to the House of Lords
from the decree of the Chancellor. *Error* may be applied to
courts of law, *appeal* to courts of equity.

A writ of error lies from inferior courts of record in England
into the Queen's Bench ; and the writ of error on any judgments of the Queen's Bench, Common Pleas, or Exchequer of
Pleas, is returnable in the Exchequer Chamber, and from thence
to the House of Lords, which is the only *final* judgment, and
conclusive upon all parties.

In *criminal* cases, judgments may be reversed by writ of
error, which lies from all inferior courts of criminal jurisdiction
to the Queen's Bench, and from the Queen's Bench to the
House of Lords.

In *equity*, decrees pronounced by the Master of the Rolls or
the Vice-Chancellors may be reversed by the Lord Chancellor,
on a *petition of appeal*. From the Lord Chancellor a petition of
appeal lies to the House of Lords.

Appeal, Lords Justices of.—*See* LORDS JUSTICES OF.

Assault and Battery.—A simple assault is an attempt
to commit an act of personal violence on another. Battery is
the beating or unauthorised touching another ; therefore, any
acts done to the person of another in a violent, rude, or revenge-

ful manner, are batteries ; a battery includes the assault. An action of *trespass* is the civil remedy for this injury, which is applicable to the assault only, though this action is generally brought to recover damages for both. Any menace or threat which hinders another in his business by occasion of the fear thereby reasonably entertained is actionable.

Archbishop.—The chief of the clergy in his province; he has supreme power under the Queen in all ecclesiastical causes, and superintends the conduct of other bishops, his suffragans. England has two archbishops—Canterbury and York. The Archbishop of Canterbury is styled Primate of *all* England, and is the first peer of the realm. The Archbishop of York is called Primate of England. Ireland has four—Armagh, Dublin, Cashel, and Tuam; of whom Armagh is Primate of all Ireland.

Archdeacon.—Is a substitute for the bishop, and has ecclesiastical jurisdiction and dignity over the clergy and laity next to the bishop throughout the diocese. He has a court where he hears ecclesiastical causes, and may inflict penance and excommunicate, subject to an appeal to the bishop. He examines candidates for holy orders, and inducts clerks upon receipt of the bishop's mandate. In law he is styled the bishop's vicar or vicegerent.

Arches Court.—A court of appeal belonging to the Archbishop of Canterbury, the judge of which is called the Dean of Arches. Its proper jurisdiction is only over the thirteen peculiar parishes belonging to the archbishop in London; but the office of Dean of the Arches having been for a long time united to that of the archbishop's principal official, the Judge of the Arches now receives and determines appeals from the sentences of all inferior ecclesiastical courts within the province. An appeal lies from this court to the Judicial Committee of the Privy Council. Its sittings are held in Westminster.

Articles of Religion.—In 1539 six articles of religion were published, viz. :—Transubstantiation, communion in one kind, vows of chastity, private masses, celibacy of the clergy, and auricular confession. In 1552, forty-two were published, but were reduced in 1562 to thirty-nine, and received the royal authority and consent of Parliament in 1571. Subscription to the articles is no longer necessary on matriculation or on taking a degree at the Universities of Oxford or Cambridge.

Articles of War.—A code of laws for the regulation of the land forces, made in pursuance of the several annual Acts against mutiny and desertion. There were formerly articles of the navy for the government of the royal fleet, but these have been repealed by the "Naval Discipline Act" in 1861.

Assizes.—A court or jurisdiction which summons a jury by a commission of assize to take the assizes. There are two commissions—a *general* commission, which is issued twice a year to the judges of the superior courts of common law at Westminster, two of whom are assigned to every circuit; and a *special* commission, which is granted to certain judges to try certain causes and crimes.

Attainder, is the corruption of the blood of a criminal capitally condemned. The Norman laws provided that by attainder of treason or felony a person forfeited his lands and *his blood became attainted,* which utterly disqualified his descendants from inheriting property. Its severity was modified in 1695; and in 1814 disinheritance was restricted to the culprit, except in cases of high treason. In 1834 further modifications were made in this Act. Two witnesses in cases of high treason are necessary where corruption of blood is incurred, unless the accused shall confess or stand mute.

Attorney-General.—A great officer of State, appointed by letters patent, and the legal representative of the Crown in the courts of law and equity. He exhibits informations, prosecutes for the Crown in criminal matters, files bills in the Exchequer in revenue causes, and informations in Chancery where the Crown is interested. The Prince of Wales and a Queen Consort have each an attorney-general. First attorney-general appointed in 1278.

Audit Office.—Established in 1785, when the auditors of imprests were abolished, and five commissioners appointed to audit the public accounts. These commissioners were subsequently increased to ten, but they are now limited to their original number—one chairman and four commissioners. They act under the Treasury, and undertake the inspection of the whole of the public accounts, and the investigation of all advances of money on behalf of the public service. Hours : ten to four. Somerset House.*

Augmentations, Exchequer Court of.—A court (now abolished) erected by Henry VIII. in 1535 to determine suits and controversies relating to monasteries and abbey lands.

Aula Regia, or Regis.—An ancient court established by William the Conqueror, and composed of all the great officers of State. It was presided over by one special magistrate, called the Chief Justiciar, and settled all business, civil and criminal, and likewise the matters of the revenue. It followed the King's household in all his expeditions. By Magna Charta it was enacted, " *communia placita non sequantur curiam nostram sed teneantur in aliquo loco certo.*" The *certain place* was established in Westminster Hall, where it now sits under the name of the Court of Common Pleas or Common Bench.

Award.—When persons refer any matter in dispute to the private decision of another party, such act is termed a submission. The party who is to decide upon such submission is the arbitrator, and the decision of such arbitrator is termed an *award.* The proper subjects of award are long and unclosed accounts ; cases in which it would be difficult to collect several witnesses so as to ensure their attendance on a trial ; cases

---

* This office is now amalgamated with the Exchequer.

between landlord and tenant upon questions of dilapidations; as to the title of small property, where the claimants are numerous; matters of privacy, arising between family connections; and executors' or trustees' accounts. Cases of slander, or criminal conversation, or where the measure of damages may influence further proceedings, or establish opinion of friends or general acquaintance as to character, are also fit subjects of arbitration.

Every agreement to submit matters to arbitration should be in writing and unconditional, or, as it is termed, *irrevocable*, and stipulated to be made a rule of some court, else it will be ineffectual.

There are two modes of enforcing obedience to the award : first, by an attachment for nonperformance of the things ordered to be done, after such award shall have been made a rule or order of any court by the usual application, and after formal demand made; secondly, by an action brought to recover damages for what is directed by the award to be done, paid, or performed; and these proceedings cannot be stayed unless it can be shown to the court of which the award is made a rule or order, that the award was not in conformity to, or that it exceeded the objects or the terms of, the submission, or that the arbitrator misconducted himself, or some equally strong case; for these agreements receive all possible sanction and assistance from the courts.

It is a very common practice, when parties refer their disputes to the decision of more than one arbitrator, to make provision for the appointment of a person to finally decide in case the arbitrators are unable to come to a decision; which person is called an "umpire."

Bail.—To set at liberty a person arrested or imprisoned, on security being taken for his appearance on a day and at a place certain, which security is called bail, because the party arrested is delivered into the hands of those who bind themselves for his forthcoming, in order that he may be safely protected from prison.

There are several kinds of bail at common law. *Common bail* is given to the sheriff after arresting a person on a bail-bond entered into by two sureties, on condition that the defendant appear at the day and in such place as the arresting process commands.

Special bail are persons who undertake generally that, if the defendant be condemned in the action, he shall satisfy the debt, costs, &c., or render himself to the proper prison, or that they will do it for him.

Bail in Error.—Bail is also given when a defendant brings a writ of error on account of some defect, real or alleged, in the proceedings of a suit in which judgment has been given against him. It is similar to the giving *special bail*, the recognisance being taken before a particular officer appointed for that purpose ; but the bail should remember that nothing *short of absolute payment of debt and costs* will relieve them from this suretiship: the render of the defendant availing them nothing.

In other cases of bail, such as attachments for contempt (not for nonpayment of money), a bail-bond is given to the sheriff, if he chooses to accept of it, for it is by no means imperative on him to take bail in these cases; and at the return of the process the bail of defendant enter into recognisances for the defendant's future appearance. The recognisances are sometimes conditioned for large sums, but are vacated on the defendant's answering the matters of the contempt, &c. Bail is often given to the sheriff on other contempts; and the bond is forfeited if the defendant is not in custody at the return of the attachment, according to the terms of the bond.

In almost all criminal cases, two justices may admit a party to bail, if the evidence be not such as to raise a strong presumption of guilt, but still afford reasonable ground of inquiry. In criminal cases where bail is required, it is taken before a justice or justices, and they have an absolute discretion in admitting parties to bail or committing them, but they are bound to take down the examination in writing.

The Court of Queen's Bench, or any judge thereof in time of vacation, may bail for any crime whatever.

Bailiwick, is a county of which the sheriff is legally the keeper, or bailiff. It is also used to signify the precinct of an exclusive jurisdiction distinct from the sheriff, though within his county. In the execution of processes relating to civil matters, this last distinction does not now exist.

Bank of England.—This bank conducts the whole banking business of the British Government. It receives and pays the greater part of the annuities which are due to the creditors of the public; it circulates Exchequer bills, and it advances to Government the annual amount of the land and malt taxes, which are often not paid until some years thereafter.

Bankruptcy, Act of.—An act the commission of which by a debtor renders him liable to be adjudged a bankrupt. Before the Bankruptcy Act, 1861, a man was not liable to be made a bankrupt unless he was a trader, and had committed an act of bankruptcy as defined by the statutes in force. By the recent Act a non-trader is now in certain cases liable to be made a bankrupt; and a debtor may be made a bankrupt in several cases, although he may not have committed any act which in terms is declared by any statute to be an act of bankruptcy. The cases in which a man may be adjudged bankrupt are specified in the "Bankrupt Law Consolidation Act, 1849," 12 & 13 Vict. c. 106; and the "Bankruptcy Act, 1861," 24 & 25 Vict. c. 134. The Bankrupt Law is a system of positive statute regulations, its character being peculiar and anomalous, and designed for the special advantage of persons with whom debts are contracted in the course of trade. It involves these three general principles: (1) a summary seizure of all the debtor's property; (2) a distribution of it among the creditors in general, instead of merely applying a portion of it to the payment of the individual complainant; and (3) the discharge of the debtor from future liability for the debts then existing.

Bankruptcy Court.—This court was erected in 1831, and consists of a chief court in London, and seven district courts held at Bristol, Exeter, Birmingham, Leeds, Liverpool, Manchester, and Newcastle-on-Tyne. Its judges are one or more commissioners appointed by letters patent under the Great Seal. Each of these courts is a court of law and equity, and has all the rights of a court of record.

Bargain and Sale.—The name of a conveyance by which freeholds were granted. It is required to be enrolled in the courts of law or chancery within six lunar months, exclusive of the day of the date.* If made of land or houses in London, it is enrolled in the Court of Hustings. This mode of conveyance has great advantages, but its publicity has brought it into disuse.

Baron.—A degree of the greater nobility of the kingdom next to a viscount. Great proprietors of land were originally termed "barons"; and their title has since been confirmed by patent or prescription, to distinguish them from the lesser barons, being the ordinary gentry, who in former days were the only proprietors of land in common with the greater barons, who were called up to Parliament. There are still barons by office, as the barons of the Exchequer, and barons of the Cinque Ports.

The present barons are:—1. By prescription; for that they and their ancestors have immemorially sat in the Upper House. 2. Barons by patent; having obtained a patent of this dignity to them and their heirs male or otherwise. 3. Barons by tenure; holding the title as annexed to land: it is said that

---

* A bargain and sale of chattels does not require to be enrolled.

it is the possession of their ancient landed territories which imparts the barony to the bishops, thereby giving them a place in the Upper House, although they hold by succession, not by inheritance. Another more favoured opinion is, that they sit in the Upper House by immemorial usage.

Baron of the Exchequer, Chief.—*See* CHIEF BARON, &c.

Barons of the Exchequer.—Are the judges of the Court of Exchequer. They were formerly barons of the realm, but now are persons learned in the laws who preside in the common law court called "The Exchequer of Pleas," at Westminster. Their office is also to look into the Crown accounts, for which reason they have auditors under them.

Baronet.—The holder of a dignity of inheritance created by letters patent, and descendible to the issue male. He takes precedence of all knights except Knights of the Garter. The order was instituted by James I. in 1611. The first baronet ever created was Sir Nicholas Bacon, of Redgrave, in Suffolk.

Barrator.—A promoter or instigator of suits and actions in disturbance of the public peace, and for his own gain, without regard to the plaintiff's right. This offence is termed BARRATRY, and is punishable by fine and imprisonment. Instances rarely occur at the present day of a prosecution.

An attorney knowingly bringing actions where nothing is due, and inciting the plaintiff thus to trouble his neighbours or others, is indictable as a barrator, or the courts will remove him, on summary application, from the roll of attornies.

Barratry, in marine insurance, is the commission of any fraudulent or illegal act by a captain or crew, to the damage of the ship, or whereby the ship may be subjected to forfeiture or detention, to the injury of the owners, freighters, or insurers. The acts done must be fraudulent in intent; for mere indiscretion or ignorance, in the absence of fraudulent motives, will not render the captain chargeable.

Barrister.—A councillor learned in the law admitted to plead at the bar of the courts, and to take upon himself the protection and defence of those who retain him. They are either utter or *outer* barristers, that is, plead *without* the bar; or Queen's counsel and serjeants-at-law, who plead *within* the bar. The judges are chosen from the serjeants-at-law.

Bath, Knights of the.—A military order of knighthood instituted by Richard II. The order received its denomination from a formerly observed custom of bathing before the knights received the golden spur. George I. revived the order by the creation of a great number of knights. This order was newly regulated in 1847 and in 1850. Motto: *Tria juncta in uno.*

Battel, Trial by.—A trial anciently allowed by our law, when the defendant in an appeal of murder might fight with the appellant, and make proof thereby of his guilt or innocence. Abolished in 1819.

Battery.—*See* ASSAULT AND BATTERY.

Benefit of Clergy.—Arose out of the great respect paid by Christian princes to the Church, and consisted in the exemption of all clergymen from criminal process before the secular judge in particular cases. Gradually, benefit of clergy extended to all who could read; and it was enacted that there should be a prerogative allowed to the clergy, that in case of any man being condemned to death who could read, the bishop might claim him as a clerk. The prisoner who could read was only burnt in the hand, otherwise he suffered death. Benefit of clergy was entirely repealed in 1827.

Bigamy.—Is the offence of polygamy, *i.e.* the having a plurality of husbands and wives at once. The law provides that the marrying another person during the life of the former husband or wife, no matter *where* the second marriage takes place, is a felony, punishable in principal and accessory with not more than seven and not less than three years' penal servitude; or imprisonment, with or without hard labour, not exceeding two years. But there are four exceptions :—1. Where the second marriage is contracted out of England by an alien. 2. Where either of the parties has been *continually* absent from the other for seven years, not knowing the other party to be living. 3. Where there is a divorce from the bond of matrimony on account of nullity. 4. Where the first marriage has been declared void.

Bill.—A document submitted to Parliament in which are contained certain propositions for its consideration. Bills are the drafts or skeletons of statutes. They are either *public*, affecting the general interests of the State, or *private*, enabling private individuals to undertake works of utility at their own risk ; and also relating to naturalisation, change of name, &c. Public bills may originate in either House, unless they be for granting supplies of any kind, when they must commence in the Commons ; so must all private bills authorising the levying of local tolls or rates. Estate, peerage, and naturalisation bills begin in the House of Lords.

Bill.—A word applied to many writings which state special or particular matters, such as a bill of complaint, or bill in chancery, a bill of indictment, bill of exceptions, bill of exchange, bill of lading, bill of charges, bill of store, bill of sufferance, &c.

Bill of Indemnity.—*See* INDEMNITY.

Bill of Rights.—A declaration delivered by the Lords and Commons to the Prince and Princess of Orange, Feb. 13th, 1688–9, and afterwards enacted in Parliament on their accession to the throne. It sets forth,

1. That the power of suspending laws, or the execution of laws, by regal authority, without consent of Parliament, is illegal.

2. That the pretended power of dispensing with laws, or the execution of laws, by regal authority, as it hath been assumed and exercised of late, is illegal.

3. That the commission for erecting the late Court of Commissioners for Ecclesiastical Causes, and all other commissions and courts of like nature, are illegal and pernicious.

4. That levying money for or to the use of the Crown, by pretence and prerogative, without grant of Parliament, for longer time or in other manner than the same is or shall be granted, is illegal.

5. That it is the right of the subjects to petition the king, and all commitments and prosecutions for such petitioning are illegal.

6. That the raising or keeping a standing army within the kingdom in time of peace, unless it be with consent of Parliament, is against law.

7. That the subjects which are Protestants may have arms for their defence suitable to their conditions, and as allowed by law.

8. That election of members of Parliament ought to be free.

9. That the freedom of speech, and debates or proceedings in Parliament, ought not to be impeached or questioned in any court or place out of Parliament.

10. That excessive bail ought not to be required, nor excessive fines imposed, nor cruel and unusual punishments inflicted.

11. That jurors ought to be duly impanelled and returned, and jurors which pass upon men in trials for high treason ought to be freeholders.

12. That all grants and promises of fines and forfeitures of particular persons before conviction are illegal and void.

13. And that for redress of all grievances, and for the amending, strengthening, and preserving of the laws, Parliament ought to be held frequently.

*   *   *   *   *   *   *

Resolved that William and Mary, Prince and Princess of Orange, be declared King and Queen of England, France, and Ireland, and the dominions thereunto belonging, to hold the crown and royal dignity of the said kingdoms and dominions to them the said prince and princess during their lives, and the life of the survivor of them ; and that the sole and full exercise of the regal power be only in and executed by the said Prince of Orange, in the names of the said prince and princess, during their joint lives ; and after their deceases, the said crown and royal dignity of the said kingdoms and do-minions to be to the heirs of the body of the said princess ; and for default of such issue to the Princess Anne of Denmark and the heirs of her body ; and for default of such issue to the heirs of the body of the said Prince of Orange. And the Lords Spiritual and Temporal, and Commons, do pray the said prince and princess to accept the same accordingly.

And that the oaths hereafter mentioned be taken by all persons of whom the oaths of allegiance and supremacy might be required by law, instead of them ; and that the said oaths of allegiance and supremacy be abrogated :—

"I do sincerely promise and swear that I will be faithful and bear true allegiance to their majesties King William and Queen Mary : So help me God."

"I do swear that I do from my heart abhor, detest, and abjure as impious and heretical, that damnable doctrine and position that princes excommunicated or deprived by the pope, or any authority of the see of Rome, may be deposed or murdered by their subjects, or any other whatsoever. And I do declare that no foreign prince, person, prelate, state, or potentate hath, or ought to have, any jurisdiction, power, superiority, pre-eminence, or authority, ecclesiastical or spi-ritual, within this realm : So help me God."

*   *   *   *   *   *   *

And for preventing all questions and divisions in this realm, by reason of any pretended titles to the crown, and for pre-serving a certainty in the succession thereof, in and upon which the unity, peace, tranquillity, and safety of this nation doth, under God, wholly consist and depend, the said Lords Spiritual and Temporal, and Commons, do beseech their majesties that it may be enacted, established, and declared, that the crown and regal government of the said kingdoms and dominions, with all and singular the premises thereunto belonging and appertaining, shall be and continue to their said majesties, and the survivor of them, during their lives, and the life of the survivor of them. And that the entire, perfect, and full exercise of the regal power and government be only in and executed by his majesty, in the names of both their majesties during their joint lives; and after their deceases the said crown and premises shall be and remain to the heirs of the body of her majesty; and for default of such issue, to her royal highness the Princess Anne of Denmark and the heirs of her body; and for default of such issue, to the heirs of the body of his said majesty: And thereunto the said Lords Spiritual and Temporal, and Commons, do, in the name of all the people aforesaid, most humbly and faithfully submit themselves, their heirs and posterities for ever; and do faithfully promise that they will stand to, maintain, and defend their said majesties, and also the limitation and succession of the crown herein specified and contained, to the utmost of their powers, with their lives and estates, against all persons whatsoever that shall attempt anything to the contrary.

And whereas it hath been found by experience that it is inconsistent with the safety and welfare of this Protestant kingdom to be governed by a popish prince, or by any king or queen marrying a papist; the said Lords Spiritual and Temporal, and Commons, do further pray that it may be enacted, that all and every person and persons that is, are, or shall be reconciled to, or shall hold communion with, the see or Church of Rome, or shall profess the popish religion, or shall marry a papist, shall be excluded, and be for ever incapable to inherit, possess, or enjoy the crown and government of this realm, and Ireland, and the dominions thereunto belonging, or any part of the same, or to have, use, or exercise any regal power, authority, or jurisdiction within the same ; and in all and every such case or cases the people of these realms shall be and are hereby absolved of their allegiance ; and the said crown and government shall from time to time descend to, and be enjoyed by, such person or persons, being Protestants, as should have inherited and enjoyed the same in case the said person or persons so reconciled, holding communion, or professing, or marrying as aforesaid, were naturally dead.

And that every king and queen of this realm who at any time hereafter shall come to and succeed in the imperial crown of this kingdom shall, on the first day of the meeting of the first Parliament next after his or her coming to the crown, sitting in his or her throne in the House of Peers, in the presence of the Lords and Commons therein assembled, or at his or her coronation, before such person or persons who shall administer the coronation oath to him or her, at the time of his or her taking the said oath (which shall first happen), make, subscribe, and audibly repeat the declaration mentioned in the statute made in the 13th year of the reign of King Charles II., intituled, " An Act for the more effectual preserving the King's person and government, by disabling Papists from sitting in either House of Parliament." But if it shall happen that such king or queen, upon his or her succession to the crown of this realm, shall be under the age of twelve years, then every such king or queen shall make, subscribe, and audibly repeat the said declaration at his or her coronation, or the first day of meeting of the first Parliament as aforesaid, which shall first happen, after such king or queen shall have attained the said age of twelve years.

* * * * * *

Provided that no charter, or grant, or pardon granted before the 23rd day of October, in the year of our Lord 1689, shall be any ways impeached or invalidated by this Act, but that the same shall be and remain of the same force and effect in law, and no other than as if this Act had never been made.

Bishops.—A bishop is the chief of the clergy within a certain district, or subdivision termed a *diocese*, and is the archbishop's *suffragan*, or assistant, in England, Wales, and Ireland.

The ecclesiastical state of England and Wales is divided into twenty-four bishoprics, besides the bishopric of Sodor and Man, the bishop of which does not sit in Parliament ; and each archbishop has within his province bishops of several dioceses.

A bishop is elected by the Queen's *congé d'élire*, or licence, to elect the person named by the Queen, in a letter missive directed to the dean and chapter ; if they fail to make election within twelve days, the Queen nominates whom she pleases, by letters patent.

A bishop, when consecrated, must be full thirty years of age.

A bishop (as well as an archbishop) has his consistory court, to hear ecclesiastical causes ; and is to visit the clergy, &c. He consecrates churches ; ordains, admits, and institutes priests ; confirms, suspends, excommunicates, grants licences for marriage, &c. He has his archdeacon, dean and chapter, chancellor, and vicar-general, to assist him ; and may grant leases for three lives, or twenty-one years, of land usually letten, reserving the accustomed yearly rents.

The chancellor to the bishop is appointed to hold his courts for him, and to assist him in matters of ecclesiastical law ; who, as well as all other ecclesiastical officers, if lay or married, must be a doctor of the civil law, so created, in some university.

The right of trial by the Lords of Parliament, as their peers, it is said, does not extend to bishops ; who, though they are Lords of Parliament (except the Bishop of Sodor and Man), and sit there by virtue of their *baronies*, which they hold in right of the Church, or, as some think, by immemorial usage, yet are not ennobled in blood, and consequently not peers with the nobility. Bishoprics may become void by death, deprivation for any very gross and notorious crime, and also by resignation.

Bishop's Court.—An ecclesiastical court held in the cathedral of each diocese, the judge of which is the bishop's chancellor, who judges by the civil canon law. If the diocese be large, he has his commissaries in remote parts, who hold consistory courts for matters limited to them by their commission.

Black Mail. A compulsory payment, formerly made in parts of Scotland by the Lowlanders to the Highlanders, for the protection of their cattle. It existed up to 1745, and rendered agricultural improvement impossible.

Black Rod, Gentleman Usher of, is chief gentleman usher to the Queen; he has his name from the *black rod*, on the top of which sits a lion in gold, which he carries in his hand. In time of Parliament he attends on the Peers, and to his custody all Peers called in question for any crime are first committed.

Blasphemy, the denying the existence of God or His Providence. Contumelious reproaches of our Saviour are offences punishable at common law; and by a statute of King James I., the prophanely or jestingly using the name of God, our Saviour, or the Holy Trinity, in any stage play, is punishable by a fine of £10. A profane scoffing at the Holy Scriptures is also blasphemy. It is punishable by fine, imprisonment, or corporal punishment.

Board of Control was established by Pitt's East India Bill, 24 Geo. III. c. 25 (May 18, 1784). Six privy councillors were appointed as commissioners to have control and superintendence of all the affairs of the British possessions in the East Indies. The Act was amended by 33 Geo. III. c. 52 (June 11, 1793), and subsequent Acts. The first president was Lord Sydney, appointed September 3, 1784. The Board of Control

G

was abolished by 21 & 22 Vict. c. 106 (August 2, 1858), when a Council of India, consisting of fifteen members and a Secretary of State for India, was appointed.

Board of Green Cloth, or Court of Marshalsea, was a court of justice, noticed as early as the time of Henry III., having exclusive jurisdiction in the King's palace and within the verge, described by 13 Rich. II. c. 3 (1390), not to exceed twelve miles of the King's lodging. Its power, confirmed by several statutes, was derived from the common law. The statute 28 Edw. I. c. 3 (1300), determined what pleas should be held in the Court of Verge; that of 2 Henry IV. c. 23 (1400), laid down regulations respecting fees. Its powers were extended to treasons, misprisions of treasons, murders, man-slaughters, bloodsheds, &c., by 33 Henry VIII. c. 12 (1542). This court was abolished by 9 Geo. IV. c. 31 (June 27, 1828).

Board of Health. The General Board of Health was established by 11 & 12 Vict. c. 63 (Aug. 31, 1848), for sanitary purposes, with the power of creating local boards in provincial towns. It was reconstructed by 17 & 18 Vict. c. 95 (Aug. 10, 1854), entitled, "An Act to make better provision for the administration of the laws relating to public health." Sir B. Hall was made president, with a salary of £2000 per annum. By 21 & 22 Vict. c. 97 (Aug. 2, 1858), all the powers of the General Board of Health were given to the privy council. Further provision for the local government of towns and populous districts in this matter was made by 21 & 22 Vict. c. 98 (Aug. 2, 1858).

Board of Trade and Plantations. Cromwell, in 1655, appointed his son Richard, with several lords of the council, merchants, &c., to consider by what means trade and navigation might be best promoted and regulated. Charles II. established a council to superintend and control the whole commerce of the nation, Nov. 7, 1660, and a council of Foreign Plantations, Dec. 1 in the same year. The boards were united in 1672, undergoing many changes until 1782, when, by 22 Geo. III. c. 82, the board was abolished. A committee of members of the privy council was ordered to be appointed for the consideration of all matters relating to trade and foreign plantations. The order of council, issued March 5, 1784, was revoked, and a new committee, appointing the board as at present constituted, was nominated Sept. 5, 1786, Lord Hawkesbury being the first president. The president and vice-president quit office on a change of government; the other appointments are permanent. This office is divided into the General, the Railway, the Marine, and the Statistical Departments. It exercises its supervision over all matters of public interest connected with the commercial enterprise of the United Kingdom. Hours, 11 to 5, Whitehall.

Borough Courts are private tribunals erected in particular districts for the convenience of the inhabitants, that they may prosecute small sums and receive justice at home. The jurisdiction of ancient courts for the trial of actions, formerly held in boroughs now governed by the operation of the Municipal Corporation Act, are preserved by the same Act, but the jurisdiction is extended to twenty pounds, under certain provisions which ensure the good regulation of such courts, and place their rules under the *surveillance* of the courts of Westminster. The judges are either a barrister of five years' standing or the recorder of the borough. The clerk of the peace summons the jury.

Borough-English. A mode of descent, or inheritance, which prevails in some ancient boroughs and copyhold manors, which is that estates shall descend to the youngest son; or if the owner has no issue, to his younger brother. If no son or brother, then the daughters or sisters jointly and severally inherit. By this custom the widow has for her dower the whole of her husband's lands holden by this tenure, instead of a third, for her life, as dower. This extended dower is called free-bench. This custom obtains in the manor of Lambeth, Surrey, in the manors of Hackney, St. John of Jerusalem in Islington, Heston, and Edmonton in Middlesex, and in other counties.

Bounty of Queen Anne, *see* QUEEN ANNE'S BOUNTY.

Budget. The annual speech, known by that name, of the Chancellor of the Exchequer. It embraces a review of the income and expenditure of the last as compared with those of preceding years. It remarks upon the financial prospects of the country; upon the intended repeal, modifications, or impositiou of taxes during the season, and gives a detail of the public expenditure during the current period, with its grounds of justification.

Burgesses generally are the inhabitants of a borough or walled town—men of trade. The term is sometimes restricted to magistrates, &c., of corporate towns, and sometimes to the representatives of such boroughs in the Commons House of Parliament.

By-Laws. The orders and regulations of corporations for the government of their members, being private laws, which may also be made by courts-leet and courts-baron, persons having right of common, &c., which are binding upon themselves, unless contrary to law or public policy, and then they are void. By-laws, by whomever made, should be reasonable and for the common benefit, not for the advantage of any particular individuals. The by-laws of some of the companies of London have lately been noticed by the courts of law, and a nice distinction has been drawn between by-laws made in *restraint* of a trade, and by-laws to *regulate* a trade. Generally speaking, by-laws imposing fines on their members for neglect of any particular duty necessary for their government, can be supported, and an action can be maintained for the penalty. By an ancient statute, by-laws of corporations should be approved of by the Lord Chancellor. With regard to corporations of towns now regulated by the Municipal Corporation Act, the council have express power by that statute to make such by-laws as to them shall seem meet for prevention and suppression of any nuisances not already made punishable in a summary manner, and to inflict a fine, not exceeding £5. These by-laws cannot be made unless two-thirds of the whole council are present; and cannot come into operation till forty days after the same have been sent to the Secretary of State, for approval by Her Majesty in Council, who may disallow the same; and after public notification thereof has been made in the borough, by affixing the same in some public place, usually the town-hall. But the by-laws must be consistent with reason and law, else no approval of Her Majesty will give them validity.

Cabinet Council. A private and confidential assembly of the most considerable Ministers of State to concert measures for the administration of public affairs. It was first established by Charles I. (*See* GREAT BRITAIN, ADMINISTRATIONS OF.)

Canon Law. A collection of ecclesiastical laws, serving as the rule and measure of Church-government. The power of making laws was exercised by the Church before the Roman Empire became Christian. The Canon-law that obtained throughout the west, till the twelfth century was the collection of canons made by Dionysius Exiguus in 520, the capitularies of Charlemagne, and the decrees of the popes from Sircius to Anastasius. The Canon-law, even when papal authority was at its height in England, was of no force when it was found to contradict the prerogative of the King, the laws, statutes, and customs of the realm, or the doctrine of the Established Church. The ecclesiastical jurisdiction of the See of Rome in England was founded on the Canon-law; and this created quarrels between Kings and several archbishops and prelates who adhered to the papal usurpation.

Besides the foreign canons, there were several laws and constitutions made here for the government of the Church; but all these received their force from the royal assent; and if, at any

time, the ecclesiastical courts did, by their sentence, endeavour
to enforce obedience to such canons, the Courts at Common
Law, upon complaints made, would grant prohibition.   The
authority vested in the Church of England of making canons,
was ascertained by a statute of Henry VIII., commonly called
the Act of the Clergy's Submission; by which they acknowledged that the convocation had always been assembled by the
King's writ; so that though the power of making canons resided
in the clergy met in Convocation, their force was derived from
the authority of the King's assenting to and confirming them.
The old canons continued in full force till the reign of James
I., when the clergy, being assembled in Convocation, the King
gave them leave to treat and consult upon canons; which they
did, and presented them to the King, who gave them the royal
assent; these were a collection out of the several preceding
canons and injunctions.   Some of these canons are now obsolete.
In the reign of Charles I. several canons were passed by the
clergy in Convocation.   "The Canon-law," says Lord Thurlow,
"prevails in this country only so far as it hath been actually
received, with such amplifications and limitations as time and
occasion have introduced.   And subject at all times to the
municipal law.   It is founded on the civil law; consequently
the tenets of that law also may serve to illustrate the received
rules of the Canon-law."

Canon. A person who possesses a prebend, or revenue
allotted for the performance of divine service in a cathedral, or
collegiate church.   Originally canons were only priests, or
inferior ecclesiastics who lived in community; residing by the
cathedral church, to assist the bishop; depending entirely on his
will; supported by the revenues of the bishopric; and living in
the same house, as his domestics, or counsellors. By degrees,
these communities of priests shook off their dependence, and
formed separate bodies, of which the bishops, however, were still
heads.   In the tenth century, there were communities or con-

gregations of the same kind, established even in cities where there were no bishops : these were called collegiates, as they used the terms congregation and college indifferently : the name chapter, now given to these bodies, being much more modern. Under the second race of the French kings, the canonical, or collegiate life, had spread itself all over the country ; and each cathedral had its chapter, distinct from the rest of the clergy. They had the name canon from the Greek κανων, which signifies three different things ; a rule, a pension, or fixed revenue to live on, and a catalogue or matricula ; all which are applicable to them.

In time, the canons freed themselves from their rules, and, at length, they ceased to live in community. However, they still formed bodies ; pretending to other functions besides the celebration of the common office in the church ; assuming the rights of the rest of the clergy ; making themselves as a necessary council of the bishop ; taking upon them the administration of a see during a vacancy, and the election of a bishop to supply it. There are even some chapters exempt from the jurisdiction of the bishop, and owning no head but their dean.

Capias ad respondendum (*that you take to answer*). Prior to Statute 1 & 2 Vict. c. 110, all personal actions were commenced in the Superior Courts of Common Law by this writ against any person whom it was intended to arrest or hold to bail. Its use is now only restricted to certain special cases, and it no longer is the commencement of the action. In form it is a command from the Queen to the sheriff to arrest the defendent till he shall have given bail in a specific action at the suit of the plaintiff, or until the defendant shall be discharged from custody. The defendant within eight days after the execution of this writ must cause special bail to be put in for him in the court from which the writ is issued.

Capias ad Satisfaciendum (*that you take to satisfy*). A writ of execution that issues on a judgment obtained, and lies where any person recovers in a personal action, as for debt,

damages, &c., in which cases this writ issues to the sheriff, commanding him to take the body of him against whom the debt is
recovered, who is to be kept in prison till he make satisfaction.*

Capias Utlagatum (*that you take the outlaw*). A writ
which lies against any one outlawed, upon any action personal or
criminal, by which the sheriff is ordered to apprehend the party
outlawed, for not appearing on the exigent, and keep him in safe
custody till the day of return, when he is ordered to present
him to the court, to be there further ordered for his contempt.

Capital Felonies are those crimes upon conviction of
which the offender is condemned to be hanged. The crimes now
punishable with death are high treason and murder. Numerous
offences formerly capital have ceased to be so by various statutes
passed in the reign of our present Queen. (*See* 24 & 25 VICT.
cc. 96, 97, 98, 100.)

Catholic Relief Bill. This bill was passed April 13,
1829. Through its introduction a different form of oath was
substituted for the oath of supremacy, and there were no offices
from which Roman Catholics were now excluded except those of
Regent, of Lord Chancellor of England and Ireland, and of
Viceroy of Ireland. By way of security, the franchise in Ireland
was raised from 40s. to 10l., and certain regulations were made
respecting the exercise of the Roman Catholic religion.

Caveat (*that he take heed*). A kind of process in law to
stop the enrolment of a decree in Chancery in order to present
a petition of appeal to the Lord Chancellor, which prevents the
enrolment for twenty-eight days. It is also entered to prevent the issuing of a lunacy commission, the probate of a will,
the licence of marriage, or an institution of a clerk to a benefice.

Central Criminal Court. This is the most important
criminal tribunal in our country. It was erected in 1834, and

---

* By 7 & 8 Vict. c. 96, s. 57, this writ cannot be issued on any judgment obtained in any of the superior or inferior courts, in any action
for the recovery of any debt under £20.

ordered to consist of the lord mayor, the lord chancellor, the judges of the three superior courts at Westminster, the judges in bankruptcy, the judges of the Admiralty, the dean of the Arches, the aldermen, recorder, and common serjeant of London, and the judges of the sheriffs' court. It tries all cases of treasons, murders, felonies, and misdemeanours committed within the city of London and county of Middlesex, and in certain specified parts of the counties of Essex, Kent, and Surrey. This court sits at the Old Bailey; and there are at least twelve sessions held every year. Several subsequent statutes have greatly augmented its jurisdiction. During every session two of the judges of the superior courts at Westminster preside here for the purpose of trying the more important offences. The remainder are tried by the recorder or common serjeant, or a judge from the sheriffs' court.

Certificate. A testimony given in writing to declare or verify the truth of anything. There are several sorts, the principal of which are :—

Certificates of acknowledgment of married women.

Annual certificate of an attorney.

Certificate of appointment of the creditors' assignees to a bankrupt's estate and effects.

Certificate of conformity of a bankrupt.

Certificates of counsel.

Certificates of the judges of the superior common law courts at Westminster.

Certificates in the customs, &c.

Certiorari, in law, a writ which issues out of Chancery, in civil cases, and the Crown side of the Queen's Bench in criminal cases, directed to the Judges or officers of an inferior court, to call up the records of a cause depending before them, in order that justice may be done. This writ is obtained upon complaint that the party who seeks it has received hard usage, or is not like to have an impartial trial in the inferior court.

Chamberlain. The Lord Chamberlain of Great Britain is the sixth high officer of the Crown, to whom belongs the government of the palace at Westminster, and upon all solemn occasions the keys of Westminster Hall and the Court of Requests are delivered to him; he disposes of the Sword of State to be carried before the Queen when she comes into Parliament; and he has the care of providing all things in the House of Lords during its sessions. He also has the power of licensing theatres, &c. The office is hereditary.

The *Lord Chamberlain of the Household* has the oversight and direction of all officers belonging to the Queen's chambers, except the precinct of the bedchamber.

The *Chamberlain of London* presides over the affairs of the citizens and their apprentices. He presents the freedom of the City to those deserving it, and keeps the City money.

Chancellor, Lord High, of Great Britain, is the highest honour of the long robe, being created by the mere delivery of the Queen's great seal into his custody; by which he becomes, *without writ or patent*, an officer of the greatest weight and power of any now subsisting in the kingdom. He is a privy counsellor by his office; a Cabinet Minister; and, according to Lord Chancellor Ellesmere, prolocutor of the House of Lords by prescription. To him belongs the appointment of all the justices of the peace throughout the kingdom. Being in former times commonly an ecclesiastic (for none else were then capable of an office so conversant in writing), and presiding over the royal chapel, he became keeper of the Sovereign's conscience; visitor, in right of the Crown, of all hospitals and colleges of the king's foundation; and patron of all the king's livings under the value of 20*l.* per annum in the king's books. He is the general guardian of all infants, idiots, and lunatics; and has the general superintendence of all charitable uses in the kingdom. And all this over and above the vast extensive jurisdiction which he exercises in his judicial capacity in the Court of Chancery. He takes precedence of every temporal lord except the royal family, and of all others except the Archbishop of Canterbury. He vacates his office with the ministry by which he was appointed. His retiring pension is 5000*l.* per annum. There is also a Lord High Chancellor of Ireland ; but the Chancellorship of Scotland was abolished at the Union.

Chancellor of a Cathedral, an officer who hears lessons and lectures read in the church, either by himself or his vicar. He corrects and sets right the reader when he reads amiss ; inspects schools ; hears causes ; applies the seal ; writes and despatches the letters of the chapter ; keeps the books ; takes care that there be frequent preachings, both in the church and out of it ; and assigns the office of preaching to whom he pleases.

Chancellor of the Duchy of Lancaster, an officer before whom the Duchy Court, or Chamber of Lancaster, is held. The court concerns only the lands holden of the Crown in right of the dukedom of Lancaster, and is quite distinct from the jurisdiction of the County Palatine. This jurisdiction comprises much property lying out of the *County* of Lancaster—in Yorkshire, Nottinghamshire, Leicestershire, Staffordshire, Essex, Herts, Northamptonshire, Monmouthshire, Derbyshire, and particularly a tract of land surrounded by Westminster (the Savoy, &c.). The proceedings of this court are the same as in the High Court of Chancery.

Chancellor of the Exchequer. A great officer, who sometimes sits with the barons of the exchequer in the exchequer chamber ; but his office, in fact, is rather with the practical management of the revenue. His name is still preserved in all bills of complaint, which are preferred to him and the barons of the exchequer on the equity side, where a jurisdiction is exercised similar to the chancery, in practice and effect ; but beyond his formal appearance on stated occasions, his judicial functions are scarcely ever called for. The Chief Baron, or other Barons, make orders, decrees, &c., although it was originally intended that the treasurer (whose office is in commission), Chancellor, and Barons should sit together.

Chancellor of the Order of the Garter, and other Military Orders, is an officer who seals the commissions and mandates of the chapter and assembly of the Knights, keeps the register of their proceedings, and delivers acts thereof under the seal of their order.

Chancellor of an University. An honorary office of great distinction. The Chancellor of Oxford is usually one of the chief nobility chosen by the students themselves in convocation. He is their chief magistrate ; his office is, *durante vitâ*, to govern the University, preserve and defend its rights and privileges, convoke assemblies, and do justice among the members under his jurisdiction. Under the Chancellor is the Vice-Chancellor, who is chosen annually, being nominated by the Chancellor, and elected by the University in convocation. He is always the head of some college, and in Holy Orders. His proper office is to execute the Chancellor's power to govern the University according to her statutes, to see that officers and students do their duty, that Courts be duly called, &c. When he enters upon his office, he chooses four pro-Vice-Chancellors out of the heads of the colleges, to execute his power in his absence. The Chancellor of Cambridge is also usually one of the chief nobility, and in most respects the same as that in Oxford ; only he does not hold his office *durante vitâ*, but may be elected every three years. Under the Chancellor there is a Commissary, who holds a Court of Record for all privileged persons and scholars under the degree of Master of Arts, where all causes are tried and determined by the civil and statute law, and by the custom of the University. The Vice-Chancellor of Cambridge is chosen annually by the Senate, out of two persons nominated by the heads of the several colleges and halls.

Chancellor's Courts. *See* UNIVERSITY COURTS.

Chancery, is the Court wherein the Lord Chancellor, or

Lord Keeper, exercises his jurisdiction, which is divided into what is termed the common law and the equitable jurisdiction. The *first* being that in which he is bound to observe the method of the common law, by issuing various writs returnable in other Courts, writs of *habeas corpus* and prohibition to inferior Courts, and taking cognizance of a variety of formular matters in respect of bankruptcy, letters patent, sureties of the peace against peers, &c. The *second* being the equitable jurisdiction, which is the most extensive, in which he proceeds by the rules of equity and good conscience, and moderates the rigour of the common law, considering rather the *intention* than the words of the law, equity being the correction of that wherein the law, by reason of its universality, is deficient. The Courts of Chancery are either superior or inferior. The superior is called the High Court of Chancery, consisting of the following tribunals, which rank in the order here placed :—

The Court of the Lord High Chancellor of Great Britain, whose name has given to these Courts their title.

The Court of the Master of the Rolls.

The Court of the two Lords Justices of Appeal (the Lord Chancellor together with these judges form the Court of Appeal in chancery).

And the separate Courts of the three Vice-Chancellors.

The inferior Courts of Chancery are :—

The Equity Courts of the Palatine counties of Durham and Lancaster.

The University Courts.

The Lord Mayor's Court in the City of London,

And the Court of Chancery in the Isle of Man.

Charter, in law, a written instrument, or evidence of things acted between one person and another. The word charter comes from the Latin *charta,* anciently used for a public and authentic act, a donation, contract, &c. Britton divides charters into those of the Sovereign, and those of private persons. 1. Charters of the Sovereign are those whereby the Sovereign passes any grant to any person or body politic, as a *charter of exemption* of privilege, &c.; *charter of pardon*, whereby a man is forgiven a felony, or other offence committed against the Crown ; *charter of the forest*, wherein the laws of the forest are comprised, such as the charter of Canutus, &c. 2. Charters of private persons, are deeds and instruments for the conveyance of lands, &c. And the purchaser of lands shall have all the charters, deeds, and evidences, as incident to the same, and for the maintenance of his title.

Charter-Land, such land as a person holds by charter ; that is, by evidence in writing, otherwise called freehold.

Charity Commission. An office instituted in 1853 to exercise control over property left in trust for various public charities in England and Wales. All proposed alterations, as well as sales or exchanges of Charity Lands, require the sanction of these Commissioners, who hold their offices independently of party changes.ˑ Hours 10 to 5, York Street, St. James's Square.

Chief Baron of the Exchequer. Is the presiding judge in the Court of Exchequer of Pleas at Westminster, with whom four *puisné* judges are associated for the administration of justice.

Chief Justice of the Common Pleas. Is the presiding judge in the Court of Common Pleas at Westminster. He has four *puisné* judges associated with him.

Chief Justice of England. Is the presiding judge in the Court of Queen's Bench at Westminster. He has four *puisné* judges associated with him.

Chiltern Hundreds. A Member of the House of Commons, not disqualified, can only vacate his seat by accepting the Stewardship of the Chiltern Hundreds, or some other nominal office, in the gift of the Chancellor of the Exchequer. The practice was instituted about 1750.

Church Discipline Act, 3 & 4 Vict. Enables the

bishop, when a clerk in holy orders is charged with any offence against the laws ecclesiastical, or there exists any scandal or evil report about him, to issue a commission to five persons, of whom one must be the vicar-general, or an archdeacon or rural dean of the diocese, to inquire into the said charge or report. Of the commission notice must be given to the person charged ; and it is to be conducted in public unless special application to the contrary is made. If the defendant admits the truth of the charge the bishop may at once pass sentence ; and if he denies the charge the bishop hears and determines the cause, and gives judgment according to ecclesiastical law. The bishop can send the case to be determined in the court of appeal of the province if he thinks fit.

Church-Rates. Rates assessed for the repairs of a parochial church by the parishioners in vestry assembled. The churchwardens are the persons who collect and levy this rate, and they are the persons whose duty it is, as ecclesiastical officers, to call the meeting, or vestry, to consider of the amount necessary. At this vestry, or meeting, the churchwardens are mere parishioners, they not being empowered to make the rate themselves ; but if they give notice of a vestry for that purpose, and if no other parishioners attend, they may alone, or with those who do attend (however few in number), make and assess the rate. The courts of law have no power to enforce the assessment of church-rates. They are recoverable in the Ecclesiastical Court, or if the arrears do not exceed £10, and no question is raised as to the legal liability, before two justices of the peace.

Churchwardens are persons appointed for the purpose of performing all acts requisite for the repairs, management, good order, and decency of behaviour in a church. The following description of persons are exempt from serving the office of churchwarden, viz. :—Aldermen, apothecaries, or members of the apothecaries' company by charter, attornies and solicitors, barristers, clergymen, clerks in court, dissenting teachers, militiamen, members of parliament, peers, physicians, prosecutors of felons, surgeons, magistrates, revenue officers, officers of the courts of law, captains of the guards, persons attendant on the Queen, officers in the army, navy, or marines, whether on full or half pay; and no person living out of the parish, although he has or occupies property within it, can lawfully be chosen churchwarden.

Cinque Ports. Five ports or havens that lie on the south-east coast of England, towards France, namely, Dover, Hastings, Hythe, Romney, and Sandwich, to which were afterwards added Winchelsea, Seaford, and Rye. They were distinguished from other ports, on account of their superior importance, in consequence of which they are governed by a *Lord Warden of the Cinque Ports*, and have divers privileges granted to them as a particular jurisdiction. All authority and jurisdiction of the Lord Warden has been lately abolished with regard to the administration of justice in actions or other civil proceedings at law or in equity.

Circuits are eight certain divisions of England and Wales appointed for the Common Law Judges, to go twice a year in the respective vacations after Hilary and Trinity Terms, to administer justice in the several counties. Two judges preside over each of the circuits, except those of North and South Wales, to each of which one judge is found sufficient.

Civil Law, is properly the peculiar law of each state, country, or city; but what we usually mean by the civil law, is a body of laws composed out of the best Roman and Grecian laws, compiled from the laws of nature and nations; and, for the most part, received and observed throughout all the Roman dominions for above 1200 years. It was first brought over into England by Theobold, a Norman abbot, elected to the see of Canterbury in 1138, who appointed a professor, Roger surnamed *Vicarius*, in the university of Oxford, to teach it to the people of this country. Nevertheless it gained ground very slowly.

King Stephen issued a proclamation, prohibiting its study; and though the clergy were attached to it, the laity rather wished to preserve the old constitution. However, the zeal and influence of the clergy prevailed; and the civil law acquired great reputation from the reign of King Stephen to the reign of Edward III., both inclusive. Many transcripts of Justinian's Institute are to be found in the writings of our ancient authors, particularly of Braeton and Fleta; and Blackstone observes, that the common law would have been lost and overrun by the civil, had it not been for the incident of fixing the Court of Common Pleas in one certain spot, and the forming the profession of the municipal law into an aggregate body. It is allowed that the civil law contains all the principles of natural equity; and that nothing can be better calculated to form good sense and sound judgment. Hence, though in several countries it has no other authority than that of reason and justice, it is everywhere referred to for authority. It is not received at this day in any nation without some alterations; and sometimes the feudal law is mixed with it, or general and particular customs; and often ordinances and statutes cut off a great part of it.

Civil List.—An annual sum granted by Parliament for the expenses of the royal household as distinguished from the general exigencies of the State. It is the provision made for the Crown out of the taxes instead of its proper patrimony, and in consideration of the assignment of that patrimony to the public use. This arrangement has prevailed from the time of the Revolution. At the commencement of the present reign a civil list was settled upon Her Majesty of £385,000 per annum; of which £60,000 is assigned for Her Majesty's Privy Purse. In return for which grant it was stipulated that the hereditary revenues of the Crown should form part of the Consolidated Fund, during the Queen's life. The Civil List is properly the whole of the Sovereign's revenue, in her own distinct capacity; and now

H

occupies the same place as the hereditary income did formerly. It is not chargeable with the public expenses of government. By the Civil List Act, the Queen is empowered to grant pensions to the amount of £1200, chargeable on her Civil List revenues, as a remuneration for those who, by their services, have merited the gratitude of their country.

Civil Service Commission.—A board instituted in 1855, by an Order in Council, to test by fixed rules the qualifications of candidates appointed to the junior situations in the Home Civil Service. No appointment is now valid unless the person nominated has received a certificate of fitness from the Commissioners. This office is composed of two commissioners, a secretary, registrar, and clerks. Hours 10 to 5, Westminster.

Clarendon, Constitutions of.—In the reign of Henry II., the power of the clergy, supported by Thomas à Becket, had reached its climax. Their authority, no longer defensive, became aggressive. A struggle ensued. On the one side were the Laws of England supported by the nobility, and on the other the Laws of Rome, advocated by the clergy. The result was the Constitutions of Clarendon, which were brought forward at a great council held at Clarendon, a village in Wiltshire, in the tenth year of the reign of Henry II., January 25, 1163-4. They are contained in sixteen articles, ten of which were solemnly condemned by Pope Alexander as hostile to the right of the clergy; and the other six he tolerated, not as good, but as less evil. These sixteen articles enact :—

I. All suits concerning advowsons to be determined in civil courts.

II. The clergy accused of any crime to be tried by civil judges.

III. No person of any rank whatever to be permitted to leave the realm without the royal licence.

IV. Laics not to be accused in spiritual courts except by legal and reputable promoters and witnesses.

V. No chief tenant of the Crown to be excommunicated, or his lands put under interdict.

VI. Revenues of vacant sees to belong to the king.

VII. Goods forfeited to the Crown not to be protected in churches.

VIII. Sons of villeins not to be ordained clerks without the consent of their lord.

IX. Bishops to be regarded as barons, and be subjected to the burthens belonging to that rank.

X. Churches belonging to the king's see not to be granted in perpetuity against his will.

XI. Excommunicated persons not to be bound to give security for continuing in their abode.

XII. No inhabitant in demesne to be excommunicated for non-appearance in a spiritual court.

XIII. If any tenant *in capite* should refuse submission to spiritual courts, the case to be referred to the king.

XIV. The clergy no longer to pretend to the right of enforcing debts contracted by oath or promise.

XV. Causes between laymen and ecclesiastics to be determined by a jury.

XVI. Appeals to be ultimately carried to the king, and no further, without his consent.

Clerk of the House of Commons.—An officer of great trust and importance, appointed by letters patent. It is his duty to make minutes of the decisions at which the House arrives ; to record its votes, resolutions, addresses, reports, &c., and to read aloud all such documents as the House may order to be read. He also performs the duty (without taking the chair) of president, or moderator, during the choice of a Speaker.

Close Rolls, or *Rotuli Litterarum Clausarum*, are a series of parchment rolls commencing with the sixth year of the reign of King John (1204), on which are recorded or enrolled all mandates, letters, and writs of a private nature. The entries on the Close Rolls are letters addressed in the, King's name to individuals for special purposes, and were *closed up* and sealed on the outside with the Great Seal. These Rolls are of infinite variety and importance. They illustrate the policy and history of foreign nations as well as our own in the thirteenth, fourteenth, and fifteenth centuries. They elucidate the laws, particular and general; the prerogatives of the Crown; the power and influence of the clergy and nobility, and the relative condition of the people, both morally and politically. Their historical value cannot be overrated. Among other entries, the early Close Rolls contain articles concerning the royal prerogative, Crown revenue, treasure trove, *donationes regis*, Magna Charta, royal marriages, jewels, tournaments, naval and military affairs, truces, &c. Concerning the Courts of Law are matters relating to politics and laws, the Chancellor of England, jurisdiction of the Courts of Chancery, King's Bench and Exchequer, appointments of Justices of the Peace, the Privy Council, and summons to the councils, &c. Under Ecclesiastical affairs are subjects of divorce, alimony, adultery, masses, papal bulls, &c. There are also various entries respecting repairs of palaces and other public buildings, the fine arts, pictures, costumes, &c. From the reign of Henry VII. to the present time, the Close Rolls appear to be limited to the enrolment of deeds and instruments, pursuant to statutes and the practice of the Courts, with other deeds enrolled for safe custody.

Cognovit, *see* WARRANTS OF ATTORNEY.

Collusion, is a deceitful agreement or contract between two or more persons, for the one to bring an action against the other to some evil purpose, so as to defraud a third person of his right, &c. This collusion is either apparent, when it shows itself on the face of the act, or, which is more common, it is secret, when done in the dark, or covered over with a show of honesty. It is a thing the law abhors; therefore, when found, it makes all things void dependent upon the same, though otherwise in themselves good.

Colony.—The formation of colonies is among the earliest events of which any historical record exists. The Phœnicians and the Carians planted several colonies in the Mediterranean, and the Greeks followed their example. The Romans began to establish colonies during the monarchical period. In modern times, the Venetians, the Portuguese, the Spanish, the French, the English, and the Dutch, have been distinguished by their attempts to form colonies. In this respect England has distanced all competitors, having succeeded in establishing the most extensive colonial empire of ancient or modern times. The following is a list of the British colonies, with the date of their settlement, capture, &c. :—

	A. D.
African Forts—Settled in	1618
Anguilla „	1650
Antigua „	1632
Ascension Island—Granted by Spain	1827
Australia, South—Settled	1834
„ West „	1829
Bahamas „	1629
Barbadoes „	1625
Barbuda—Settled	1628
Berbice—Capitulated	Sept. 1803
Bermudas—Settled	1609
British Columbia—Settled	1858
British Guiana—Capitulated	Sept. 1803
Canada, Lower „	Sept. 18, 1759
„ Upper „	Sept. 8, 1760
Cape Breton Island—Settled	1584
Cape Coast Castle—Ceded by the Dutch	1672
Cape of Good Hope—Capitulated	Jan. 10, 1806
Ceylon—Capitulated	Sept. 17, 1795

A.D.

Demerara   „   .   .   .   .   Sept. 1803
Dominica—Ceded by France 1763
Essequibo—Capitulated   .   .   .   Sept. 1803
Falkland Islands—Settled   .   .   .   1833
Gambia—Settled   1631
Gibraltar—Capitulated .   .   .   Aug. 4, 1704
Gold Coast—Settled 1661
      Do.   (Danish)—Ceded   1850
Gozo—Capitulated   .   .   .   .   Sept. 1800
Grenada—Ceded by France 1763
Heligoland—Ceded   1807
Honduras—Ceded 1670
Hongkong   „   1842
Jamaica—Capitulated   1655
Lagos—Ceded   1861
Malacca—Received from the Dutch in exchange
      for Sumatra .   .   .   .   April 9, 1825
Malta—Capitulated   .   .   .   Sept. 1800
Mauritius   „   .   .   .   . Dec. 3, 1810
Montserrat—Settled   1632
Natal—Settled 1824
Nevis—Settled   1628
New Brunswick—Settled   1622
Newfoundland—Settled 1608
New South Wales—Settled   1788
New Zealand   „   1839
Nova Scotia—Settled 1622
Prince Edward's Island—Taken from the French 1758
Prince of Wales Island—Purchased by the East-
      India Company 1786
Queensland, N. S. Wales—Settled   .   . . 1860
South Australia—Settled   1836
West Australia   „   1829

A. D.

Sierra Leone—Settled 1787

„ Transferred to Government . 1807

Singapore—Treaty . . . . Feb. 26, 1819

St. Helena—Taken from the Dutch . . . 1673

„ Transferred to Government . . 1836

St. Christopher's, or Kitt's—Settled . . . 1623

St. Lucia—Capitulated . . . June 22, 1803

St. Vincent—Ceded by France 1763

Tobago—Ceded by France 1763

Tortola—Settled 1666

Trinidad—Capitulated . . . Feb. 18, 1797

Vancouver—Settled 1848

Van Diemen's Land—Settled 1804

Victoria, *see* Hongkong.

Victoria—Settled 1836

„ Erected into a separate colony . . 1836

Virgin Islands 1666

Colonial Office.—In 1660, Charles II. established a Colonial Office, under the title of the " Council of Foreign Plantations," but it was abolished in 1675. Commissioners of Trade were again instituted by William III.; but the first Secretary of State for the Colonies was not appointed till 1768. Subsequently, this office was suppressed, and its duties transferred to the Home Department. In 1794 a third Secretary of State was created for the department of War, and in 1801 the management of all colonial affairs was transferred to him. The duties of this secretary are now entirely confined to colonial matters, and consist in exercising a watchful supervision of the interests of our colonies, in administering their laws and customs, in appointing their governors, and in directing their government. The Secretary of State for the Colonies is assisted in the discharge of his duties by two under-secretaries and other officials. Hours, 11 to 5. Downing Street.

Common Law.—An ancient collection of unwritten maxims and customs of British, Saxon, and Danish origin, which has subsisted immemorially in this kingdom. It includes those principles and rules of action applicable to the government and security of person and property which do not rest for their authority upon any express declaration of the will of the legislature. The common law is divided into three kinds :—1. General customs, or those applicable to and governing the whole kingdom, comprehending the law of nations and the law merchant ; 2. Particular customs affecting the inhabitants of particular districts ; 3. The civil and canon laws, *i.e.*, the ecclesiastical military, maritime, and academical laws.

Common Pleas, Court of.—One of the three Superior Courts of common law at Westminster, presided over by a Lord Chief Justice and four *puisné* judges. All controversies between subject and subject according to law are here debated. Real actions are pleaded here, and this court may grant prohibitions. Its jurisdiction is altogether confined to civil matters, having no cognisance in criminal cases. It was the ancient *Aula Regia*.

Commons, House of, *see* PARLIAMENT.

Conscience, Courts of.—Tribunals for the recovery of small debts in the City of London and other towns. The County Courts have generally superseded them.

Consistory Court.—A court of every diocesan bishop, held in his cathedral, for the trial of all ecclesiastical causes arising within his diocese. The bishop's chancellor is the judge, and from his sentence an appeal lies to the archbishop of each province respectively.

Consolidated Fund.—A repository of public money, now comprising the produce of customs, excise, stamps, and several other taxes. It constitutes almost the whole of the public income of the United Kingdom of Great Britain and Ireland.

This fund is pledged for the payment of the whole of the interest of the national debt. It is liable to several specific charges imposed upon it, such as the Civil List, the salaries of the judges and ambassadors, &c.

Conspiracy.—The term used for an unlawful confederacy to prejudice a third person. Formerly, and in its strict legal sense, it was used for an agreement of two or more falsely to prosecute another for felony, which is a crime not very frequent now. There must be two at least to form a conspiracy. Combinations or confederacies, which are entered into for the purpose of wronging third persons, are of various natures, and, consequently, these offences bear different shades of guilt; but, ordinarily speaking, all conspiracies, combinations, and confederacies are misdemeanors, punishable by fine and imprisonment.

Constable, or petty constable as he is termed, to distinguish him from the high constable or bailiff of a hundred or other district, is a very ancient officer, appointed in every village or township throughout the kingdom for the purpose of keeping the peace, or more practically speaking for the purpose of taking into custody those who commit breaches of the peace or more serious offences. The office of a constable is chiefly to obey the warrants and precepts of the justices of the county, or those who *back* any warrant to be executed by him in the limit of his power, within the village, township, or parish, or other place for which he is chosen or appointed. Special constables are appointed on particular occasions.

Constable, Lord High, *see* LORD HIGH CONSTABLE.

Consul.—An officer appointed by government to reside in foreign countries for the purpose of extending and facilitating commerce and communication between the two countries. Also, merchants or other persons appointed by foreign princes to reside here for the same purpose. The duties of British consuls abroad and their fees are regulated by the statute

6 Geo. IV. c. 87, s. 20. A foreign consul resident here is not protected from arrest as an ambassador's servant.

Control, Board of, *see* BOARD OF.

Conventicle Act.—An Act passed in 1664, which enacted that wherever five persons above those of the same household should assemble in a religious congregation, every one of them was liable for the first offence to be imprisoned three months, or pay £5; for the second offence, six months, or pay a fine of £10; and for the third offence, transportation for seven years, or pay a fine of £100. It was repealed by 52 Geo. III. c. 155.

Convocation, an assembly of the clergy of England, by their representatives, for the consultation of ecclesiastical matters. It is held during the session of parliament, and consists of an Upper and a Lower House. In the Upper sit the bishops, and in the Lower the inferior clergy, who are represented by their proctors; consisting of all the deans and archdeacons, of one proctor for every chapter, and two for the clergy of every diocese. The Lower House chooses its prolocutor; whose business it is to take care that the members attend, to collect their debates and votes, and to carry their resolutions to the Upper House. The convocation is summoned by the Queen's writ, directed to the archbishop of each province, requiring him to summon all bishops, deans, archdeacons, &c.

The power of the convocation is limited by a statute of Henry VIII. They are not to make any canons or ecclesiastical laws without the king's licence; nor, when permitted to make any, can they put them in execution, but under several restrictions. They have the examining and censuring of all heretical and schismatical books and persons, &c., but from its judicial proceedings there lies an appeal to the Sovereign in Council. The clergy in convocation, and their servants, have the same privileges as members of parliament. Since the year 1665, when the convocation of the clergy gave up the privilege of taxing themselves to the House of Commons, they seldom have been allowed to do any business. Convocation by express licence from the Sovereign may legislate by making canons. However, except in one instance in 1861, it has long ceased to exercise any legislative power.

Copyhold Inclosure and Tithe Commission.— In the year 1851 the Tithe, Copyhold, Inclosure and Drainage Commissioners were all merged into one department. This office facilitates the inclosure of all waste lands not within a prescribed distance of any city or town ; it assists towards the commutation of tithes, and of any rent fines payable to lords of the manor. It regulates also the advancement of public money for the improvement of land by drainage. The commissioners, of which there are three, hold their offices independently of party changes. Hours 10 to 4. St. James' Square.

Copyhold.—A tenure of lands in England, for which the tenant or owner has nothing to show but the copy of the rolls made by the steward who holds the lord's court, which rolls contain special entries and memoranda of the admission of a tenant, his surrender to the use of another, or alienation, his death, and the claim and admission of the heir or devisee. There are two sorts of copyhold. The first, which is styled ancient demesne, or a customary freehold, subject only to a very small quit-rent, and an occasional nominal heriot. The second, a base tenure or mere copyhold, holden, as the copy says, "at the will of the lord," and subject to a two years' value as a fine on death, or alienation, or heriot, and a yearly quit-rent superadded. The " will of the lord" is now practically a nullity, it being qualified by " the custom of the manor."

The statute 21 & 22 Vict. c. 94, has tended greatly to diminish various grievances, and to facilitate enfranchisement with regard to this tenure. A copyhold commission, consisting of three commissioners, has been instituted to carry out the provisions of this act.

Copyright.—Is the exclusive privilege allowed by law to

an author, of printing, selling, and publishing his own original work. The 5 & 6 Vict. c. 45, provides that the copyright of every book which shall be published in the life time of its author, shall endure for his natural life and for seven years longer; or if the seven years expire before the end of forty-two years from the first publication, it shall endure for such period of forty-two years. When the work is posthumous, the copyright shall endure for forty-two years from the first publication, and shall belong to the proprietor of the author's manuscript. The title of the work must be entered at Stationers' Hall.

Corn Laws.—The earliest enactments on this subject were to forbid the exportation of corn, while its importation was freely admitted; but in later times the policy of the legislature was altogether different. The first statute extant on corn is in 1360, which forbids its exportation, except to certain places where it was necessary to the king's interest, and to be named by him. At a later period, in the reigns of Richard II. and Henry VI., this policy was reversed, and liberty given to export to any places; agriculture seems to have much declined in England towards the end of the reign of Henry VIII. and in that of Edward VI., which was probably owing to the great change of property consequent on the dissolution of the abbeys and religious houses. Thus the statute 25 Henry VIII., c. 2, positively forbids the exportation of corn; and the statute 5 and 6 Edw. VI., c. 5, entitled "An Act for the Maintenance and Increase of Tillage and Corn," attempted to make the cultivation of corn compulsory, by exacting a fine of 5s., payable by each parish on every acre of land in each deficient in tillage when compared with the quantity that had been tilled at any period after the accession of Henry VIII.

The act of Henry VIII., forbidding the exportation of corn, was repealed in the reign of Mary; but the price at which exportation was allowed was gradually raised, till, in 1670, it was enacted that wheat might always be exported as long as it was under 53s. 4d. a quarter. At the same time heavy import duties were imposed ; and the design of the legislature seems to have been to keep wheat at an average of about 53s. 4d. Regulations were also made respecting the home-trade in corn ; and in the reign of Elizabeth it was made an offence to buy corn in one market and sell it in another. By a bill passed in 1773 importation was allowed at the nominal duty of 6d. whenever the price of wheat should be above 48s. Subsequently, in 1791 and 1804, this price was raised to 54s. and 63s. ; and in 1815 the importation of wheat for home consumption was positively forbidden when the price was under 80s., and other corn in proportion. Various modifications were introduced between that time and 1829, when the principle of a graduated duty or sliding scale was introduced ; the duty, when the price was 62s., being 24s. 8d., and gradually diminishing as the price advanced, till at 73s. and upwards it fell to 1s. The operation of this principle, however, was found to be inconvenient and unsalutary ; and at length, by Peel's bill of 1846, the trade in corn was ultimately left entirely free.

Coroner.—An ancient officer, whose duty is chiefly to make inquiry or inquisition upon violent or unnatural deaths, to perform certain acts relating to the execution of process when the sheriff is a party, and to inquire concerning shipwrecks and treasure trove. Coroners are chosen by the freeholders of a county in a full county court, summoned by the sheriff, who is the judge, upon receipt of the Sovereign's writ for that purpose. There are usually four or six appointed for every county in England. By 7 & 8 Vict. c. 92, coroners may be appointed for districts within counties, instead of the county at large. The Crown and certain lords of franchises may appoint coroners for certain precincts by their own grant and without election. The coroner, when elected, is chosen for life, or during good behaviour, or till incapacity : he is generally

a man of substance and repute, and very often a lawyer by profession, the office requiring adequate legal information.

Corporations, Municipal.—Bodies politic, authorised
by the Queen's charter, to have a common seal, one head officer
or more, and members, who are able to grant or receive in law
any matter within the compass of their charter.

The *Corporation Act* was passed in 1661. In it a religious
test was combined with a political test. All corporate officers
were required to have taken the Sacrament of the Lord's
Supper, "according to the rites of the Church of England,"
within one year before their elections, and, upon being elected,
to take the oaths of allegiance and of supremacy. Repealed by
9 Geo. IV. c. 17.

Council of India.—*See* INDIA COUNCIL.

County Courts.—Instituted in 1846 for the recovery of
debts under £20, superseding courts of requests. The counties
of England and Wales are divided into sixty districts, each dis-
triot having a County Court, and a barrister as judge, and juries
sworn when necessary. In 1850 their jurisdiction was extended
to sums not exceeding £50, and their proceedings were facilitated in 1852 and 1854. An Act was passed in 1865 conferring
on these Courts equity powers in cases relating to sums under
£500, like those of the Court of Chancery.

Court Baron.—A Court incident to every manor, ordained for the maintenance of the services and duties stipulated
for by lords of manors, and for determining actions of a personal nature when the debt or damage is under forty shillings.
It cannot fine or imprison.

Courts of Equity are the Courts of the Lord Chancellor, the Vice-Chancellors, and the Master of the Rolls. Their
office is to correct the operations of the literal text of the law,
and supply its defects by reasonable construction not admissible
in a Court of law.

Court of Honour.—A Court of chivalry, in which the

Lord High Constable was a judge. It was called *Curia Militaris* in the time of Henry IV.

Court Leet.—A Court belonging to a hundred, for punishing nuisances, false weights, and offences against the Crown. The steward is the judge, and all persons residing within the hundred (peers and clergymen excepted) are obliged to do suit within this Court.

Court of Quarter Sessions.—A Court held in every county once in every quarter of a year, whose jurisdiction is over the smaller felonies and misdemeanours, and certain matters more of a civil than criminal nature. The custody of its rolls is entrusted to a special officer called *custos rotulorum.*

Courts of Requests (also called COURT OF CONSCIENCE). —First instituted in 1493 for the recovery of small debts ; they were superseded in 1847 by the County Courts, with the exception of those of the City of London.

Cruelty to Animals.—By the Act 24 & 25, Vict. c. 97, the unlawful and malicious killing, maiming or wounding of cattle is felony. It is punishable by penal servitude for a term not exceeding fourteen years, and not less than three, or by imprisonment for any term not exceeding two years, with or without hard labour or solitary confinement.

Curfew.—A Norman institution, introduced by William the Conqueror. On the ringing of the curfew at eight o'clock in the evening all fires and candles were to be extinguished under a severe penalty. It was abolished in 1100.

Custom-House.—The house or office where exports and imports are entered, and where the duties, drawbacks, and bounties payable or receivable, are settled ; and where ships are, as it is termed, *cleared out.* The principal office is in Thames Street, near the Tower, London. There are minor or subordinate custom-houses in seaport towns. The Board of Customs consists of six Commissioners, and a large working staff of clerks. Hours ten to four, but in some departments nine to six.

Customs are duties charged on commodities export or import. The Customs are regulated by various Acts, in which specific directions are given for the entry, discharging, and shipping of all goods, inwards and outwards, with certain probibitions and restrictions as to the import and export of certain goods ; also for regulating the coasting trade, which term designates all trade by sea from any one part of the United Kingdom to any other part thereof. In 1853 the several acts then in force for the management of the Customs were consilidated.

Custos Rotulorum (the Keeper of the Rolls). Is the principal justice of the peace within the county, but he is rather an officer than a judge.

Danegelt.—An annual tax laid on the Anglo-Saxons, first of 1s. afterwards 2s. for every hide of land through the realm, for maintaining such a number of forces as were thought sufficient to clear the British seas of Danish pirates, which in early times greatly annoyed our coasts. Danegelt was first imposed as a standing yearly tax on the whole nation, under King Ethelred, A.D. 991. That prince, much distressed by the continual invasions of the Danes, to procure a peace, was compelled to charge his people with heavy taxes, called *danegelt.* At first he paid £10,000, then £16,000, then £24,000, after that £36,000, and lastly, £48,000. Edward the Confessor remitted this tax : William I. and II. reassumed it occasionally. In the reign of Henry I. it was accounted among the king's standing revenues ; but King Stephen, on his coronation-day, abolished it for ever. No church or church-land paid a penny to the *danegelt;* because, as it is set forth in an ancient Saxon law, the people of England placed more confidence in the prayers of the church than in any military defence they could make.

Deacon.—A minister in the church, whose office is to assist the priest in divine service. He may perform any of the divine offices except pronouncing the absolution and consecrating the Holy Eucharist. No one can be ordained deacon under twenty-

three years of age, except specially admitted by the Archbishop
of Canterbury. A deacon is not capable of any ecclesiastical
promotion; but he may be chaplain to a family, curate to a
beneficed clergyman, or lecturer to a parish church.

Dean.—An ecclesiastical dignitary. Deans are of six kinds.
Deans of Chapters, who are either of cathedral or collegiate
churches. *Deans of Peculiars,* who have sometimes both jurisdiction and cure of souls, and sometimes jurisdiction only.
Rural Deans, who are deputies of the bishop to inspect the conduct of the parochial clergy, to examine candidates for confirmation, &c., and who are endowed with an inferior degree of judicial authority. *Deans in the Colleges of our Universities,* who are
officers appointed to superintend the behaviour of the members
and to enforce discipline. *Honorary Deans,* as the Dean of the
Chapel Royal St. James's, &c. ; and *Deans of Provinces,* thus the
Bishop of London is Dean of the province of Canterbury.

The statute 3 & 4 Vict. c. 113, provides that the old deaneries,
except in Wales, shall henceforth be in the direct patronage of
the Queen ; and no person shall be capable of becoming dean,
archdeacon, or canon, until he has been six years in priest's
orders. A dean must reside at least eight months in the year.

Declaration of Right.—*See* BILL OF RIGHTS.

Deed is the general term applied to a contract under seal,
and has its essence by sealing, signing, and delivery ; which last
is the manual or constructive giving it to the party, with or to
whom the deed is made, and is generally presumed to be done
where other essentials concur. Deeds are of various natures :
deeds of lease, assignment, covenant, settlement, &c. A deed
must be written on parchment or paper duly stamped, and
must not be interlined or altered *after* the delivery. Some
deeds are required to be enrolled at length, as deeds of bargain
and sale ; some only should have a *memorial, i.e.,* a memorandum, containing the date, parties, and land or property
conveyed, enrolled.

Defamation.—*See* LIBEL.

Defendant.—Is the person sued in a personal action or suit, or indicted for a misdemeanour. He who is sued in a real action is called the tenant; the former term is, however, the one most commonly used.

Defender of the Faith (*Fidei Defensor*), a peculiar title belonging to the king of England, first conferred by Leo X. on King Henry VIII. for writing against Martin Luther; it was afterwards confirmed by Clement VII. On Henry's suppressing the houses of religion at the time of the Reformation, the Pope not only deprived him of his title, but deposed him from his crown also; though in the thirty-fifth year of his reign, his title, &c., was confirmed by Parliament, and has continued to be used by all succeeding kings to the present time. Chamberlayne says, the title belonged to the kings of England before that time, and for proof of which appeals to several charters granted to the University of Oxford.

Delegates, High Court of.—Was formerly the great court of appeal in all ecclesiastical causes. These delegates were appointed by the king's commission under his great seal, issuing out of Chancery, to represent his royal person, and hear all appeals to him made by virtue of the statute 25 Henry VIII. c. 19. This commission was usually filled by lords spiritual and temporal, judges of the courts at Westminster, and doctors of the civil law. Appeals to Rome were always looked upon by the English nation, even in the times of Popery, with an evil eye, as being contrary to the liberty of the subject and the independence of the whole realm; and were first introduced in very turbulent times, in the sixteenth year of King Stephen (A.D. 1151), at the same period that the civil and canon laws were first imported into England. But in a few years after, to obviate this growing practice, the constitutions made at Clarendon expressly declare, that appeals in causes ecclesiastical ought to lie from the archdeacon to the diocesan; from the diocesan to the archbishop of the province; and from the archbishop to the king; and are not to proceed any farther without special license from the crown. The advantage however that was given in the reign of King John, and his son Henry III. to the encroaching power of the Pope, who was ever desirous of improving all opportunities of extending his jurisdiction to Britain, at length riveted the custom of appealing to Rome in causes ecclesiastical so strongly, that it never could be thoroughly broken off, till the grand rupture happened in the reign of Henry VIII., when all the jurisdiction usurped by the Pope in matters ecclesiastical was restored to the crown, to which it originally belonged. This court was afterwards abolished, and the Judicial Committee of the Privy Council constituted the Court of Appeal in ecclesiastical causes.

Demain, or *Demesne*, in law, is commonly understood to be the lord's chief manor-place, with the lands thereto belonging, which he and his ancestors have, time out of mind, kept in their own manual occupation.

Demurrage, in commerce, an allowance made to the master of a ship by the merchants, for staying in a port longer than the time first appointed for his departure. The claim for demurrage ceases as soon as the ship is cleared out and ready for sailing, even if she be detained by tempestuous weather.

Demurrer, in law, a stop put to any action upon some point of difficulty which must be determined by the court before any further proceedings can be had in the suit.

Denizen, in law, an alien made a subject by letters-patent; or who has acquired the privileges of a natural born subject pursuant to 7 & 8 Vict. c. 66. A denizen is in a kind of middle state between an alien and a natural born subject, and partakes of both of them. He may take lands by purchase or devise, which an alien may not; but cannot take by inheritance; for his parent, through whom he must claim, being an alien, had no inheritable blood, and therefore could convey none to the son; and, upon a like defect of blood, the issue of a denizen born before denization cannot inherit to him; but his issue born after may. A denizen is not excused from paying the alien's duty, and some other mercantile burdens. No denizen can be of the Privy Council, or either House of Parliament, or have any office of trust, civil or military, or be capable of any grant of lands, &c., from the crown.

Deodand.—Any personal chattel which was forfeited by "moving to the death" of a person. In strictness, if the thing which kills was in motion, not only that part which gave the wound (as the wheel which runs over a man's body and kills him), but all things which moved with it and helped to make the load more dangerous (as the cart and loading, which increase the pressure of the wheel) were forfeited. Where a thing not in motion was the occasion of a man's death, as if a man fell from a cart wheel, the thing alone, *i.e.*, wheel, was forfeited. The deodand, viz., the produce of the sale, generally belonged or was forfeited to the Crown, but, by prescription or custom, it might belong to the lord of a manor or franchise; in either case it was, by ancient law, to be laid out in *pious*, *i.e.*, charitable, uses, not for superstitious or even religious purposes. This forfeiture was abolished by 9 & 10 Vict. c. 62.

Deponent.—A person who makes an affidavit; a witness; one who gives his testimony in a court of justice.

Deposition, in law, the testimony given in court by a witness upon oath. It is also used for the sequestering or depriving a person of his dignity and office.

Deprivation, in the common law, the act of bereaving, divesting, or taking away a spiritual promotion or dignity: as when a bishop, vicar, prebend, or the like, is deposed or deprived of his preferment, for some matter, or fault, in fact, or in law. Deprivation is of two kinds : *a beneficio, et ab officio.*

Deprivation *a beneficio* is, when for some great crime a minister is wholly and for ever deprived of his living or preferment: which differs from suspension, in that the latter is only temporary.

Deprivation *ab officio*, is when a minister is for ever deprived of his order: which is the same, in reality, with what we otherwise call *deposition* and *degradation;* and is usually for some heinous crime, and is performed by the bishop in a solemn manner.

Detinue, in law, a writ or action that lies against one who has goods or other things delivered to him to keep, and afterwards refuses to deliver them. In this action, the thing detained is generally to be recovered, and not damages; but if one cannot recover the thing itself, damages may be recovered for the thing, and also for the detainer. Detinue lies for any thing certain and valuable, wherein one may have a property or right; as for a horse, cow, sheep, hens, dogs, jewels, plate, cloth, bags of money, sacks of corn, &c.

Diocese.—The circuit of every bishop's jurisdiction; it is divided into archdeaconries, each archdeaconry into rural deaneries, and rural deaneries into parishes. A table of the English and Welsh dioceses and their jurisdictions is subjoined.

	Diocese.	Jurisdiction.
PROVINCE OF CANTERBURY.	Canterbury (Archdiocese).	All Kent (except the city of Rochester and deanery of the same), the parishes of Addington and Croydon, together with the district of Lambeth Palace, in the county of Surrey.
	Bath and Wells	Nearly the whole of the county of Somerset.
	Chichester	The whole county of Sussex.
	Ely	Nearly the whole of Cambridgeshire, Huntingdonshire, and Bedfordshire, and part of Norfolk and Suffolk, adjacent to Cambridgeshire.
	Exeter	Cornwall and Devonshire, and the Scilly Islands.

Diocese.	Jurisdiction.
Gloucester and Bristol	Gloucestershire and city of Bristol, a part of Wiltshire adjacent to Gloucestershire, and the parish of Bedminster.
Hereford . . .	Herefordshire and parts of Salop, Monmouth, Radnor and Worcester shires.
Lichfield . . .	Staffordshire, and the greatest part of Derby shire, Warwickshire, and Salop.
Lincoln . . .	Lincoln and Nottingham shires.
London . . .	London, Middlesex, and parishes in counties of Surrey, Essex, and Kent, about ten miles round London.
Norwich . . .	All Norfolk and Suffolk, with the exception of the Archdeaconry of Sudbury.
Oxford . . .	Oxfordshire, Buckinghamshire, Berkshire, and parts of Wiltshire.
Peterborough . .	Northampton, Rutland, and Leicester shires.
Rochester . . .	The deanery and city of Rochester in Kent; Hertfordshire and Essex, except the parishes in the latter within eight or ten miles of London.
Salisbury . . :	All Dorsetshire ; the parishes of Holwell (Somerset) and Thornecomb (Devon); and parts of Wiltshire and Berkshire.
Winchester . .	Surrey (except certain parishes near London), Hants, Guernsey, and Jersey.
Worcester. . .	Nearly all Worcestershire, the archdeaconry of Coventry, and parts of Staffordshire and Gloucestershire.
St. Asaph . .	The whole counties of Flint and Denbigh, and parts of the counties of Salop, and Montgomery.
Bangor . .	The whole counties of Anglesea, Carnarvon, and Merioneth, and part of Montgomery.
Llandaff . .	The counties of Glamorgan and Monmouth.
Saint David's .	Parts of Caermarthenshire, Pembrokeshire, Brecknockshire, Radnorshire, Cardiganshire, Montgomeryshire, and Herefordshire.
York (Archdiocese) .	All the county of York not in the diocese of Ripon.
Durham . . .	The counties of Durham, Northumberland, and the district called Hexhamshire.
Carlisle . . .	The counties of Cumberland and Westmoreland, and the deaneries of Furness and Cartmel in Lancashire.
Chester . . .	The county of Cheshire, with the archdeaconry of Liverpool.
Manchester . .	Almost the whole of Lancashire.
Ripon . . .	The greater part of the West Riding of Yorkshire.
Sodor and Man . .	The Isle of Man.

THE PROVINCE OF CANTERBURY.

WALES.

PROVINCE OF YORK.

Divorce.—Divorces are of two kinds, namely, *à mensâ et thoro* (from bed and board), and *à vinculo matrimonii* (from the bond of marriage). A divorce from bed and board does not dissolve the marriage ; for the cause of it is subsequent to the marriage, and supposes the marriage to be lawful : this divorce may be by reason of adultery in either of the parties, for cruelty of the husband, &c. And as it does not dissolve the marriage, so it does not debar the woman of her dower, or bastardise the issue, or make void any estate for the life of husband and wife. A divorce from the bond of marriage, absolutely dissolves the marriage, and makes it void from the beginning, the causes of it being *precedent* to the marriage, as precontract with some other person, consanguinity or affinity within the Levitical degrees, &c. This divorce enables the parties to marry again ; but this is not the case with respect to a divorce from bed and board only. By 20 & 21 Vict. c. 85, the Court for Divorce and Matrimonial Causes has been established, abolishing the power of the ecclesiastical court in these matters. This court is presided over by three judges, the judge of the Probate Court being one. Various recent acts have amended and extended its jurisdiction.

Doctors' Commons.—Soon after the accession of Henry VIII., in 1509, some civilians privileged to plead in the Court of Arches formed a plan of association, by which they were to occupy contiguous houses and board in common. The spot first selected by them is not recorded ; but in February, 1568, Dr. Henry Hervie procured a lease of Montjoy House and other tenements, which he devoted to the accommodation of the advocates, and which received the title of Doctors' Commons. The original edifice was destroyed in 1666 by the great fire of London. The courts were held in Essex House, Strand, until the college was rebuilt in 1672. They were incorporated in June, 1768, as " The College of Doctors of Law, exercent in the Ecclesiastical and Admiralty Courts." Doctors'

Commons consisted of five courts; viz., the Court of Arches, the Prerogative Court, the Court of Faculties or Dispensations, the Consistory Court, and the High Court of Admiralty. The new courts of Divorce and Matrimonial Causes and of Probate came into operation in January, 1858.

Domesday, or Doomsday, Book, a most ancient record, made in the time of William I., containing a survey of all the lands of England. It consists of two volumes, a greater and a less. The first is a large folio, written on 382 double pages of vellum, in a small but plain character; each page having a double column. Some of the capital letters and principal passages are touched with red ink; and the names of towns, manors, &c., have strokes of red ink run across them, apparently for the purpose of catching the eye. This volume contains the description of 31 counties. The other volume is in quarto, written upon 450 double pages of vellum, but in a single column, and in a large but very fair character. It contains the counties of Essex, Norfolk, Suffolk, part of the county of Rutland included in that of Northampton, and part of Lancashire in the counties of York and Chester. This work, according to the red book in the Exchequer, was begun by order of William the Conqueror, with the advice of his Parliament, in the year of our Lord 1080, and completed in the year 1086. The reason given for taking this survey, as assigned by several ancient records and historians, was, that every man should be satisfied with his own right, and not usurp with impunity what belonged to another. But, besides this, it is said by others, that now all those who possessed landed estates became vassals to the king, and paid him so much money by way of fee or homage in proportion to the lands they held. This appears very probable, as there was at that time extant a general survey of the whole kingdom, made by order of King Alfred.

For the execution of the survey recorded in Domesday Book, commissioners were sent into every county and shire; and juries summoned in each hundred, out of all orders of freemen, from barons down to the lowest farmers. These commissioners were to be informed by the inhabitants, upon oath, of the name of each manor, and that of its owner; also by whom it was held in the time of Edward the Confessor; the number of hides; the quantity of wood, of pasture, and of meadow-land; how many ploughs were in the demesne, and how many in the tenanted part of it; how many mills, how many fish-ponds or fisheries belonged to it; with the value of the whole together in the time of King Edward, as well as when granted by King William, and at the time of this survey; also whether it was capable of improvement, or of being advanced in its value; they were likewise directed to return the tenants of every degree, the quantity of lands then and formerly held by each of them, what was the number of villains or slaves, and also the number and kinds of their cattle and live stock. These inquisitions being first methodised in the county, were afterwards sent up to the King's Exchequer. So minute was the survey that the writer of the contemporary portion of the Saxon chronicle records; "So very narrowly he caused it to be traced out, that there was not a single hide, nor one virgate of land, nor even an ox, or a cow, nor a swine was left that was not set down."

For some reason left unexplained, many parts of England were unsurveyed. Northumberland, Cumberland, Westmoreland, and Durham are not described in the survey. Lancashire does not appear under its proper name: but Furness and the northern part of the county, as well as the south of Westmoreland, with a part of Cumberland, are included within the West Riding of Yorkshire. That part of Lancashire which lies between the Ribble and Mersey is subjoined to Cheshire; and part of Rutlandshire is described in the counties of Northampton and Lincoln.

The authority of Domesday Book is never permitted to be called in question; and always, when it has been necessary to distinguish whether lands were held in ancient demesne, or in any other manner, recourse has been had to Domesday Book, and to that only, to determine the doubt. From this definitive authority, from which, as from the sentence pronounced at *domesday*, or the day of judgment, there could be no appeal, the name of the book is said to have been derived. But Stowe assigns another reason for this appellation, namely, that Domesday Book is a corruption of *domus Dei book*, a title given it because heretofore deposited in the King's treasury, in a place of the church of Westminster or Winchester, called *domus Dei*.

Domesday Book is now preserved in Her Majesty's Record Office.

Dower, is a third part or other customary share of such lands of inheritance whereof the husband was owner during the marriage, which the wife is to enjoy during her life, unless she acknowledges a deed parting with this right, which attaches on all land not conveyed to the husband in a special manner, for the purpose of barring this right, or where the wife has not released it before marriage in consideration of a jointure or other provision, whether he sold it during the marriage or not. But women married after the 1st of January, 1834, cannot claim dower out of land disposed of by their husbands in their lifetime, or by their will. Again, any partial incumbrances effected by their husbands are good against dower. Husbands also may defeat their wives' dower by any prospective instrument during the marriage, or by will; so that in the marriages taking place on or after the 1st of January, 1834, this estate will not so frequently attach.—*See* HUSBAND AND WIFE.

Duchy of Lancaster.—*See* LANCASTER.

Duchy Court of Lancaster.—A tribunal of special jurisdiction, held before the chancellor of the duchy or his deputy, concerning all matters of equity relating to lands holden of the Crown in right of the duchy of Lancaster. The proceedings in this court are the same as on the equity side of the Court of Chancery.

Duel.—*See* MURDER.

Duke.—The highest title of honour next to the Prince of Wales. It is a mere title of dignity, without giving any territory or jurisdiction over the place whence the title is taken.

Durham, County Palatine of.—This jurisdiction, which was vested until a very recent period in the Bishop of Durham for the time being, is now transferred to the Crown by 6 Will. 4, c. 19 (June 21, 1836).

Earl, a British title of nobility, next below a marquis, and above a viscount. The title is so ancient that its original cannot be clearly traced out. This much, however, seems tolerably certain, that among the Saxons they were called *ealdormen*, *quasi* elder men, signifying the same with *senior* or *senator* among the Romans; and also *schiremen*, because they had each of them the civil government of a several division or shire. On the irruption of the Danes they changed their names to *eorels*, which, according to Camden, signified the same in their language. In Latin they are called *comites* (a title first used in the empire), from being the king's attendants. After the Norman conquest they were for some time called *counts*, from the French; but they did not long retain that name themselves, though their shires are from thence called *counties* to this day. At present the title is accompanied by no territory, private or judicial rights, but merely confers nobility and an hereditary seat in the House of Lords. In writs, commissions, and other formal instruments, the Queen, when she mentions any peer of the degree of an earl, usually styles him "trusty and well-beloved *cousin*," an appellation as ancient as the reign of Henry IV., who being either by his wife, his mother, or his sisters, actually related or allied to every earl in the kingdom, artfully and constantly acknowledged that connection in all his letters and other public acts; whence the usage has descended to his successors, though the reason has long ago failed.

Earl Marshal of England.—A great officer of state, who had anciently several courts under his jurisdiction, as the Court of Chivalry and the Court of Honour. Under him is the Heralds' College. This office is of great antiquity, and has been for several ages hereditary in the family of the Howards. Roger de Montgomery, Marshal of the Norman army at the Conquest, is said to have been the first Marshal of England.

East India Company.—This celebrated association for the purpose of carrying on trade with the East Indies was formed in London A.D. 1599, and obtained its charter Dec. 31, 1600. In 1635 a rival company was established by Sir William Courten and chartered by Charles I., but the two associations united in 1649. In 1657, Cromwell renewed their charter, which was confirmed by Charles II. in 1661, and again in 1677. In 1694 the East-India trade was thrown open, but in 1698 a new company obtained a monopoly, in exchange for a loan to Government of £2,000,000. In 1702, however, the old and new companies amalgamated, and formed the "United Company of Merchants of England trading to the East Indies." In 1772 the company was compelled to apply for a loan, and in 1784 the Board of Control was erected by 24 Geo. III. c. 25, to regulate the civil and military government of the company's territories. By 53 Geo. III. c. 155, s. 7 (July 21, 1813), the importation of any goods but tea from any place except China was declared free to all British subjects, and the commercial character of the company was abolished by 3 & 4 Will. IV. c. 85 (Aug. 28, 1833). The number of directors was reduced from twenty-four to eighteen by 16 & 17 Vict. c. 95 (Aug. 20, 1853), and the government of India was finally transferred from the company to the Crown by 21 & 22 Vict. c. 106 (Aug. 2, 1858), which vested in Her Majesty all the rights formerly exercised by the company.—*See* INDIA, COUNCIL OF.

Easter Dues are small sums of money paid to the parochial clergy by the parishioners at Easter as a compensation for personal tithes or the tithe for personal labour.

Ecclesiastical Commission Office.—This office was established in 1834 for the purpose of equalising the incomes derived from bishoprics, church livings, and clerical offices; for the general management of church property, and to organise a proper distribution of the church funds. The chief dignitaries of Church and State are *ex officio* ecclesiastical commissioners, but the two paid commissioners are *de facto* the heads of this department. Hours 10 to 5. Whitehall.

Ecclesiastical Corporations.—Ecclesiastical corporations are such bodies whose members are entirely spiritual persons. Sole corporations are composed of bishops, certain deans and prebendaries, and all archdeacons, rectors, and vicars; corporations aggregate are composed of deans and chapters. They are erected for the furtherance of religion and to perpetuate the rights of the church. The ordinary is their visitor by the common law. The Pope formerly, and now the Crown, as the supreme ordinary, is the visitor of the archbishop or metropolitan. The metropolitan has the charge and coercion of all his suffragan bishops, and the bishops in their several dioceses are, in ecclesiastical matters, the visitors of all deans and chapters, of all parsons, and of all other spiritual corporations.

Ecclesiastical Courts.—In the time of the Anglo-Saxons there was no sort of distinction between the lay and the ecclesiastical jurisdiction; the County Court was as much a spiritual as a temporal tribunal; the rights of the church were ascertained and asserted at the same time, and by the same judges, as the rights of the laity. For this purpose the bishop of the diocese, and the alderman, or in his absence the sheriff of the county, used to sit together in the County Court, and had there the cognizance of all causes, as well ecclesiastical as civil; a superior deference being paid to the bishop's opinion in spiritual matters, and to that of the lay-judges in temporal. This union of power was very advantageous to them both: the presence of the bishop added weight and reverence to the sheriff's proceedings, and the authority of the sheriff was equally useful to the bishop, by enforcing obedience to his decrees among such refractory offenders as would otherwise have despised the thunder of mere ecclesiastical censures. But so moderate and rational a plan was wholly inconsistent with those views of ambition that were then forming by the Court of Rome. It soon became an established maxim in the Papal system of policy that all ecclesiastical persons, and all ecclesiastical causes, should be solely and entirely subject to ecclesiastical jurisdiction only; which jurisdiction was supposed to be lodged in the first place in the Pope, by divine indefeasible right and investiture from Christ himself, and through him in all inferior tribunals.

It was not, however, till after the Norman conquest that this doctrine was received in England; when William I. was at length prevailed upon to establish this fatal encroachment, and separate the ecclesiastical court from the civil; whether actuated by principles of bigotry, or by those of a more refined policy, in order to discountenance the laws of King Edward abounding with the spirit of Saxon liberty, is not altogether certain. But the latter, if not the cause, was undoubtedly the consequence, of this separation: for the Saxon laws were soon overborne by the Norman justiciaries, when the County Court fell into disregard by the bishop's withdrawing his presence, in obedience to the charter of the Conqueror, which prohibited any spiritual cause from being tried in the secular courts, and commanded the suitors to appear before the bishop only, whose decisions were directed to conform to the canon law. King Henry I. at his accession, among other restorations of the laws of King Edward the Confessor, revived this of the union of the civil and ecclesiastical courts, which was, according to Sir Edward Coke, after the great heat of the Conquest was past, only a restitution of the ancient law of England. This however was ill relished by the Popish clergy, who, under the guidance of Archbishop Anselm, very early disapproved of a measure that put them on a level with the laity, and subjected spiritual men and causes to the inspection of the secular magistrates; and, therefore, in their synod at Westminster, 3 Hen. I., they ordained that no bishop should attend the discussion of temporal causes, which soon dissolved this newly effected union. And when, upon the death of King Henry I., Stephen was brought in and supported by the clergy, we find one article of the oath which they imposed upon him was, that ecclesiastical persons and ecclesiastical causes should be subject only to the bishop's jurisdiction. And as it was about that time that the contest and emulation began between the laws of England and those of Rome, the temporal courts adhering to the former and the spiritual adopting the latter, as their rule of proceeding, this widened the breach between them, and made a coalition afterwards impracticable; which probably would else have been effected at the general reformation of the church.

The Ecclesiastical Courts are the Archdeacon's Court, the Consistory Courts, the Court of Arches, the Court of Peculiars, the Prerogative Courts of the two archbishops, the Faculty Court, and the Privy Council, which is the Appeal Court. In July, 1830, a commission was appointed to inquire into their practice and jurisdiction, which recommended sundry important changes in 1832. The Probate and Divorce Court, established by 20 & 21 Vict. c. 77, s. 3 (Aug. 25, 1857), abolished all the authority of the Ecclesiastical Courts in matters relating to wills, &c.

Ecclesiastical Titles Bill.—In consequence of the Papal bull of Sept. 30, 1850, by which an attempt was made to establish a Roman Catholic hierarchy in England, Lord

John Russell, then Prime Minister, introduced a measure into parliament Feb. 7, 1851, which was read for the third time, and passed July 4. By this Act the Papal brief was declared null and void, and a fine of £100 was imposed on all such as should endeavour to carry it into effect.

Education.—Among the ancient Greeks and Romans, education was chiefly carried on in the schools of philosophy. The Britons left all learning to the Druids. The Saxon children were taught to repeat the psalms and other books by heart, reading being still uncommon in the time of Alfred. The English language was not spoken in the twelfth century; but after the Norman period children learned their lessons in English, and afterwards translated them into French. Reading and writing became the chief branches of education in the fourteenth century. The following are some of the most important dates connected with the subject :—

A.D.

880. Alfred the Great invites learned foreigners to establish schools in his dominions.

1070. Westminster School is founded about this year.

1198. Sampson, abbot of St. Edmund's, founds a school at Bury St. Edmund's for forty poor boys.

1387. Winchester School is founded by William of Wykeham.

1441. Eton College is founded by Henry VI.

1552. Christ's Hospital, or the Blue-coat School, is founded.

1560. Westminster School is re-founded by Queen Elizabeth.

1567. Rugby School is founded.

1585. Harrow School is founded.

1690. The first mutual-improvement society is established in London, under the title of the Society for the Reformation of Manners.

1698. The Society for Promoting Christian Knowledge is founded.

A.D.

1783. Sunday schools are established by Mr. Robert Raikes.

1785. The Society for the Support and Encouragement of Sunday Schools is founded.

1788. The first Reform School is established by the Philanthropic Society.

1803. The Sunday School Union is established.

1805. Joseph Lancaster founds the British and Foreign School Society.

1807. Mr. Whitbread proposes the establishment of parochial schools, on the monitorial system, to the House of Commons, by whom it is rejected.

1811. Andrew Bell founds the National School Society; and the Rev. Mr. Charles establishes the first adult school at Bala, in Wales.

1818. A committee of the House of Commons publishes its reports on the state of endowed schools in England.

1823. The first mechanics' institution is established at London.

1825. The Society for the Diffusion of Useful Knowledge is founded.

1837. The first "Ragged" School is opened at Westminster.

1839. The Council of Education is appointed.

1843. The Field Lane Ragged School is opened.

1844. The Ragged School Union is formed.

1857. June 18. The convocation of the Oxford University passes a statute authorising middle-class examinations. June 22. An educational congress is held in London, under the presidency of the Prince Consort.

1858. June 21. Middle-class examinations commence at Oxford.

1859. July 6. Her Majesty appoints a Committee of Council on Education to superintend the application of any sums of money voted by Parliament for the purpose of promoting public education.

1861. July 21. Minute of the Committee of Council on Education, establishing a revised code of Regulations, to come into operation after March 31, 1862.

1864. November 14. First Meeting of the Royal Commission appointed to inquire into the State of Education in Scotland, in Edinburgh.

Ejectment. In English law a writ or action which lies for the lessee for years, on his being ejected or put out of his land, before the expiration of his term, either by the lessor or a stranger. It may also be brought by the lessor against the lessee, for rent in arrears, or holding over his term, &c. Ejectment of late years is become an action in the place of many real actions; and this is now the common action for trial of titles, and recovering of lands, &c., illegally held from the right owner.

Eleemosynary Corporations are those constituted for the perpetual distribution of the free alms, or bounty, of the founder of them to such persons as he has directed. Of this kind are all hospitals for the maintenance of the poor, sick, and impotent; and all colleges, both *in* our universities and *out* of them which are founded for two purposes: 1. For the promotion of piety and learning by proper regulations and ordinances. 2. For imparting assistance to the members of those bodies, in order to enable them to prosecute their devotion and studies with greater ease and assiduity. All these eleemosynary corporations are, strictly speaking, lay, and not ecclesiastical, even though composed of ecclesiastical persons, and although they in some things partake of the nature, privileges, and restrictions of ecclesiastical bodies. Accordingly they are not subject to the jurisdiction of the Ecclesiastical Courts, or to the visitations of the ordinary or diocesan in their spiritual characters.

Embezzlement. The pilfering or purloining money or property entrusted to any one as a servant or agent, or for a particular purpose. Clerks and servants receiving and embezzling the money or property of their employers shall be deemed to have stolen the same, and shall be punished by penal servitude for a term not exceeding fourteen, nor less than three years, or by imprisonment not exceeding two years. With respect to clerks and servants, it must be noted that to bring a servant or clerk within the law, it must be shown that he was authorised to receive it ; and if a person, who, not being a clerk or servant, in a single instance is requested to receive money, receives and embezzles it, he cannot be convicted of embezzlement. Embezzlement by any officer or servant of the Banks of England or Ireland is a felony, punishable by penal servitude for life or not less than three years, or imprisonment not exceeding two years.

Emblements. When a tenant from year to year, or any person whose tenancy is not determined by the tenor of the lease or agreement under which he holds the land, sows the land, the tenant or executors shall reap the crops which have been so sown ; but it is otherwise in respect of leaseholders, or those whose tenancies expire at a particular day, as at the end of the lease or other specific time agreed on at the commencement of the tenancy, except by custom as to *way-going crops, &c.* These crops are termed *emblements.*

Ember Days. Pope Calixtus I. (A.D. 218—223) appointed certain fast-days for imploring the Divine blessing on the fruits of the earth and on the ordinations of priests, which were celebrated at these times. From the custom of strewing ashes or embers upon the head on these occasions, the days were called ember days, and the weeks in which they fell ember weeks. They occur four times a year, being the Wednesday, Friday, and Saturday after the first Sunday in Lent, after Whitsunday, after September 14 (the Feast of Holy Cross), and after December 13 (the Feast of St. Lucia). They are now chiefly noticed because the canon appoints the Sundays next after the ember weeks for the purposes of ordination : though the bishops may ordain on any Sunday or holiday if they please.

Emigration was placed under the regulation of a Government commission in 1831. It was one of the modes of relief proposed by the Poor Law Amendment Act, 4 & 5 Will. IV., c. 76, s. 62 (August 14, 1834), and in January, 1840, was placed under the supervision of commissioners, appointed under the royal sign manual, as the Land and Emigration Board. The conveyance of emigrants from the United Kingdom was at first regulated by 5 & 6 Will. IV. c. 53 (August 31, 1835), which was amended by the Passengers Act, 5 & 6 Vict. c. 107 (August 12, 1842).

England, Bank of. *See* BANK OF.

Enlistment. The enlistment of British subjects to serve in foreign armies was prohibited by 59 Geo. III. c. 69 (July 3 1819). By 5 & 6 Will. IV., c. 24 (August 21, 1835), enlistment of sailors was limited to five years ; and by 10 & 11 Vict. c. 37 (June 21, 1847), military service was restricted to ten years in the infantry, and twelve years in the cavalry, artillery, and marines.

Entail is an estate-tail " a freehold of inheritance, limited to a person and the heirs of his body general or special, male or female." The custom of confining the succession to property in this manner resulted from the desire of the nobility to retain their possessions in their own families. It was commenced by the second statute of Westminster, 13 Edw. I. c. 1 (1285). Owing to the inefficacy of attainders of treason when estates were protected by entails, they were evaded in 1472 by a decision that common recoveries should constitute a bar to an entail. By 26 Henry VIII., c. 13 (1534), high treason confiscates entailed property to the Crown ; and by 21 James I. c. 19, s. 12 (1623), entailed estates were permitted to be sold in cases of bankruptcy. This latter Act was repealed by 6 Geo. IV., c. 16, s. 65 (May 2, 1825), which was again supplanted by 3 & 4 Will.

IV., c. 74, ss. 55—65 (August 28, 1833), and 12 & 13 Vict. c. 106, s. 208 (August 1, 1849). Leases made by tenants in tail are regulated by 19 & 20 Vict. c. 120 (July 29, 1856).

Equity is, in a general sense, the virtue of treating all other men according to reason and justice, or as we would gladly be treated ourselves when we understand aright what is our due. Equity, in jurisprudence, is defined a correction or qualification of the law, generally made in that part wherein it fails or is too severe. It likewise signifies the extension of the words of the law to cases unexpressed, yet having the same reason ; so that where one thing is enacted by statute, all other things are enacted that are of the like degree. Equity is of two kinds. The one abridges and takes from the letter of the law : the other enlarges and adds to it ; and statutes may be construed according to equity, especially where they give remedy for wrong, or for expedition of justice. Equity seems to be the interposing *law of reason*, exercised by the Lord Chancellor in extraordinary matters to do equal justice ; and by supplying the defects of the law, gives remedy in all cases.

Equity, Courts of.—*See* COURTS OF EQUITY.

Escheat, in law, signifies any lands or tenements that casually fall to a lord within his manor. It is the determination of the tenure or dissolution of the mutual bond between the lord and tenant, from the extinction of the blood of the latter by either natural or civil means ; if he died without heirs of his blood, or if his blood was corrupted and stained by commission of treason or felony ; whereby every inheritable quality was entirely blotted out and abolished. In such cases the land escheated or fell back to the lord of the fee ; that is, the tenure was determined by breach of the original condition, expressed or implied in the feodal donation. In the one case, there were no heirs subsisting of the blood of the first feudatory or purchaser, to which heirs alone the grant of the feud extended ; in the other, the tenant, by perpetrating an atrocious crime, showed that he was no longer to be trusted as a vassal, having forgotten his duty as a subject; and therefore forfeited his feud, which he held under the implied condition that he should not be a traitor or a felon. The consequence of which in both cases was, that the gift being determined, resulted back to the lord who gave it. The following interests do not escheat: —Gavelkind, a rent-charge; a right of common, free warren, or any kind of inheritance which does not lie in tenure; a trust estate; an estate given to a corporation; and money to be laid out in land.

By 13 & 14 Vict., c. 60, beneficiaries and mortgagors were protected from the ordinary law of escheat in the event of a trustee or mortgagee dying heirless and intestate.

Escheator.—An officer formerly appointed by the Lord Treasurer, &c. in every county, to make inquests of titles by escheat, which inquests were to be taken by good and lawful men of the county impannelled by the sheriff.

Esquire.—This title is of considerable antiquity, and, like armiger, scutifer, scutarius, and _écuyer_, is derived from the shield, and other portions of the knight's arms which the esquire used to carry. Selden states that it was first used to express the next rank below a knight, about A.D. 850, and it is said to have been applied to other persons than attendants upon knights as early as 1245. Esquires may be divided into four classes.

I. The younger sons of peers and their eldest sons.

II. The eldest sons of knights and their eldest sons.

III. The chiefs of ancient families are esquires by prescription.

IV. Esquires by creation or office.

Estate, in law, signifies the title or interest that a person has in lands, tenements, or other effects: comprehending the whole in which a person has any property, and will pass the same. Estates are either real or personal, and may be divided into the following classes:—

I. Freeholds of inheritance.

II. Freeholds not of inheritance.

III. Estates for years, or at will, or at sufferance ; and

IV. Estates upon condition.

A fee-simple is the amplest estate our law admits of.

Estates of the Realm, are the three branches of the Legislature—the Lords Spiritual, the Lords Temporal, and the Commons.

Estrays are such valuable animals as are found wandering in a manor or lordship, the owner whereof is not known. In which case the law gives them to the sovereign, but they most commonly belong to the lord of the manor by special grant from the Crown. Estrays must, however, be publicly proclaimed, and a year and a day elapse before they belong to the sovereign or his substitute. The doctrine of estrays applies only to animals *domitæ naturæ.*

Evidence, that perception of truth which arises either from the testimony of the senses or from an induction of reason. Evidence, in law, signifies some proof by testimony of men upon oath, or by writings or records. It is called evidence, because thereby the point in issue in a cause to be tried is to be made evident to the jury. "The rules of evidence are the same in civil and criminal courts, for a fact must be established by the same evidence, whether it be followed by a civil or a criminal consequence."

Exchange.—That species of mercantile transactions by which the debts of individuals residing at a distance from their creditors are satisfied without the transmission of money. Par of Exchange of any two countries means the equivalency of a certain amount of the currency of the one in the currency of the other, supposing the currencies of both countries to be of the precise weight and purity fixed by their respective mints.

Exchequer, Barons of the.—*See* BARONS OF THE EXCHEQUER.

Exchequer Bills.—Promissory notes due at certain dates, and bearing interest, issued by Government when in want of money. The daily transactions between the Bank and Government are chiefly carried on through their intervention.

Exchequer Chamber.—This court was erected by 31 Edward III. stat. 1, c. 12 (1357), to discuss questions which other courts find doubtful, and to serve as a tribunal of appeal from the Court of Exchequer. By 27 Eliz. c. 8 (1585), its jurisdiction was extended over erroneous judgments in the Court of King's Bench, and it was confirmed and further regulated by 31 Eliz. c. 1 (1589). The constitution of this court was again altered by 11 Geo. IV. and 1 Will. IV. c. 70, s. 8 (July 23, 1830).

Exchequer, Chancellor of the.—*See* CHANCELLOR.

Exchequer (Comptroller-General of the).—On the suppression of the offices of Auditor, Tellers of the Exchequer, and Clerk of the Pells, by 4 Will. IV. c. 15, s. 1 (May 22, 1834), the same act provided for the discharge of their respective functions by creating a Comptroller-General, with a regular staff of clerks and assistants. This office controls and records the details of the national revenue. The duties connected with the preparation of Exchequer Bills devolve also upon this department. It is now amalgamated with the Audit Office.

Exchequer (Court of).—This court was appointed by William I., A.D. 1079, to take cognizance of matters connected with the revenue. It also exercised jurisdiction over common-plea suits until a separate court was erected for their decision by Magna Charta, in 1215. The name was derived from the table at which its sittings were held, which is described as " a four-cornered board, about ten feet long and five feet broad, fitted in manner of a table to sit about ; on every side whereof is a standing ledge, or border, four fingers broad. Upon this board is laid a cloth, bought in Easter term, which is of a black

colour, rowed with strekes, distant about a foot or a span."
On the squares of this chequered cloth counters were placed, to
assist in making the needful computations. Barons of the
exchequer were first appointed July 6, 1234, and chief barons
March 8, 1312. By 9 Edward III. stat. 1, c. 5 (1335), justices
of assize, &c., were ordered to send all their records to this
court annually at Michaelmas, and by 31 Edward III. stat. 1,
c. 12 (1357), the Lord Chancellor and Lord Treasurer were authorised to examine its erroneous judgments. As a court of
revenue, it ascertains and enforces by proceedings appropriate
to the case, the proprietary rights of the Crown against the
subjects of the realm. As a court of common law it admini-
sters redress between subject and subject in all actions whatever, except real actions. It is a court of record, and its judges
are five in number, consisting of one chief and four *puisné*
barons. Its equitable jurisdiction, except when it sits as a
court of revenue, was transferred to the Court of Chancery by
5 Vict. c. 5.

Excise, or a duty levied upon articles of consumption,
produced within the state in which the tax is levied, was introduced at Rome by Augustus, after the civil wars, B.C. 28. An
attempt, made in 1626, to introduce excise duties into England,
proved unsuccessful. The Long Parliament levied the first
excise duties in England, May 16, 1643. Wines, ale, beer,
cider, perry, and tobacco were the articles taxed. By 12
Charles II. c. 24 (1660), excise duties were levied as part of the
revenues of the crown. The malt duty was first levied in 1695.
A large number of articles on which excise was formerly levied
are now exempted. In 1823, the Irish and Scotch Boards of
Excise were incorporated with the English establishment,
and in 1849, the Board of Excise was united with that of
Stamps and Taxes, under the name of the Board of Inland
Revenue.

Exclusion Bill.—The first Exclusion Bill committed in

the House of Commons, May 21, 1679, by 207 against 128, was lost by the dissolution of that Parliament, May 27. A second measure "for securing the Protestant religion by disabling James, Duke of York, to inherit the imperial crown of this realm," passed the House of Commons Nov. 11, 1680; and was rejected in the House of Lords, on the motion for its first reading, Nov 15. Charles II. sent a message to the Commons, refusing to pass a bill of exclusion, Jan. 7, 1681. In the new Parliament summoned to meet at Oxford, March 21, 1681, the Commons ordered, March 28, that the bill for excluding James, Duke of York, was to be read a third time the next day. Charles II. at once dissolved the Parliament.

Excommunication.—An ecclesiastical censure divided into the greater and the lesser. By the greater a person was cut off from the communion of the Church, and rendered incapable of any legal act. By the lesser he was debarred from the services of the Church. It was formerly employed to enforce the decrees and orders of the Ecclesiastical Courts; but in all cases of contempt of court it has been abolished—the writ now *de contumace capiendo,* issuing from the Court of Chancery, having the same effect as the former writ *de excommunicato capiendo.*

Executive.—That branch of the government which puts the laws into execution. The body that deliberates and enacts laws is legislative; the body that judges and applies the laws in particular cases judicial, and the body that superintends the enforcement of them, the executive.

Executor, a person nominated by a testator, to take care to see his will and testament executed or performed, and his effects disposed of according to the tenor of the will, after his decease.

Extradition.—The act of sending by authority of law a person accused of crime to a foreign jurisdiction, where the act was committed, for his trial. It is usually the subject of international treaty. Conventions have been entered into by England with France and Denmark, for the apprehension and extradition of persons charged with murder, forgery, or fraudulent bankruptcy; and with the United States of America for the apprehension and extradition of persons charged with those offences, and also with piracy, arson, or uttering forged paper. Various Acts of Parliament have been passed for carrying into effect those conventions; see 6 and 7 Vict. c. 75; 8 and 9 Vict. c. 120; and 25 and 26 Vict. c. 70.

Eyre.—The court of justices itinerant.

Fabric Lands.—Lands given to provide for the rebuilding or repair of cathedrals and churches. Formerly, almost every one gave something by his will to be applied in repairing the fabric of the cathedral or parish church where he lived.

Faculties, Court of.—A jurisdiction belonging to the archbishop. It does not hold pleas in any suits, but creates rights to pews, monuments, and particular places, and modes of burial. It can also grant licences of various descriptions, as a licence to marry, &c.

Feasts.—Anniversary days of rejoicing either on a civil or religious occasion. Feasts among us are either immoveable or moveable. Immoveable Feasts are those constantly celebrated on the same day of the year; the principal of these are Christmas Day or the Nativity, the Circumcision, Epiphany, Candlemas, or the Purification; Lady Day, or the Annunciation; All Saints, and All Souls; besides the days of the several apostles, St. Thomas, St. Paul, &c., which with us are feasts, though not *feriæ*. Moveable Feasts are those which are not confined to the same day of the year. Of these the principal is Easter, which gives law to all the rest, all of them following, and keeping their proper distances from it; such are Palm Sunday, Good Friday, Ash Wednesday, Sexagesima, Ascension Day, Pentecost, and Trinity Sunday. The four feasts which the English laws take special notice of are, the Annunciation of the blessed

Virgin Mary or Lady Day, the 25th of March; the nativity of
St. John the Baptist, held on the 24th of June; the Feast of
St. Michael the Archangel, on the 29th of September; and that
of St. Thomas the Apostle, on the 21st of December : on which
quarterly days rent on leases is usually reserved to be paid.

Fee simple.—A freehold estate of inheritance, absolute
and unqualified. It stands at the head of estates as the highest
in dignity and the most ample in extent; since every other
kind of estate is " derivable thereout and mergeable therein."
It may be enjoyed not only in land but also in advowsons,
commons, and other hereditaments, as well as in personalty. A
fee simple is generally without condition and unrestrained,
except by the laws of escheat and the canons of real property
descent. It is not confined to any particular line of heirs, but
descends to the owner's heirs general, whether lineal or collateral,
paternal or maternal, male or female, born or unborn.'

Fee tail.—*See* TAIL.

Felo de se.—One who feloniously commits self-murder.
The barbarous mode of burying such persons is abolished ; the
only legal consequences of the crime are now forfeiture and
deprivation of Christian burial.

Felony.—All crimes (not mere misdemeanors, however high)
above simple larceny to treason. In its original signification
it meant the penal consequences resulting from the commission
of certain offences, *i. e.*, the forfeiture of the offender's lands and
goods at common law, but now it imports the offence itself.

Feoffment.—The name of a conveyance of freehold lands,
now not much in use, because it must be accompanied by an
open and known delivery of possession at the time of executing
the deed, termed " livery of seisin." It is mostly used for gifts,
or where no pecuniary consideration is given or money paid, as
where corporate property is vested in a certain number of
persons of whom very few survive, the survivors by this deed
enfeoff some new nominees.

Feudal system.—Whilst the barbarous tribes which overran Europe after the fall of the Roman empire were wandering from clime to clime in search of subsistence, every individual claimed an equal share of liberty. But when they were settled in the possessions won with their swords, they found new cares devolve upon them, and the necessity of a new system of polity. Having abandoned their life of wandering and brigandage, it became necessary not only to cultivate the land for a subsistence, but to be prepared to defend it both against the attempts of the ancient possessors to regain, and of fresh swarms of wanderers to seize it. Still retaining their military character, and ignorant alike of systems of finance and the expedient of a standing army, each man held himself in readiness to obey the call to service in the field. The superior officers, who held large territories directly from the Prince, were bound to appear with a proportionate number of followers; and these followers held their lands from their immediate lord on the same condition. The possessions held by these tenures were called *fiefs*, or *beneficia*. The vassal who held them was not only bound to mount his horse and follow his lord, or suzerain, to the wars, but also to assist him with his counsel, and to attend as an assessor in his courts of justice. More special and definite services were—to guard the castle of his lord a certain number of days in the year; to pay a certain sum of money when his suzerain's eldest son was made a knight, and his eldest daughter was married; and to contribute to his ransom in case he was taken prisoner in war. In return for these services the lord was bound to afford his vassal protection in case of his fief being attacked; whilst the defence of each other's person was reciprocal. The natural consequence of this was the system called "sub-infeudation," by which the immediate holder parcelled out portions of his fief to others on the same conditions of tenure by which he held it himself. These sub-tenants owed to him the same duties which he owed

to his lord ; and he held his own court of justice, in which he
exercised jurisdiction over his vassals.   The few lands that
remained free, that is, which were not bound to render service
to a superior lord, or suzerain, though liable to burthens for the
public defence, were called *allodial* in contradistinction to *feudal.*
The ceremony by which the vassal acknowledged his feudal
dependence and obligations was called homage, from *homo,* a man,
because the vassal became the man of his lord.   Homage was
accompanied with an oath of fealty on the part of the vassal,
and investiture on the part of the lord, which was the conveying
of possession of the fief by means of some pledge or token.
Homage was of two kinds, liege and simple.   Liege homage (from
Lat. *ligare,* Fr. *lier,* to bind) not only obliged the liege man to
do personal service in the army, but also disabled him from
renouncing his vassality by surrendering his fief.   The liege
man took the oath of fealty on his knees without sword and
spurs, and with his hands placed between those of his lord.
The vassal who rendered simple homage had the power of
finding a substitute for military service, or could altogether
liberate himself by the surrender of his fief.   In simple homage
the vassal took the oath standing, girt with his sword and with
his hands at liberty.   The aristocratical nature of feudalism
will readily be inferred from the preceding description.   The
great chief, residing in his country-seat, which he was commonly
allowed to fortify, lost in a great measure his connection or
acquaintance with the Prince, and added every day new force
to his authority over the vassals of his barony.   They received
from him education in all military enterprises ; his hospitality
invited them to live and enjoy society in his hall ; their leisure,
which was great, made them perpetual attendants on his person,
and partakers of his country sports and amusements ; they
had no means of gratifying their ambition but by making a
figure in his train ; his favour and countenance was their
greatest honour ; his displeasure exposed them to contempt

and ignominy; and they felt every moment the necessity of his protection, both in the controversies which occurred with other vassals, and, what was more material, in the daily inroads and injuries which were committed by the neighbouring barons. From these causes not only was the royal authority extremely eclipsed in most of the European states, but even the military vassals, as well as the lower dependants and serfs, were held in a state of subjection, from which nothing could free them but the progress of commerce and the rise of cities, the true strongholds of freedom.

The introduction of feudalism was one of the principal changes effected in England by the conquest. The King became the supreme lord of all the land; whence Coke says, "All the lands and tenements in England in the hands of subjects are holden mediately or immediately of the King; for in the law of England we have not properly allodium." Even the Saxon landholders who were not deprived of their lands were brought under the system of feudal tenure, and were subjected to services and imposts to which they were not before liable; but most of the manors were bestowed upon the Normans, who thus held immediately of the King, and were hence called *Tenants in Capite* or *Tenants in chief.* But though the Anglo-Saxon thane was thus reduced to the condition of a simple freeholder, or franklin, and though the Norman lord perhaps retained a certain portion of his estate as demesne land, yet the latter had no possessory right in the whole, and the estate was not therefore so profitable to him as might at first sight appear. The tenant-in-chief was bound to *knight service*, or the obligation to maintain, forty days in the field, a certain number of cavaliers completely equipped, raised from his under-tenants. Even religious foundations and monasteries were liable to this service, the only exception being the tenure of *frankalmoign*, or free alms. Every estate of twenty pounds yearly value was considered as a knight's fee, and was bound to furnish a soldier. The tenants-in-chief appear from Domesday-Book to have amounted in the reign of William the Conqueror to about 1400, including the numerous ecclesiastical foundations. The number of *mesne* lords, or those holding fiefs not directly from the King, was about 8000. There were peculiarities in the feudal system of Normandy itself which were introduced by William into England. According to the generally received principle of feuds, the oath of the vassal was due only to the lord of whom he immediately held. But William exacted the oath of fealty from all the landowners of England, as well those who held *in capite* as the under-tenants. In doing this he seems to have been guided by the custom of Normandy, where the Duke had immediate jurisdiction over all his subjects. Hence William's power was much greater than that of the feudal sovereigns of the continent, and the constitution approached more to an absolute despotism. The great fiefs of England did not, like those of France, date their origin in a period when the power of the vassal who received them was almost equal to that of the sovereign who bestowed them; but being distributed on the same occasion, and almost at the same time, William took care not to make them so large as to be dangerous to himself; for which reason also the manors assigned to his followers were dispersed in different counties. Hence the nobles in England never attained that pitch of power which they possessed in Germany, France, and Spain; nor do we find them defying the sovereign's jurisdiction, as was very common in those countries, by the right of carrying on private wars among themselves.[*]

Fiat (*let it be done*).—A decree. A short order or warrant of some judge for making out and allowing certain processes.

Fieri Facias (*that you cause to be made*).—A judicial writ that lies for him who has recovered any debt or damages

---

[*] Dr. Smith's Hume condensed.

in the Queen's Courts. It is a command to the sheriff, that of the goods and chattels of the party he cause to be made the sum recovered by the judgment together with interest at 4 per cent., and have the money and the writ itself before the Queen or her justices, if in the Common Pleas; or her barons if in the Exchequer at Westminster, immediately after the execution of the writ, to be rendered to the party who sued it out. Under this execution all personal goods and chattels to the value of £5, except wearing apparel, can be taken, and also any bank notes, cheques, bonds, &c.

Fine, in law, has divers applications. Sometimes it is used for a formal conveyance of lands or tenements, or of any thing inheritable, being *in esse temporis finis,* in order to cut off all controversies. Others define it to be a final agreement between persons, concerning any lands or rents, &c., of which any suit or writ is depending between them in any court. Fine sometimes signifies a sum of money paid for entering lands or tenements let by lease; and sometimes a pecuniary mulet for an offence committed against the Queen and her laws, or against the lord of the manor.

Fines and Recoveries.—*See* RECOVERIES.

Fire Policy.—A contract in writing effected by an insurance office, by which in consideration of a single or periodical payment of premium, the company engages to pay an assured person such loss as may arise by fire to his property described in the policy within the period therein specified, to an amount not exceeding a particular sum fixed for that purpose by such policy.

First Fruits.—The first year's profits of every clergyman's benefice, otherwise called *annates* or *primitiæ.* By 2 & 3 Anne, the first fruits of all benefices, (except those under the value of £50 per annum, which are exempted from the payment of first fruits,) were vested in trustees to form a perpetual fund called Queen Anne's Bounty, for the augmentation of poor livings.

Fishery, &c.—All persons who peaceably demean them-

selves have a right to take fish in great rivers, being arms of
the sea, and where the tide ebbs and flows; indeed there are
few navigable rivers where the public have not a right of free
fishery. Where the right to the soil of the river, *i.e.*, the ground
over which the river flows, is in the queen, it is pretty certain
that the subject may fish there, but where the soil is the property of another, as it generally is in a private river, there no
one can lawfully fish unless he is interested in a right of common
of "piscary" (the legal term for fishery), or can by prescription
claim a particular right to fish in exclusion of others, or without
leave first obtained of the owners of the adjoining lands, the
ownership of the ground evidencing a presumptive right, the
disturbance whereof is a trespass for which an action will lie.
By custom or prescription, many persons, such as the owners or
occupiers of neighbouring land, or the inhabitants of a township
or city, may have an exclusive right of fishery in a river,
although the ground or soil belongs to the owners of the land
on both sides, and sometimes an individual may claim an exclusive right by prescription to have a several fishery, *i.e.*, a right
of exclusive fishing in creeks or arms of the sea, where otherwise
all would be entitled in common. Unless the privileges of
lords of manors or claims by prescription interfere, every one
has a right to take fish left on the shore between high and low
water mark. However, no trespass must be committed on the
lands of another, in the assertion of this right. With respect
to fish as private property, by being enclosed in ponds or private waters, the law provides by statute 7 & 8 Geo. IV., c. 27 :
1. That the taking or destroying fish in water running through
or in land adjoining, or belonging to the dwelling-house of any
person who is the owner of such water or has a right of fishing
therein, is a misdemeanour ; 2. The taking, or attempting to
take, or destroy fish in any other water, but which shall be
private property, or in which there shall be any private right of
fishery, is an offence punishable summarily before one magis-

trate with a penalty of £5. But if any person by angling in the day time take, or attempt to take, or destroy fish in the first-mentioned water, he is liable, on summary conviction before a magistrate, to a penalty of £5 ; if in the second and last-mentioned water, £2 : and power is given to seize the rods, lines, and fishing tackle for the use of the owner, but this seizure exempts the angler from the payment of any penalty or damages for such angling. Acts tending to the destruction of fish ponds and dams, or the fish therein, are classed as malicious injuries, and punishable accordingly. Various statutes have been passed for the preservation of salmon and river fish, commencing at the reign of Edward I., many of them local, but all empowering justices and lords of court leets to inflict penalties for injuries done to the fry of fish, and taking fish out of season or unsizable.

Five Mile Act.—An oppressive statute passed in 1665, obliging nonconformist teachers, who refused to take the non-resistance oath, not to come within five miles of any corporation where they had preached since the Act of Oblivion (unless travelling), under the penalty of £50. Repealed in 1689.

Flotsam.—Goods floating upon the sea, which belong to the Crown, unless claimed by the true owners thereof within a year and a day.

Foreign Office.—Previous to the year 1782 the two principal secretaries were known as Secretaries of State for the Northern and Southern Departments respectively. In this year, however, a re-division of the duties was made, under which arrangement the Northern became the Foreign, and the Southern, the Home Department. The Secretary of State for Foreign Affairs is the official channel of communication between Great Britain and other countries; all treaties and alliances are made through him, and it is part of his duty to extend his protection to English subjects residing abroad. All ambassadors and consuls are under his control. The Foreign Secretary is assisted in the discharge of his duties by two Under-Secretaries, and a staff of officials. Hours, twelve to seven. Temporary office, Whitehall Gardens.

Foreign Enlistment Act.—An Act passed in 1819, prohibiting British subjects from enlisting in the service of a foreign power without licence from the King or Privy Council. It also forbids the fitting out of ships for any foreign power to be employed against any power with whom our Government is at peace.

Foreigners are amenable to our laws whilst residing in England. It is no defence for a foreigner charged with a crime committed in England that he did not know he was doing wrong, the act not being criminal in his own country.

Forest Laws.—Ancient statutes exercised with great rigour after the Norman Conquest for the preservation of the hunting of the king. By these laws any one who killed the beasts of the chase in the royal forests was punished with death. Under King John the laws were extended to include all the winged creation. Magna Charta greatly mitigated their severity.

Forfeiture of Goods was formerly the punishment o all felonies; to which was superadded some other punishment of a corporal nature, generally death; and it still attaches on all felonies above petty larceny, and upon cases of *felo de se;* the law contemplating the act of suicide as a felony committed by a man upon himself. Lands are forfeited now, as far as regards the profits, during the life of the offender · and are absolutely forfeited by the owner's committing murder or treason : but suicides, strictly so termed, do not forfeit lands, or any interest therein. A person outlawed for murder or treason forfeits lands and goods ; and a person outlawed for debt also forfeits the profits of his land and all his goods, which are distributed by the treasury among the creditors prosecuting the outlawry. In manslaughter the offender forfeits goods and chattels. After a conviction by judgment, or outlawry for high treason, or murder, a commission issues to nominees of the attorney, to inquire what lands or tenements the offender had, at the time of the treason, or murder committed, and to seize them for the use of the sovereign. The goods of a felon cannot be seized before forfeiture; but they may be inventoried. There are two instances in which a person forfeits goods and chattels, and the profits of his lands during life; namely, the drawing a weapon on a judge in Court, and striking any one in the presence of the Queen's Courts of Justice. In præmunire a party forfeits lands absolutely, and goods and chattels.

Forgery is the making, or alteration of, any instrument, with a fraudulent intent; and the uttering a forged instrument, with perfect knowledge of its being forged, is also forgery; and, with very few exceptions, rendered equally penal with the act of forgery itself. Therefore, not only the fabrication of the *whole* of a written instrument, but a fraudulent insertion, alteration, or erasure, even of a letter, in any material part of a true instrument, is a forgery; and it matters not, whether the signature be true and the matter contained in the instrument false, or *vice versâ*. The making of a false instrument in the name of a fictitious person, is as much forgery, as if it were made in the name of a person known to be in existence. The laws respecting this crime were very indefinite until the passing of 5 Eliz. c. 14 (1562), which rendered forgers liable to pay double costs and damages; to be set in the pillory, and have their ears cut off, and nostrils slit and seared; to forfeit to the Crown all their revenues of lands and tenements, and to suffer imprisonment for life. In 1634 it was made a capital offence, and in 1722 to forge letters of attorney for the transfer of stock was made felony, without benefit of clergy, by 8 Geo. 1, c. 22. All capital forgeries were collected into one act by 11 Geo. 4 & 1 Will. 4, c. 66, which was amended by 2 & 3 Will. 4, c. 123, and again amended by 24 & 25 Vict. c. 98. Capital punishment is abolished in all cases of forgery, and the punishment is now penal servitude, the length of which varies according to the nature of the offence, from life to three years, or imprisonment for not more than two years.

Franchise is an incorporeal hereditament synonymous with liberty—a royal privilege subsisting in the hands of a subject. It arises either from royal grants or from prescription. Franchise is also the right of voting at an election for a member of Parliament.

Frank-pledge.—A surety to the Sovereign for the good behaviour of freemen. Living under frank-pledge has been termed living under law.

Freehold, Frank Tenement, is land, or tenement, which a man holds in fee-simple, fee-tail, or for term of life. Freehold is of two kinds, in deed and in law. The first is the real possession of land or tenement in fee, fee-tail, or for life: the other is the right a man has to such land or tenement before his entry or seizure. A freehold, by the common law, cannot commence *in futuro*, but it must take effect presently, either in possession, reversion, or remainder. Whatever is part of the freehold goes to the heir; and things fixed thereto may not be taken in distress for rent, or in execution, &c. No man shall be disseised of his freehold by Magna Charta, but by judgment of his peers, or according to the laws of the land: nor shall any distrain free-holders to answer for their freehold, in anything concerning the same, without the Sovereign's writ. Freehold estates, of certain value, are required by statutes to qualify jurors, electors of the knights of the shire in Parliament, &e.

Friendly Societies, or Benefit Clubs, are associations chiefly among the lower classes of tradesmen, " for the purpose of mutual relief, and maintenance of the members, their wives, or children, relations, or nominees, in sickness, infancy, advanced age, widowhood, or any other natural state or contingency, whereof the occurrence is susceptible of average, or for any other purpose which is not illegal." They are regulated by various statutes, which, in encouraging associations of the above nature, extend the subjects of relief to losses by fire, shipwreck, substitutes, if drawn for the militia; a weekly allowance, if reduced to the workhouse, or imprisoned for debt; and for any contribution towards an annual feast, or for any reasonable or lawful purpose; but these last-named subjects are to be separately and distinctly contributed to, as an extra subscription, and not to be identified with the primary purposes for which these societies are erected. Also, the money payable on the death of a member may be disposed of by will at his pleasure. The. only restriction in their formation is the enrolment and approval of their rules by the barrister appointed to certify their correctness and freedom from irregularity or erroneous principles *See* 18 & 19 Vict. c. 73, amended by 23 & 24 Vict. c. 58.

Fund, in general, signifies any sum of money appropriated for a particular purpose. Thus, that part of the national revenue which is set aside for the payment of the national debt, is called the sinking fund. But, when we speak of the funds, we generally mean the large sums which have been lent to Government, and constitute the national debt; and for which the lenders, or their assignees, receive interest from revenues allotted for that purpose. The term stock is used in the same sense, and is also applied to the sums which form the capital of the Bank of England, &c. The funding system appears to have originated at Venice, where it was established as early as A.D. 1172. In 1600 it was introduced into Holland, in 1672 into France by Louvois, and in 1689 into England. In this country the legal percentage was at first six per cent.; but by 12 Anne, st. 2, c. 16 (1713), it was reduced to five per cent. The legal restriction to five per cent. for interest was abolished by 17 & 18 Vict. c. 90 (1854).

A.D.

1716. The sinking-fund is established.

1726. Bank annuities are created.

1747. Three per cent. reduced annuities.

A.D.

1751. Three per cent. consols.

1758. Three-and-a-half per cent. annuities.

1761. Long annuities are created.

1762. Four per cent. consols.

1771. New three-and-a-half per cent. annuities.

1796. Five per cent. annuities.

1818. Three-and-a-half per cents.

1822. The five per cents are reduced to four per cents.

1823. The "dead weight" annuity created. It will expire in
     1867.

1824. Reduced three-and-a-half per cents.

1830. New five per cent. annuities.

1844. New annuities.

1853. New annuities at two-and-a-half per cent., and new
     three-and-a-half per cent. annuities.

1860. The long annuities expire.

Dividends on Consols, New $2\frac{1}{2}$ per Cents, New $3\frac{1}{2}$ per Cents,
and New 5 per Cents, are payable Jan. 5 and July 5. Dividends on the Reduced 3 per Cents and New 3 per Cents are
payable April 5 and Oct. 10.

Game are hares, pheasants, partridges, grouse, heath or
moor-game, black game, and bustards. The taking of which is
regulated, and the selling legalised, by Act 1 & 2 Will. 4, c. 32.
Any person is at liberty to kill game on his own land, or on that
of another person, with the leave of the person entitled to the
game, upon obtaining a game certificate, for which 3l. 13s. 6d.,
or for a menial gamekeeper 1l. 5s., is payable to the collector of
the Queen's taxes of the place where the applicant resides. The
restrictions as to time or season are, Sunday or Christmas Day,
under a penalty of 5l., with costs, for each offence, recoverable
before two magistrates ; and with regard to season, the taking
or killing partridges between the 1st of February and the 1st of
September ; pheasants, between the 1st of February and the

1st of October ; black-game (except in Somerset, or Devon, or in the New Forest, Hants), between the 10th of December and the 20th of August, and in Somerset, Devon, and the New Forest, between the 10th of December and the 1st of September ; grouse, or red-game, between the 10th of December and the 12th of August ; or bustards, between the 1st of March and the 1st of September, subjects the party to a penalty of 1*l.* for every head of game, with costs of conviction, recoverable before two magistrates. Hares may be killed all the year round. Poisoning game subjects the party to a penalty not exceeding 10*l.*, with costs, recoverable in like manner. Any person not having the right of killing game upon the land, or permission from the person having such right, taking or destroying the eggs of any bird of game, swan, wild duck, teal, or widgeon, or having the same in his possession, is liable, on conviction before two magistrates, for every egg taken, destroyed, or found in his house or possession, 5*s.*, and costs. The enabling all certificated persons to kill game only gives them power to sport on their own land, or that of another, with leave of the person entitled to the game. Persons killing or taking game without a certificate are subjected to a penalty of 5*l.*, in addition to the penalties imposed for not taking out a certificate. If an occupier kill or take game, or permit others to do so, he is liable for the penalty of 2*l.* for the pursuit, in addition to a penalty of 1*l.* for every head of game ; and the persons to whom he gave permission are also liable for any proceeding the landlord may institute for the trespass. Various statutes have recently been passed regarding this subjcet. See 2 & 3 Vict. c. 35 ; 11 & 12 Vict. c. 29 ; 23 & 24 Vict. c. 90 ; and 24 & 25 Vict. c. 96.

Gaming.—The passion for play has in all ages been common among the wealthy and unemployed, and frequently even among the poorer classes. Tacitus mentions the excess to which it was carried by the ancient Germans, who frequently staked their freedom on the hazard of the die, and suffered themselves to be sold as slaves to liquidate their gaming debts. Justinian's Code (A.D. 528) contains several enactments for its suppression. The Romans were immoderately addicted to it in the latter days of the Republic and the Empire. The practice was introduced very early into England. The first statute directed against it (33 Henry 8, c. 9, 1541), prohibited the keeping of gaming-houses under a penalty of 40s. per day, and the frequenting of such places under forfeiture of 6s. 8d. By 16 Car. 2, c. 7 (1664), any person winning money by fraud, cozenage, or deceit, was to forfeit treble the value of his gains; and by 9 Anne, c. 14 (1710), any one who had lost at one sitting, and paid, the sum of ten pounds, might sue the winner, and recover the same with treble its value, and the costs of the suit. The game of passage, and all other games played with dice, except backgammon, were prohibited by 13 Geo. 2, c. 19 (1740), and gaming-house keepers were subjected to imprisonment with hard labour by 3 Geo. 4, c. 114 (Aug. 5, 1822). The police are entitled to enter all gaming-houses, and arrest the frequenters, by 2 & 3 Vict. c. 47, s. 48 (Aug. 17, 1839), and most of the former statutes on the subject were consolidated, repealed, or amended by 8 & 9 Vict. c. 109 (Aug. 8, 1845), which is now the principal statute respecting gaming. Betting-offices were suppressed by 16 & 17 Vict. c. 119 (Aug. 20, 1853), and the opposition of constables in their efforts to enter a house was made proof that the said house is a common gaming-house, by 17 & 18 Vict. c. 38 (July 24, 1854).

Gaol.—A strong place for the confinement of offenders against the law. Every county of England and Wales must maintain one common gaol at its own expense; and at least one house of correction at the expense of every county and division having a distinct commission of the peace. Every prison must possess a resident keeper, and resident matron to superintend the female prisoners; also a visiting chaplain and surgeon; and must be visited three times a year by two or more justices of the peace appointed at the quarter sessions for that purpose

The Queen's Prison, Millbank, Parkhurst, and Pentonville Prisons are subject to separate and specific regulations.

Gaol Delivery.—A commission to the judges empowering them to try and deliver every prisoner who may be in gaol when they arrive at the assize towns, whenever or before whomsoever indicted, or for whatever crime committed.

Garter (Order of the).—King Edward III., wishing to emulate the example of the renowned Arthur, and found an order of chivalry which should become as famous as the Round Table, issued letters, Jan. 1, 1344, in which he invited knights of all nations to take part in a grand tournament to be celebrated at Windsor on Monday, Jan. 18. According to Selden, the order of the Garter was founded April 23, 1344 ; but Ashmole considers it to have originated in 1349 or 1350. The companions were not chosen till July, 1346, and Sir Harris Nicolas is of opinion that the order was not definitely established until the latter part of 1347. The earliest delivery of mantles to the knights was in September, 1351, and in May, 1418, the office of Garter King of Arms was created. The collar and George of the order were granted by Henry VII. about 1497, and new statutes were adopted in 1522. The star was granted by Charles I. in 1626. The order of the Garter was reconstituted Jan. 17, 1805, and made to consist of the Sóvereign and twenty-five knights companions, with such lineal descendants of George III. as may be elected, and the Prince of Wales.

Gavelkind.—A custom which holds in Kent, concerning the descent of lands in most parts of that county, whereby the lands of the father are equally divided at his death amongst all his sons, or the land of the brother among all the brothers, if the brother has no issue. Females inherit jointly and severally as at common law. Many parts of Kent are *disgavelled* by various statutes, and the mode of descent rendered conformable to the course of inheritance at common law, but it still prevails to a considerable extent. The widow of a *gavelkind man*, as he is termed, takes a life interest in the half of her husband's gavelkind lands, and the husband is tenant by courtesy of his wife's land, whether he has issue by her or not. This custom cannot be avoided by making a will, for the custom cannot be separated from the land : as the term is, the custom runs with the land.

General Quarter Sessions of the Peace, Courts of.—Tribunals held in every county, before two or more justices of the peace, once in every quarter. When held otherwise than quarterly, they are called "The General Sessions of the Peace." Their jurisdiction is now confined to the trial of smaller felonies and misdemeanours within their respective counties—viz., offences relating to game, highways, bastards, servants' wages, &c. *See* 5 & 6 Vict. c. 38 ; 7 & 8 Vict. c. 71 ; and 22 & 23 Vict. c. 4.

General Register Office.—At the dissolution of the monasteries parish registers were first kept in England. In 1694 a registration act was passed for the purpose of imposing a war-tax on marriages, births, and burials. Under the Registration Act (6 & 7 Will. 4, c. 86), a registrar-general was first appointed ; and this act, amended by 1 Vict. c. 22, governs the department at the present time. Certified copies of the registers of all the births, deaths, and marriages in England and Wales are forwarded to this office by the various local superintending registrars. These registers are indexed, and here are prepared the weekly returns of mortality, and the various monthly and annual statistical reports. Hours : 10 to 4. Somerset House.

General Warrant.—A process which formerly issued from the office of the Secretary of State to arrest, without naming any one in particular, the author, printer, and publisher of such seditious libels specified in it. Declared illegal by the House of Commons in 1766.

Gentleman Usher of Black Rod.—*See* BLACK ROD.

Gentleman.—This name is derived from the Latin *gentilis*, which signified such as were of the same family or *gens*, and is a corruption of the French *gentilhomme*. It exists in some form in all the Romance languages, and is defined by Selden as "one that either from the blood of his ancestors, or the favour of his Sovereign, or of them that have power of sovereignty in them, or from his own virtue, employment, or otherwise according to the laws and customs of honour in the country we speak of, is ennobled, made gentle, or so raised up to an eminency above the multitude, perpetually inherent in his person, that by those laws and customs he be truly *nobilis* or noble, whether he have any of the precedent titles or not fixed besides on him."

Goods and Chattels.—The denomination of things personal as distinguished from things real, or lands, tenements, and hereditaments.

Grace, Days of.—Time of indulgence and respite granted to an acceptor for the payment of his bill of exchange. It was originally a favour, but custom has now rendered it a legal right. The number of these days varies according to the ancient custom or express law prevailing in each particular country. In England three days are allowed.

Grand Jury.—An inquisition composed of not less than twelve and not more than twenty-three good and lawful men of a county, who inquire and execute all those things commanded them by the Queen. They ought to be freeholders, but to what amount is uncertain.

Great Britain.—This name was first applied to England, Wales, and Scotland, at the union of the two crowns, Oct. 24, 1604, when James I. was proclaimed King of Great Britain, France, and Ireland. A national flag for Great Britain was announced by royal proclamation, April 12, 1606. The legal application commenced at the legislative union, agreed upon by the commissioners July 22, 1706, when it was provided that the two States should form one "United Kingdom of Great Britain." An act passed (6 Anne, c. 11) to carry out the union received the royal assent March 6, 1707 (*see* UNION OF ENGLAND AND SCOTLAND). It took effect from May 1, 1707, and a proclamation, July 28, appointed the national flag. It was the same as the one agreed upon in 1606, which had fallen into disuse.

Great Britain, Administrations of. — Hallam states :—" According to the original constitution of our monarchy, the King had his privy council, composed of the great officers of State, and of such others as he should summon to it, bound by an oath of fidelity and secrecy, by whom all affairs of weight, whether as to domestic or exterior policy, were debated, for the most part in his presence, and determined, subordinately of course to his pleasure, by the vote of the major part. It could not happen but that some councillors, more eminent than the rest, should form juntos or cabals, for more close and private management, or be selected as more confidential advisers of their Sovereign ; and the very name of a cabinet council, as distinguished from the larger body, may be found as far back as the reign of Charles I. But the resolutions of the Crown, whether as to foreign alliances or the issuing of proclamations and orders at home, or any other overt act of Government, were not finally taken without the deliberation and assent of that body whom the law recognised as its sworn and notorious councillors. This was first broken in upon after the Restoration. . . . Thus by degrees it became usual for the ministry or cabinet to obtain the King's final approbation of their measures before they were laid, for a merely formal ratification, before the council. . . . During the reign of William III. this distinction of the cabinet from the privy council, and the exclusion of the latter from all business of state, became more fully established." Thus it was not until after the Revolution that the cabinet council, as distinguished from the privy council, was formed. Monarchs had, indeed before that time, been in the habit of seeking advice from particular members of the privy council, and too frequently from favourites. In the earlier days of cabinets, ministers were only accountable for their own departments, and did not necessarily retire when their leaders or colleagues were dismissed. Nor did the minister who was considered the chief always preside over the Treasury. The office of Prime Minister is of more recent date. The practice for ministers presiding over particular departments of the Government to form themselves into what is now termed an administration, under the control of a chief, cannot be said to have been established until the reign of Queen Anne. The following is a list of the administrations that have held office from the commencement of her reign till the present time :—

Godolphin	1702	Rockingham (*second*) . .	1782
Harley	1710	Shelburne	1782
Shrewsbury . .	1714	Coalition	1783
Halifax	1714	Pitt (*first*) . . .	1783
Carlisle . . .	1715	Addington . . .	1801
Walpole (*first*) . .	1715	Pitt (*second*) . . .	1804
Stanhope . . .	1717	"All the Talents" . .	1806
Sunderland . . .	1718	Portland . . .	1807
Walpole (*second*) . .	1721	Perceval . . .	1809
Wilmington . . .	1742	Liverpool . . .	1812
Pelham . . .	1743	Canning . . .	1827
Broad-Bottom Administra-		Goderich . . .	1827
tion	1744	Wellington . . .	1828
Long-lived Administration .	1746	Grey	1830
Broad-Bottom Administra-		Melbourne (*first*) .	1834
tion restored . .	1746	Peel (*first*) . . .	1834
Newcastle . . .	1754	Melbourne (*second*) .	1835
Devonshire . . .	1756	Peel (*second*) . . .	1841
Newcastle and Pitt, after-		Russell (*first*) . .	1846
wards Lord Chatham (*first*)	1757	Derby (*first*) . . .	1852
Bute	1762	Aberdeen . . .	1852
Grenville . . .	1763	Palmerston (*first*) . .	1855
Rockingham (*first*) . .	1765	Derby (*second*) . .	1858
Chatham (*second*) . .	1766	Palmerston (*second*) . .	1859
Grafton . . .	1767	Russell (*second*) . .	1865
North	1770	Derby (*third*) . . .	1866

Great Seal of England. — The earliest English monarch who is known to have made grants under seal is Edgar (A.D. 957 to 975), but the institution of the Great Seal is usually attributed to Edward the Confessor (1041 to 1066). The custody of the great seal is the prerogative of the Lord Chancellor, but as there is sometimes an interval between the death of that officer and the appointment of his successor, a Keeper of the Great Seal was appointed to act in such cases. His dignity was declared equal to the Lord Chancellor's by 5 Eliz. c. 18 (1562). Commissioners of the Great Seal were appointed in 1689, and authorised by 1 Will. & Mary, c. 21 (1688). By the union between England and Scotland it is provided that there should be one great seal for the United Kingdom of Great Britain, which should be used for sealing all public acts of state, &c. which relate to the United Kingdom: and that a seal in Scotland should be kept and made use of for all things relating to private rights, &c. within Scotland. It was also enacted at the union of England and Ireland, that the great seal of Ireland may be used within Ireland as before the union, if the Crown thinks fit.

Green Cloth, Board of.—*See* BOARD OF.

Groom of the Stole.—An officer of the Royal Household who has charge of the King's wardrobe.

Guardian, in law, a person who has the charge of anything; but more commonly it signifies one who has the custody and education of such persons as have not sufficient discretion to take care of themselves and their own affairs, as children and idiots. The business of a guardian is to take the profits of the minor's lands to his use, and to account for the same: he ought to sell all moveables within a reasonable time, and to convert them into land or money, except the minor is near of age, and may want such things himself; and he is to pay interest for the money in his hands, that might have been so placed out. He is to sustain the lands of the heir, without making destruction of anything thereon, and to keep it safely for him; if he commits waste on the lands, it is a forfeiture of the guardianship. Where persons, as guardians, hold over any land, without the consent of the person who is next entitled, they shall be adjudged trespassers, and shall be accountable.

Guardian of the Spiritualities.—The person to whom the spiritual jurisdiction of any diocese is committed, during the time the see is vacant. A guardian of the spiritualities may likewise be either such in law, as the archbishop is in any diocese within his province; or by delegation, as he whom the archbishop or vicar-general for the time appoints. Any such guardian has power to hold courts, grant licences, dispensations, &c.

Gypsies were for a long period supposed to be of Egyptian origin, their very name being a corruption of the word Egyptians; but it is now generally believed that they are the descendants of some Hindoo Pariahs who were exiled from their country by Tamerlane at the commencement of the fifteenth century. They first appeared in Europe, in the Danubian provinces, in 1417. In 1418 they are found in Switzerland, and in 1422 in Italy. They appeared in France in 1427, in Spain in 1447, in England about 1512, and in Sweden in 1514. By 22 Hen. VIII., c. 10 (1530), they were ordered to quit the country, and severe ordinances were also issued against them by 1 & 2 Phil. & Mary, c. 4 (1554), and 5 Eliz., c. 20 (1562), which made their continuance in England for more than a month a capital felony. In 1560 they were expelled from France, and in 1591 from Spain; but, in spite of all legislative enactments, they still exist in all the countries of Europe. The oppressive statutes against them in this country were repealed by 23 Geo. III., c. 51 (1783), by 1 Geo. IV., c. 116 (July 25, 1820), and by 19 & 20 Vict. c. 64 (July 21, 1856).

Habeas Corpus Act.—This celebrated statute confirmed and rendered more available a remedy which had long existed. "The writ of *Habeas Corpus*, requiring a return of

M

the body imprisoned and the *cause* of his detention, and hence anciently called *corpus cum causâ*, was in familiar use between subject and subject in the reign of Henry VI. Its use by a subject against the Crown has not been traced during the time of the Plantagenet dynasty ; the earliest precedents known being of the date of Henry VII." The privilege of *Habeas Corpus* was twice solemnly confirmed in the reign of Charles I., first by the Petition of Right (1628), and secondly by the statute abolishing the star chamber and other arbitrary courts (1640). But as Charles II. and his ministers still found means to evade these enactments, the celebrated statute was passed in 1679, known as *the* Habeas Corpus Act. Its principal author was Lord Shaftesbury, and it was for many years called " Lord Shaftesbury's Act." It enacts :—

I. That on complaint and request in writing by or on behalf of any person committed and charged with any crime (unless committed for treason or felony expressed in the warrant ; or as accessory or on suspicion of being accessory before the fact to any petit treason or felony ; or upon suspicion of such petit treason or felony plainly expressed in the warrant ; or unless he is convicted or charged in execution by legal process), the Lord Chancellor, or any of the judges in vacation, upon viewing a copy of the warrant or affidavit that a copy is denied, shall (unless the party has neglected for two terms to apply to any Court for his enlargement) award a *habeas corpus* for such prisoner, returnable immediately before himself or any other of the judges ; and upon the return made shall discharge the party, if bailable, upon giving security to appear and answer to the accusation in the proper court of judicature.

II. That such writs shall be indorsed as granted in pursuance of this Act, and signed by the person awarding them.

III. That the writ shall be returned and the prisoner brought up within a limited time according to the distance, not exceeding in any case twenty days.

IV. That officers and keepers neglecting to make due returns, or not delivering to the prisoner or his agent within six hours after demand a copy of the warrant of commitment, or shifting the custody of the prisoner from one to another without sufficient reason or authority (specified in the Act), shall for the first offence forfeit £100, and for the second offence £200 to the party grieved, and be disabled to hold his office.

V. That no person once delivered by *habeas corpus* shall be re-committed for the same offence, on penalty of £500.

VI. That every person committed for treason or felony shall, if he requires it, the first week of the next term, or the first day of the next session of *oyer* and *terminer*, be indicted in that term or session, or else admitted to bail, unless the king's witnesses cannot be produced at that time; and if acquitted, or not indicted and tried in the second term or session, he shall be discharged from his imprisonment for such imputed offence; but that no person, after the assizes shall be open for the county in which he is detained, shall be removed by *habeas corpus* till after the assizes are ended, but shall be left to the justice of the judges of assize.

VII. That any such prisoner may move for and obtain his *habeas corpus* as well out of the Chancery or Exchequer as out of the King's Bench or Common Pleas; and the Lord Chancellor or judges denying the same on sight of the warrant or oath that the same is refused, forfeits severally to the party grieved the sum of £500.

VIII. That this writ of *habeas corpus* shall run into the counties palatine, cinque ports, and other privileged places, and the islands of Jersey and Guernsey.

IX. That no inhabitant of England (except persons contracting or convicts praying to be transported, or having committed some capital offence in the place to which they are sent) shall be sent prisoner to Scotland, Ireland, Jersey, Guernsey, or any places beyond the seas within or without the king's dominions, on pain that the party committing, his advisers, aiders, and assistants, shall forfeit to the party aggrieved a sum not less than £500, to be recovered with treble costs; shall be disabled to bear any office of trust or profit; shall incur the penalties of *præmunire;* and shall be incapable of the king's pardon.

The Habeas Corpus Act was confined to criminal cases, but by the 56 Geo. III., c. 100, was extended not only to cases of illegal restraint by subject on subject, but also to those in which the Crown has an interest, as in instances of impressment or smuggling.

Hanaper Office.—Was an office of the Court of Chancery, where writs relating to the business of the subject, and their returns, were kept *in hanaperio* (in a hamper), whilst those relating to the crown in a little bag. Hence the names Hanaper and Petty Bag Office. Abolished in 1842.

Health, Board of. *See* Board of.

Heir.—One who succeeds by descent to an estate of inheritance. The various kinds of heirs may be classed and defined thus :—

Heir apparent.—He whose right or inheritance is indefeasible, provided he outlive the ancestor.

Heir by custom.—He who is heir by a particular and local custom.

Heir by devise.—He who is made by will the testator's heir or devisee, and has no other right than the will gives him.

Heir general or heir-at-law.—He who after his father's or ancestor's death has a right to inherit all his lands, &c.

Heir presumptive.—He who if the ancestor should die immediately would, in the present circumstances of things, be his heir; but whose right of inheritance may be defeated by the contingency of some nearer heir being born.

Heir of the blood and inheritance.—A son who may be defeated of his inheritance by his father's displeasure.

Heir special.—An heir who is not heir at common law, as an heir by gavelkind, borough-English, &c.

Ultimus hæres.—He to whom lands come by escheat or forfeiture for want of proper heirs, or on account of treason or felony.

Heir-loom in our law-books, signifies such goods and personal chattels as are not inventoried after the owner's decease, but necessarily come to the heir along with the house. Heir-loom comprehends divers implements ; as tables, presses, cupboards, bedsteads, furnaces, wainscot, and such like. These articles are never inventoried after the decease of the owner, but accrue by custom, not by common law, to the heir, with the house itself. The ancient jewels of the Crown are held to be heir-looms, and are not devisable by will, but descend to the next successor.

Heptarchy.—This word, which signifies the government of seven rulers, is applied to the divisions of England under the Saxons. The first Saxon monarchy in England was that of Kent, founded A.D. 455. The erection of Sussex into a kingdom in 491 established the *Duarchy*, which became a *Triarchy* on the foundation of Wessex in 519. The commencement of the states of Essex and East Angles, in 527, made it a *Pentarchy*, which became a *Hexarchy* when Ida founded Bernicia, in 547, and a *Heptarchy* on the establishment of the British kingdom of Deira, in 559. An eighth state, Mercia, formed in 586, constituted the *Octarchy*, which continued till 670, when the union of Deira and Bernicia into the single kingdom of Northumbria restored the Heptarchy. The seven kingdoms were gradually united into one by Egbert and his successors.

Herald.—An officer whose business it is to register genealogies, adjust ensigns armorial, regulate funerals, &c. The three chief heralds are called kings-of-arms ; of whom [A] Garter is the principal, instituted by Henry V. His office is to attend the knights of the Garter at their solemnities, and to marshal the funerals of the nobility. [B] Clarencieux King of Arms, instituted by Edward IV. ; so called from the Duke of Clarence. He is to marshal and dispose the funerals of the inferior nobility on the south side of the Trent. [C] Norroy King of Arms, holds a similar appointment on the north side of the river Trent. These two last are called provincial heralds. Besides the kings of arms there are six subordinate heralds—York, Lancaster, Chester, Windsor, Richmond, and Somerset. At the accession of George I. two new heralds were added to the above, Hanover and Gloucester. To the superior and inferior heralds are annexed four others, called marshals or pursuivants of arms, viz., Blue Mantle, Rouge Croix, Rouge Dragon, and Portcullis. Lord Lyon's office in Scotland, and Ulster King of Arms in Ireland, are distinct and independent.

Hereditament is a very comprehensive term, including whatever may be inherited, be it corporeal or incorporeal. Corporeal hereditaments consist wholly of substantial and permanent objects, all of which may be comprehended under the general denomination of land. An incorporeal hereditament is a right issuing out of a thing corporeal, whether real or personal, or concerning or annexed to the same—such as rights of way, advowsons, rights of common, annuities, &c.

Heresy.—An opinion of private individuals different from that of the orthodox church. Queen Elizabeth repealed all former statutes relating to heresy, leaving the jurisdiction of this subject as it stood at common law. Heresy now consists of such tenets as have been heretofore so declared (1) by the words of the canonical Scriptures ; (2) by the first four general councils, or such others as have only used the words of the Holy Scriptures ; or (3) which shall hereafter be so declared by Parliament with the assent of the clergy in convocation. By statute 9 & 10 Will. III., c. 32, if any person educated in the Christian religion, or professing the same, shall by writing, printing, teaching, or advised speaking, deny the Christian religion to be true, or the Holy Scriptures to be of Divine authority, or maintain that there are more Gods than one, he shall incur sundry civil disabilities, and on a second conviction shall be imprisoned for three years.

Heriot is a due to the lord of a manor, rendered at the death of a copyhold tenant, or on a surrender or alienation of his estate, being the best beast or goods found in the possession of the tenant deceased, or otherwise according to custom. The copyholder who holds by a free tenure, not a base tenure, as the mere copy holder, seldom pays a heriot, but only something certain in the name of a heriot, such as a penny, &c. For heriots, the lord may either seize, distrain, or bring action of debt : the seizure may be out of the manor, but the distress (which may be of any third party, goods, or beasts upon the land) must be made within the manor, viz., on the land itself.

High Commission Court.—This tribunal was erected in 1559 to vindicate the dignity and peace of the Church by reforming the ecclesiastical state, and all manner of errors, heresies, abuses, &c. The powers of this court were directed to unconstitutional purposes, and it was therefore abolished in 1641 by Charles I.

High Constable of England, Lord.—This officer existed in the Anglo-Saxon period of our history. His jurisdiction was defined by 8 Rich. II., c. 5 (1385). The Duke of Buckingham, tried and executed for high treason, May 21, 1521, forfeited the office, and it has never been revived, except upon great occasions, as the coronation or the like. The Lord High Constable and the Earl Marshal were judges of the Court of Chivalry, called in the reign of Henry IV. Curia Militaris.

High Steward of England, Lord.—The office of Lord High Steward is of great antiquity, having existed before the time of Edward the Confessor, and the holder of which was at that period the first great officer of the Crown. It was for many years hereditary in the family of the Earls of Leicester, but on the attainder of Simon of Montfort in 1265 it was abolished, and is now only revived for the special occasions of a coronation or the trial of a peer. On the 12th of January 1559, Henry, Earl of Arundel, was created High Steward for the coronation of Queen Elizabeth, Jan. 15, to hold that office from "the rising of the sun on the same day to the setting thereof." Whenever a grand jury finds a true bill against a peer on a charge of treason or felony, a commission is issued constituting a Lord High Steward, with authority to try the accused.

High Treasurer of England, Lord.—This, the third great officer of the Crown, had the custody of the royal Treasury, and of the foreign and domestic documents kept there. The office is held during pleasure. The first Lord High Treasurer was Odo, Earl of Kent and Bishop of Bayeux, in the reign of William the Conqueror. For many years the office was held by ecclesiastics, the first lay treasurer being Richard, Lord Scroop, in 1371. The Duke of Shrewsbury, appointed by Queen Anne, July 29, 1714, and who resigned office a few days afterwards, was the last High Treasurer of England. Since that time the office has always been vested in commissioners, the chief of whom is the First Lord of the Treasury, and generally, though not necessarily, head of the Government.

Homage.—*See* FEUDAL SYSTEM.

Home Office.—The present organisation of the Home Office took place in 1801 ; before that year it had been united with the Foreign and Colonial departments. The Secretary of State for the Home Department has direct control over all matters relating to the internal affairs of Great Britain. He controls the administration of criminal justice, and the whole police force as well as the county constabulary. All official communications from the Cabinet to the vice-regal court of Ireland are made through this department, and the Home Secretary is consulted by the Lord Lieutenant on all matters of moment connected with that country. He is assisted in the discharge of his official duties by two under-secretaries, and various other officials. Hours : 11 to 5, Whitehall.

Homicide, signifies in general, the taking away of any person's life. It is of three kinds ; *justifiable, excusable,* and *felonious.* The first has no share of guilt at all ; the second very little ; but the third is the highest crime against the law of nature that man is capable of committing.

Honour, Maids of.—Ladies in attendance upon the Queen ; they are six in number, and receive salaries of £300 a year each.

Honourable.—A title of quality given to the younger children of Earls, and the children of Viscounts and Barons. Also to persons enjoying offices of trust and honour.

House of Commons.—The earliest instance of the assembly of knights, citizens, and burgesses as members of parliament, occurred Jan. 20, 1265, the parliament of 1258 having been exclusively composed of barons. They were not again summoned till the parliament of Nov. 12, 1294, and were established as a necessary part of the legislature by the declaratory statute of York, in 1322. Various statutes have been passed to regulate the amount of property necessary to enable a man to sit in the House of Commons, all of which were repealed by 21 Vict. c. 26 (June 28, 1858). The House of Commons has frequently changed its place of assembly. Our earliest knowledge on this point is that the parliament of April 30, 1343, met in the Painted Chamber, Westminster. In 1376 the Chapter-house is mentioned as the usual meeting-place, and in 1547 Edward VI. granted St. Stephen's chapel for the purpose. This building was destroyed by fire Oct. 16, 1834, and the Commons took possession of their new house Nov. 4, 1852. The following table exhibits the number of representatives now composing the House of Commons :—

ENGLAND AND WALES.

Knights of shires 160
Citizens and burgesses 340
—— 500

SCOTLAND.

Knights of the shires 30
Citizens and burgesses 23
—— 53

IRELAND.

Knight of shires 64
Citizens and burgesses 41
—— 105

Total of the United Kingdom 658

House of Lords.—The bishops and archbishops of England have composed a portion of the great council of the nation from the time of the Saxons, and they, with the barons, formed the king's council from the Conquest to the reign of John. The personal privilege of the peers was determined in 1341. The House of Lords was abolished by the Long Parliament, Feb. 6, 1649, but constituted part of the first parliament after the Restoration, April 25, 1660. The House of Lords has had various places of assembly. The first record on the subject states that in 1343 it met in the White Chamber, Westminster. The Painted Chamber was also a frequent place of assembly. Its place of meeting is first styled the " House of Lords" in 1543. The old palace of Westminster having been destroyed by fire, Oct. 16, 1834, the present Houses of Parliament were erected in its stead. The peers took possession of their new house April 15, 1847. The number of members in the House of Lords is always liable to increase, owing to the royal prerogative of creating new peerages. The following is a statement of its present numbers :—

LORDS SPIRITUAL.

2 Archbishops (English).

24 Bishops (English).   The Bishop of Sodor and
 Man and the Junior Bishop have no seat.

1 Archbishop (Irish).

3 Bishops (Irish).

———

30

LORDS TEMPORAL.

4 Princes of royal blood.

20 Dukes.

21 Marquesses.

128 Earls.

30 Viscounts.

231 Barons.

———

434

Total of the House of Lords 464.

The House of Lords is the Supreme Court of Judicature in the kingdom.

Hundred, HUNDREDUM, or *Centuria,* a part or division of a county.   It was anciently so called from its containing a hundred families, or from its furnishing a hundred able men for the King's wars.   After King Alfred's dividing this kingdom into counties, and giving the government of each county to a sheriff, these counties were divided into hundreds, of which the constable was the chief officer.   The grants of hundreds were at first made by the King to particular persons : but they are not now held by grant or prescription, their jurisdiction having devolved to the county court ; a few of them only excepted, that have been by privilege annexed to the crown, or granted to some great subjects, and still remain in the nature of a franchise.

Hundred-Court.—This was only a larger *Court-Baron,*

being held for all the inhabitants of a particular hundred
instead of a manor.   The free suitors were here also the judges,
and the steward the registrar, as in the case of a court-baron.
It was likewise no court of record ; resembling the former in all
points, except that in point of territory it was of a greater jurisdiction.   This court is said by Sir Edward Coke to have been
derived out of the county court for the ease of the people, that
they might have justice done them at their own doors, without
any charge or loss of time : but its institution was probably
coeval with that of hundreds themselves.   The court is become
obsolete.

Husband and Wife.—The law of England considers marriage in no other light than as a civil contract,
although it is accompanied with a religious ceremony and
formalities.

By marriage, the husband and wife are one person in law ;
that is, the very being or legal existence of the woman is
deemed suspended during marriage, or at least is incorporated
and consolidated into that of the husband, under whose protection she performs every thing.   Owing to this fictitious
unity, it is a rule of *law*, that a 'married woman cannot
possess *personal* property ; so every thing of that nature to
which she is entitled at the time of her marriage, and which
accrues in her right, whether by gift, bequest, or otherwise,
during the marriage, vests solely in the husband ; he takes
it free from any right of survivorship in the wife ; he may
dispose of it during his life, or bequeath it at his death ; and,
if he does not dispose of it, his executors and administrators,
and not his wife exclusively, although she may survive him,
will be entitled thereto.   All sums of money which the wife
earns by her own skill and labour belong to the husband, and
after his death they form part of his estate, though the wife
survive.   All money lent by the wife, or which another may
receive on her account during the marriage, belongs likewise to

the husband, and he alone is the proper person able to sue for it. But with respect to a certain kind of personal property called choses in action, the husband's interest is of a more limited nature than it is in other personalty.

Choses in action are mere rights arising from contracts expressed or implied, which must be asserted at law for the purpose of being reduced into possession, or, more plainly speaking, those things of which the possession can, in case of refusal, be recovered by legal process, being outstanding dues, such as money due on simple contract, specialty, damages for breach of contract, reversionary interests in personal property, &c. When these rights belong to a woman at the time of her marriage, or come to her since, they are only the husband's conditionally, *i.e.*, provided he get them into absolute possession in her lifetime, which if he does not do, and she die first, his right would only accrue as her administrator; but, if he should die first, she would be entitled, by what is termed her right of survivorship absolutely, even if she had concurred in the sale or mortgage of them by her husband; though, after they are reduced into possession, the sale by the husband seems good enough at law; yet in this last case the wife's concurrence is necessary to bar her of her right of settlement or equitable relief or allowance.

With respect to leases, and what are termed chattels real, the husband has power to dispose of them during her life, and, if he survive, they are his absolutely; they are, while he and the wife are both alive, liable for his debts, and subject to an outlawry obtained against him. If the wife survive, of course they belong to her. The husband is entitled to all rents due in his wife's right, in the same way as to her leases, and by his surviving he will be entitled to the arrears accrued due before and since the marriage; if she survive, she is entitled by her right of survivorship. After the death of the wife, the husband is entitled to administration of her personal property. After the death of the husband, the wife can, with the next of kin or reserving their right, take out administration.

With regard to a wife's unsettled real property, she cannot deal with it during the marriage except with her husband, its management devolving upon her husband, who may apply the proceeds of it to his own use. After his death the estate remains entire to her or her heirs, should she die before him, unless by the birth of a child, born alive and capable of inheriting the property, the husband become entitled to a previous estate for life, which is termed tenancy by the courtesy of England. This tenancy, however, only entitles the husband to a bare estate for life, in which he is restricted from impoverishing or wasting the estate, and cannot anticipate the profits by granting leases upon fines, though of course there is nothing to prevent his taking a fine upon a lease for his own life, reserving a nominal rent.

Four things must concur to render this estate for life perfect : 1. The marriage, which must be lawful. 2. The title or possession of the wife. 3. The birth of such issue, which by course of law would inherit the land. 4. The death of the wife. This tenancy does not attach as a legal or necessary consequence upon lands of copyhold tenure ; it generally holds by custom. The custom of gavelkind in Kent allows of this life-tenancy, but it is only half the land, and is forfeited by the husband's marrying again. The wife may, with the concurrence of the husband, convey her inheritable estate to a purchaser, by acknowledging the same before a judge, master in chancery, or commissioner, and being examined privately as to her consent. The husband and wife are restricted from granting unreasonable leases, tending to deteriorate an entailed estate, viz., leases for not more than twenty-one years, or longer than three lives. On the other hand, the husband, in recompense of the benefit he derives from courtesy, &c., is bound to discharge all obligations entered into by the wife before marriage ; for otherwise her creditors might lose their just debts ; but this responsibility is confined to the wife's engagements while unmarried ; for if made during a former marriage, her aftertaken husband is not liable for them, upon the principle that during marriage she is incapable of making any contract. And again, this liability on the part of the husband lasts only as long as the marriage ; for, should she die before her husband has paid the debts, he is released from further responsibility ; and should he die before the recovery of them, *i.e.*, before judgment obtained, she alone will be liable, and the husband's estate exonerated. Yet for debts contracted by her during the time she was unmarried, in consideration of the personal fortune he has received with her, he may be liable as her administrator ; for if there is any outstanding property not realised (choses in action) they are assets in the husband's hands as such administrator ; and to those debts he will be liable in that character, not as husband, as far as those assets or property will extend, but no further. And, lastly, the husband is liable to debts contracted by his wife as executrix before marriage, either by waste or mismanagement ; consequently the husband is chargeable therewith, and, upon a judgment in an action sued against them for such a cause, he may be taken in execution after her decease.

Although the contract of a married woman is absolutely void, yet with respect to certain contracts, namely, such as relate to suitable necessaries for her husband's family, she will be regarded as his agent, generally constituted for that purpose ; a presumption perfectly accordant with his own liability, and the duty of both, and which consequently implies his assent ; for, with respect to other contracts, she is not his agent, unless his authority be expressly proved ; yet an implied assent will be disproved by evidence that a positive order or notice was given by the husband, that his wife should not be trusted by the party seeking to charge him, except where the husband has improperly turned her out of doors, or abandoned her, in which case a promise will be implied, notwithstanding the husband's notice ; for otherwise the wife might suffer intolerable hardships. The chief point to be considered by tradesmen is, are the things purchased necessaries ? If they are such, it matters not whether the husband and wife cohabit : the husband is liable, unless the goods be furnished under his express notice to the contrary, or credit be given to the wife alone, or the tradesman is fairly presumed cognisant of particular circumstances, such as a separate allowance to the wife, previous and abundant supply to the wife by the husband, &c. However, the case of desertion, and notice not to trust given by the husband, is no reason why the husband should not be liable for her maintenance and necessaries duly furnished : if the things purchased are not necessaries, or not suitable to the apparent situation in life of the wife, which of course follows that of the husband, then it is incumbent on the tradesman supplying them to make inquiry as to the power of the wife to bind the husband, and to prove the husband's express direction to her to make the purchase, or, at least, that he saw her use the articles bought without expressing any disapprobation.

If a wife have illegally absented herself from her husband's house, or conducted herself extravagantly when there, and is likely to endeavour to obtain necessaries or goods on the credit of her husband, he may, and should, in order to protect himself from liability, give a public notice in the *Gazette*, or newspapers circulated in the neighbourhood, prohibiting third persons from trusting her on his credit. A man is responsible for necessaries or goods furnished to any woman whom he represents to be his wife, and whom he permits to use his name. However it should be remembered, that, if action be brought against a man for goods furnished to a woman after she has ceased to cohabit with the defendant, the plaintiff cannot recover, if there be proof that they never were married, though they may have lived together as man and wife for several years, and she may have been always introduced into society by him as his wife. And if a man, being already married, marries a second woman, he will be liable for necessaries furnished to the second wife during their cohabitation ; and he cannot discharge himself by proof of the previous marriage. But, if it could be proved that a person bringing an action in such a case knew of the celebration of the first marriage, such knowledge would be a bar to the action.

Not only clothes, meat, medicine, and lodging, but proper legal advice, in a suit necessarily instituted against the husband, are necessaries with which the law says, a husband is bound to provide his wife ; and for which, if another should supply her, he is liable to pay. The law in estimating what are necessaries, with a view of charging the husband, does not take account of the fortune brought by the wife, but only considers what the husband's circumstances were at the time when the articles were supplied. It is also decided, that a woman of her own authority may borrow money for necessaries, so as to charge her husband. The liabilities to which a husband is subject in respect of his wife, whether for debts contracted by her during the existence of the marriage, or for necessaries, cease altogether when the Divorce Court pronounces the marriage void from the beginning ; or if she elope from her husband, though not guilty of adultery, without sufficient cause ; or if she be separated provided the husband pays her an adequate allowance. Although a married woman is by the common law generally incapable of suing or being sued, yet there are a few necessary exceptions to this rule. The wife of a person transported for any period, however short, or imprisoned by a commutation of punishment, voluntarily exiled, an alien, enemy, or a foreigner, who has left England, is in each of these cases equally capable of suing and being sued as a *feme sole, i.e.* single woman.

By 20 & 21 Vict. c. 57, it is lawful for every married woman

N

by deed to dispose of every future or reversionary interest in
any personal estate whatsoever to which she is entitled under
any instrument made after the 31st December, 1857, and also
to release or extinguish any power which may be vested in or
reserved to her in regard to any such personal estate as fully
and effectually as she could do, as if she were a *feme sole*, provided her husband concurs in the deed by which the same shall
be effected, or that she be not restrained legally from alienating
the same.   The same Act however prevents her from disposing
of any interest in personal estate settled upon her by any
settlement on the occasion of her marriage.   By the Bankrupt
Law Consolidation Act, 1849, the Courts of Bankruptcy may
summon the wife of a bankrupt and examine her for the
discovery of the estate, &c., of such bankrupt kept or disposed
of by such wife in her own person, or by her own act, or by
any other person; and if she refuse to attend or to answer to
the satisfaction of the Court, she will incur the same penalty
as any other person.   By the Small Debts Act, 9 & 10 Vict. c.
95, all parties to any proceedings in the County Courts, their
wives and all other persons, may be examined on behalf of the
plaintiffs or defendants upon oath or affirmation.   On a wife's
petition to the Divorce Court for dissolution of marriage on the
ground of adultery and cruelty, or of adultery and desertion,
husband and wife, by 22 & 23 Vict. c. 61, are competent and
bound to give evidence of or relating to cruelty or desertion.

Although a married woman has no personal property during
her marriage, unless her husband be transported, or any circumstance occur by which she is presumed single, yet, on her
husband's death, previous interests, which had lain dormant,
revive, and come into operation, and she takes all her bonds,
bills, debts, and mortgages to herself absolutely, and also all
her leases which have not been disposed of by the husband in
his lifetime.   In addition to her own property, she is entitled
to what is called her paraphernalia, her jointure, and dower, or

thirds. Paraphernalia are the furniture of her chamber, in London called "the widow's chamber," her wearing-apparel, and ornaments of her person, being jewels or pearls, the quantity of which last seems to depend upon her husband's circumstances ; the general rule being, that, if he dies solvent, she may retain all, otherwise she relinquishes the most valuable, or much the greatest part. Wearing-apparel is always exempt from claims of creditors ; and, as personal estate is the fund for payment of debts in exoneration of the real estate, the widow may recover from the heir the amount which she has to pay in consequence of her husband's specialty creditors out of her paraphernalia, which otherwise would have been payable out of the real estate.

Pin-money is an annual income settled by the husband before marriage on his intended wife, or gratuitously allowed by the husband for the wife's private expenditure : this is usually secured by a covenant on the part of the husband, with nominees of the wife, being trustees, who can, if withheld, sue the husband for arrears ; but the arrears cannot, unless frequently from time to time demanded, be carried back beyond a year ; nor can arrears, under any circumstances, be recovered, where the husband has been compelled to supply her with the articles which it was the object of that allowance to furnish her with, viz., clothes and ornaments. Pin-money is forfeited by elopement, leaving home without good cause, and adultery ; and the trustees will be prevented from using legal measures to enforce payment by an injunction.

Jointure is a provision for the wife, made by the husband out of his land or houses, in case she survives her husband : it is generally executed by a settlement by deed, and in ancient practice gave the husband and wife a joint interes (hence the term) during their lives in the land or houses settled. The effect of a jointure is to bar the wife's dower or thirds in her husband's lands.

Dower is an estate for life which the widow acquires in a certain portion (generally a third, but by the custom of various manors it is half, and then called free-bench, sometimes the whole,) of her husband's freehold or copyhold land of inheritance, to the intent she may properly maintain and bring up the children. This legal provision for the wife may be lost by the act of the wife : as if she elopes, and is not afterwards reconciled to her husband ; by her obtaining a divorce from the bond of marriage ; by withholding the title-deeds of the property from the heir or devisee ; by acknowledging a conveyance of the land with her husband. Dower is also now void against creditors of the husband. Jointure is more advantageous for the wife, not only for its certainty, but because it cannot be forfeited if the marriage be valid. Dower is subject to a variety of contingencies, but few of them attach in respect of women married after December 31, 1833. With respect to the dower of those women married before January 1, 1834, dower attaches on all real property acquired by their husbands, unless they took it by a particular form of conveyance which excludes the wife; and is only forfeitable by elopement, or lost by their joining in and acknowledging a conveyance with their husbands, or accepting a certain provision. If a married woman should by any accident lose her jointure, she is entitled to her dower, subject to the restrictions imposed by the late law, if she was married on or after January 1, 1834.

As to equitable provision, the Court of Chancery will, in all cases where the husband requires its assistance in obtaining his wife's property, compel him to settle some part of it upon his wife, and children by her ; or, where the wife parts with her estate for the purpose of relieving her husband, a commensurate provision will be secured by the interference of the Court out of the husband's property : but these equitable claims of the wife can be waived by her upon a competent provision, or by specially releasing and giving up her right thereto, unless she is a ward of the Court, or a clandestine marriage has taken place. But it must be noticed that it is only in cases of legacies and trusts, and where the husband has not obtained the property, that the Court will interfere ; and if the husband does not apply for the principal, but is content with the interest, to which he is undoubtedly entitled, the Court will not compel him to make a settlement. The Court will interfere as against assignees, if the husband be bankrupt or insolvent : for, as the assignees could not obtain the fund without the interference of the Court, the Court will dictate the terms upon which the fund shall be paid them. When a married woman has her property in the hands of the Court, the Court will also secure her a separate allowance in case her husband illtreat or desert her.

Married women, who have been wards in chancery, and over whose property the Court of Chancery exercises special jurisdiction, have their property secured to them by settlement made under the direction of the Court. If a husband, on his marriage, make an adequate settlement on his wife, she has no claim for any further allowance, for by that act he becomes in equity the purchaser of her fortune ; but with respect to future property, of any very great amount, the Court will still exercise its jurisdiction, if the fund comes under the distribution of the Court, though perhaps not so strictly as where no settlement was ever made.

A wife is excused in law from criminal misconduct ; but to this the crimes of manslaughter, murder, and treason are exceptions. Adultery or criminal conversation with another man is left by our law to the punishment of the Divorce Courts ; but, as adultery is a wrong to the husband, the law gives a remedy for it by action, in which, upon the trial, all circumstances of aggravation or extenuation are brought forward ; for the jury are to collect, from a review of those circumstances, the extent of the real injury sustained by the husband in his peace of mind and happiness, and give damages accordingly. A husband can obtain a divorce in the Divorce Courts for the adultery of his wife ; but, if she can show a case of recrimination, he will not be permitted to have the relief he seeks for.

Idiots and Lunatics, are those incapable of transacting the ordinary business of life. The administration of idiots' and lunatics' estates is in virtue of personal authority given by the Crown, viz., a special commission under a warrant of the Queen's sign manual, countersigned by the Lords of the Treasury, not directed to the Court of Chancery, but to a certain great officer of the Crown, not of necessity the person who has the custody of· the Great Seal, though it is usually given him in consideration of its being his duty, as Chancellor, to issue the commissions on which the inquiry as to the facts of idiotcy or lunacy is to be obtained. This warrant confers no jurisdiction, but only a power of administration ; which power is now exercised by the Lord Chancellor and the two Lords Justices of Appeal.

The rules of equity and law are identical as to what amounts to insanity. In the case of a lunatic the Crown is but a trustee of his estate, but in the case of an idiot the Crown is absolutely entitled to the profits subject to the idiot's maintenance—a claim, however, which the Crown seldom accepts. A lunatic is never considered in law to be incurable.

Instead of a special commission, a general commission is issued to the two Masters in Lunacy to inquire into the lunacy of all persons whose cases shall be referred to them by the Lord Chancellor under a separate order in each case obtainable upon petition. The mode of inquiry without a jury as to lunatics in confinement formerly authorised by Lord Ashley's Act is now discontinued, and the inquiry conducted in the same manner whether the lunatic be confined or no. The practice in lunacy is regulated by 16 & 17 Vict. c. 70 ; amended by 18 Vict. c. 13 ; by the Lunacy Regulation Act, 1862, 25 & 26 Vict. c. 86 ; and the General Orders, Nov. 7, 1853.

Impeachment.—A prosecution by the House of Commons before the House of Lords of a commoner for treason or other high crimes and misdemeanors, or of a peer for any crime. It is a proceeding of great importance, involving the exercise of the highest judicial powers of Parliament. In modern times it has been rarely resorted to, but in former periods of our history it was of frequent occurrence. The last memorable cases of impeachment are those of Warren Hastings in 1788, and Lord Melville in 1805. In a bill of attainder the Commons are the judges as well as the Lords.

Imprisonment.—A restraint or detention of the person. None shall be imprisoned but by the lawful judgment of his peers, or by the law of the land — *Magna Charta;* and no person is to be imprisoned but as the law directs.

False Imprisonment, is arresting or imprisoning without just cause, contrary to law ; or where a person is unlawfully detained, without legal process. If a person be any way unlawfully detained, it is false imprisonment ; and considerable damages are recoverable in these actions. If a person be imprisoned on any by-law of a corporation, &c., it is false imprisonment ; because a by-law to imprison is against Magna Charta. If a justice of peace commit a person without just cause, it is false imprisonment ; and a constable cannot imprison a man at his pleasure, to compel him to do anything required by law, but is to carry him before a justice. When any justice sends for a man, and commits him to gaol without any examination, the party may have action of false imprisonment against him ; and if a justice of peace sends a general warrant to arrest a person, and say not for what, action lies against him, but not against the officer. If an arrest is made by one who is no legal officer, or not named in the warrant, it is false imprisonment, for which action lies. An action of false imprisonment lies against a bailiff for arresting a person without warrant, though he afterwards receives a warrant ; and so it is if he arrest one after the return of the writ is passed, or without showing the warrant. If a sheriff, or any of his bailiffs, arrest a man out of his county' or after the sheriff is discharged from office, or a person arrest one on a justice's warrant, after his commission is determined, &c., it will be false imprisonment. And if the sheriff, after he has arrested a man lawfully, when a legal discharge comes to him, do not discharge the party, he may be sued by this action.

In case the plaintiff in a suit brings an unlawful warrant to a sheriff, and shows him the defendant, requiring him to make the arrest; or if he bring a good warrant, and direct the sheriff to a wrong man, &c., for this the action for false imprisonment will lie against both. If a warrant be granted to arrest or apprehend a person, where there are several of the name, and the bailiff or other officer arrests a wrong person, he is liable to action of false imprisonment; and he is to take notice of the right party at his peril. A man arrested on a Sunday, or after the sheriff's officer has broken into his house, may bring his action for false imprisonment against the sheriff's bailiff; but the party arrested will not be released, except the Court will notice the arrest on the Sunday, &c., as an irregularity, and then, it seems, the party must waive his action. Mere irregularities in lawful process against the person may be considered as wrongful imprisonments, and the judges will discharge the party, if he agree to waive his right of action. If a bailiff demand more than his just fees, when offered him, and keep a person in custody thereupon, it is false imprisonment, and punishable; and if a sheriff or gaoler keep a prisoner in gaol after his acquittal, for anything except for lawful fees, it is unlawful imprisonment. Unlawful or false imprisonment is sometimes called duress of imprisonment, where one is wrongfully imprisoned till he seals a bond, &c. All persons concerned in a wrong imprisonment can be sued in action of false imprisonment, and the party grieved may sue any one of them for it. The power of imprisonment for small debts is now limited to cases of fraud, breach of trust, &c. *See* 22 & 23 Vict. c. 57.

Income and Property Tax. — The first income-tax was levied in 1512 to defray the expenses of the war with France. It was imposed upon the commons, who were rated at two-fifteenths, and the clergy at two-tenths. Mr. Pitt's income-tax was also levied to defray the expense of a French war, by 39 Geo. III. c. 13 (Jan. 9, 1799). It imposed a graduate l series of rates on all incomes of £60 per annum and upwards, and was repealed by 42 Geo. III. c. 42 (May 4, 1802). It was, however, virtually restored by the Property-Tax Act, 43 Geo. III. c. 122 (Aug. 11, 1803), which imposed a rate on all incomes above £60 per annum, 5 per cent. on incomes of £150 being the standard. The rate was increased to $6\frac{1}{2}$ per cent. by 45 Geo. III. c. 15 (March 18, 1805), and to 10 per cent. by 46 Geo. III. c. 65 (June 13, 1806). This tax expired in 1816, Government being defeated, on the motion for its renewal, by a majority of thirty-seven, on the 19th of March. Sir Robert Peel's rate of sevenpence in the pound was levied by 5 & 6 Vict. c. 35 (June 22, 1842), for three years. It was continued three years longer by 8 & 9 Vict. c. 4 (April 5, 1845), and again for three years by 11 & 12 Vict. c. 8 (April 13, 1848). It was renewed for one year by 14 & 15 Vict. c. 12 (June 5, 1851), and for another year by 15 & 16 Vict. c. 20 (May 28, 1852). By 16 & 17 Vict. c. 34 (June 28, 1853), it was arranged for the rate to undergo a gradual diminution, and to expire in seven years, and the tax was also extended to Ireland ; but in consequence of the Russian war the plan was abandoned, and a double rate was imposed by 17 & 18 Vict. c. 10 (May 12, 1854). An addition of twopence in the pound on incomes of more than £150, and of three halfpence on those between £150 and £100, was imposed by 18 & 19 Vict. c. 20 (May, 25, 1855). These rates were reduced to sevenpence and fivepence in the pound by 20 Vict. c. 6 (March 21, 1857), and increased to ninepence and sixpence-halfpenny by 22 & 23 Vict. c. 18 (Aug. 13, 1859). By 23 Vict. c. 14 (April 3, 1860), they were further increased to tenpence and sevenpence. A select parliamentary committee to inquire into the present mode of assessing and collecting this tax, with a view to its more equitable adjustment, was appointed Feb. 19, 1861. Reduction of the income-tax from sevenpence to sixpence, and from tenpence to ninepence (April, 1862). The rate of sevenpence on all incomes; those under £100 exempted (June, 1863). The rate of sixpence on all incomes with some exceptions (May, 1864). The rate of fourpence on all incomes with same exceptions (May, 1865).

Indemnity, Act of.—An Act of indemnity, passed May 20, 1690, exempted from penal consequences the instruments of Popery and arbitrary power during the reign of James II. In addition to the regicides, thirty-five persons were by name exempted in this Act. Various statutes render it incumbent upon most Government officers to take certain oaths as a necessary qualification for their office ; but as this would prove very troublesome in many instances, an Act of indemnity is passed every year to exempt persons from any omission in this respect. Indemnity bills are also passed to release Government or its agents from the consequences of illegal acts which circumstances may have rendered necessary. Bills of this kind were passed on behalf of the advisers of the embargo on the exportation of corn, Dec. 16, 1766 ; also to indemnify officers who arrested persons during the suspensions of the Habeas Corpus Act, April 10, 1801, and March 10, 1818 ; and for the violations of the currency laws by the suspension of the Bank Charter Act in 1848 and 1857).

India Office.—In 1858, by 21 & 22 Vict. c. 106, the Government, in the place of the East India Company, assumed the entire administration of the British Empire in India. By this Act the Secretary of State for India has all the powers hitherto exercised by the Company and the Board of Control.

He is assisted by two under-secretaries, and the council, in the discharge of his official duties, together with a large staff of officials. Hours, 11 to 5. Westminster.

India, Council of.—This council for the government of India, erected by 21 & 22 Vict. c. 106 (Aug. 2, 1858), to supersede the Board of Control, consists of fifteen members, eight of whom are appointed by the Queen, and seven by the directors of the East India Company. They receive an annual salary of £1200, retain their office during good behaviour, and are not permitted to sit in Parliament. The first meeting of this council was held in 1858.

Indictment, is a formal inquisition or accusation made by twelve men at the least, called a grand jury, whereby they find and present; namely, notify, that such a person, of such a place, in such a county, and of such a quality or situation in life, has committed such a treason, misdemeanor, felony, trespass, or other offence, against the peace of the Queen (namely, the general peace, of which the Queen, as chief magistrate, is the conservatrix), her Crown and dignity (mere words of form and respect). Before the jury have inquired into the facts, it is termed a " bill," but after they have come to the conclusion that the matters should be answered and disproved, it is termed an indictment, and thereupon is a matter of record, and the party is arraigned upon it. So a coroner's inquisition is a matter of record, because found by the oath of twelve men at the least ; and the party may be arraigned upon it, as upon an indictment, an indictment being but an inquiry, legally termed an " inquisition ; " and, by the law, no man can be put upon his trial for a felony but by an indictment, or something equivalent thereto ; for lesser offences he may be tried by information. Indictments must not only be precise in form as to name, place, date, and fact, but the offence itself must also be set forth with clearness and certainty ; and, in some crimes, particular words of art must be used, which are so appropriated by the law to express the precise idea which it entertains of the offence, that no other words, however synonymous they may seem, are capable of doing it.

Induction, *inductio,* *i.e.* a leading into. The giving a parson possession of his church. After the bishop has granted institution, he issues out his mandate to the archdeacon to induct the clerk, who thereupon either does it personally, or usually commissions some neighbouring clergyman for that purpose. It is induction which makes the parson a complete incumbent.

Infant.—A person under the age of twenty-one years; whose acts the law in many cases pronounces void, or null, or voidable, *i.e.* such as are beneficial to him or her, and which may be ratified, after the infant's attaining full age, or set aside, at the infant's option. However, many acts of considerable importance may be done by minors in relation to their persons or affairs. (*See* AGE.)

By the custom of gavelkind, which holds in some parts of Kent, and in some manors near London, an infant at fifteen may sell his lands; and similar customs are said to exist elsewhere. By the custom of London, an infant unmarried, and above the age of fourteen, may bind himself apprentice to a freeman of London with proper covenants; which covenants, by the custom, shall be as binding as if he were of full age. Infants under twenty-one are privileged in some cases as to misdemeanors so as to escape fine or imprisonment, particularly in cases of omission, as for not repairing a highway, bridge, or the like; but for misdemeanors evidencing moral turpitude there is no favour shown them. The incapacity of infancy does not attach upon the Queen, mayors of corporations, or heads of public bodies, lords of manors, and peers, in respect of their appointing chaplains (even if not ten years of age), or patrons of churches.

An infant cannot be an attorney, steward of a manor, bailiff, factor, receiver, or hold any official situation of discretion or trust, though it seems as to some situations or offices which may be executed by deputy, or which only require skill or diligence, there is an exception; such as the offices of park-keeper, gaoler, forester, &c. The rule is positive as to excluding infants from places of public and pecuniary trust. An infant cannot be a common informer; for an informer must sue in person, not by attorney, which an infant cannot do. Infants cannot be jurors or members of Parliament. The incapacities of infants are but after all so many privileges; for, though he may not alien or charge his property, he may inherit, acquire, purchase, and obtain any property whatever, and may avoid his contracts when he comes of age, if he finds them disadvantageous, save those for necessaries, and in the case where he has paid money with his own hand. By the Infants' Marriage Act (18 & 19 Vict. c. 43) it is enacted that from and after the 2nd of July, 1855, it shall be lawful for an infant (who if a male has attained the age of twenty, or if a female of seventeen) upon contemplation of his or her marriage, with the sanction of the Court of Chancery, to make a valid settlement of all or any part of his or her property, such settlement to be considered as effective as if the person executing the same were of full age.

Infanticide.—The killing of a child after it is born. In every case in which an infant is found dead, and its death becomes an object of judicial investigation, the questions to be determined are—

What is the age of the child?

Was the child born alive?

If born alive, how long had it lived?

If born alive, by what means did it die?

If it be proved that its death was owing to violence, and suspicion falls upon the mother, it is to be ascertained—

Whether she has been delivered of a child?

Whether the signs of delivery correspond as to time, &c., with the appearances developed in the child ?

The usual defences for this crime are that the woman was ignorant of her condition, or laboured under *puerperal mania*.

In formâ pauperis. Every poor person is entitled, if he have cause of action, to have writs according to the nature of the case without paying fees, and the judges may assign him counsel and attorney, who act gratis. The party applying must swear that he is not worth £5 excepting his wearing apparel. This concession is only granted to plaintiffs at common law, and not to defendants in civil actions ; it is, however, extended to defences in prosecutions. In the Divorce or Probate Courts the applicant must declare he is not worth £25 after payment of debts, excepting his wearing apparel. No person suing *in formâ pauperis* is entitled to costs from the opposite party, unless by order of the Court or a judge.

Injunction, is a writ issuing out of a Court of Equity, and is said to be—1st, Remedial or preventive ; 2nd, Judicial or decretal.

1st. Courts of Equity have assumed the right to interfere (in cases where the Courts of Common Law cannot assist), by restraining the commission of a wrongful act, to which an action at law might afford but a very unsatisfactory remedy, or where damages are not capable of complete proof, or the wrongdoer is insolvent, or where the consequences of the wrong committed or apprehended would be incalculable, or not easily repaired. The cases in which applications are mostly made are those of irreparable waste, plain nuisance, infringement of a clear copyright, forcible entry, wasteful trespass, executors wasting property, the danger of a bill being unjustly negotiated by partners or others, and to stay proceedings at law manifestly unjust ; and in similar cases where prevention, absolute or conditional, is necessary.

2nd. With regard to the *judicial* injunction. This process issues subsequent to a decree made in a suit where all the parties are regularly and formally before the Court ; it is, in fact, an order directing the defendant or other party to the suit to deliver up possession, or to continue in possession of lands, &c., and is in the nature of a writ of execution ; the first injunction enjoining a party not to do such a thing, the second enjoining that such a thing be done. Great caution, however, has always been exercised in granting injunctions at the commencement of a suit. Injunctions as preventive processes do not restrict the plaintiff from prosecuting his legal remedy ; they rather act in concurrence with other remedies, and afford the complaining party his full measure of relief. The Court generally exercises its discretion as to costs, which, however, ordinarily follow the event of the application. The Patent Law Amendment Act, 1852, enacts that in any action for the infringement of letters patent, in any of the Superior Courts, such Court on the application of the plaintiff or defendant is to make an order for an injunction, inspection, or account, together with such necessary directions as may seem fit. By the Common Law Procedure Act, 1854, it is provided that in all cases of breach of contract or other injury, the injured party may claim a writ of injunction against the repetition or continuance of such breach of contract or other injury, together with a claim for damages or other redress.

Inland Revenue Offices.—The Inland Revenue Department comprises Excise, Stamps, and Taxes. Excise applies chiefly to duties levied upon articles of consumption of home production. The duties on certain foreign articles formerly part of the Excise duties, are now transferred to the Customs. Excise duties were first levied in 1626. The Stamp duty was imposed in the reign of William and Mary in 1694. The Income-Tax was introduced in 1799 by Pitt. Formerly each of the departments was under a separate Board of Commissioners ; in 1834 the Board of Stamps was united with the

Board of Taxes ; and in 1848 the Board of Stamps and Taxes was consolidated with that of the Excise.   The Board of Inland Revenue, under a chairman, deputy-chairman, and four commissioners, with their various staff of officials, controls the whole duties of Stamps, Taxes, and Excise.   Hours 10 to 4.   Somerset House.

Insolvency.—The state of a person who has not property sufficient for the full payment of his debts.   The various Acts for the relief of insolvent debtors were repealed by the Bankruptcy Act, (24 & 25 Vict. c. 134).   Insolvent debtors are now amenable to the Bankruptcy laws.

Installation.—The ceremony of investing with any charge or office, as the placing a bishop into his see, a dean or prebendary into his stall, or a knight into his order.

Institution, is a writing made by the bishop, whereby a clergyman is approved to be inducted to a rectory or parsonage i. e., the bishop, having upon examination found the clerk presented capable of the benefice, admits and institutes him.   On such institution, the clerk or clergyman, who is then called the parson, has a right to enter on the parsonage-house and glebe, and to take the tithes, but he cannot grant, let, or do any act to charge them till he is inducted into the living.   By the institution he is only admitted to pray and preach, and upon formal induction he is entitled to the freehold and profits of the rectory or cure.   Taking a reward for institution incurs a forfeiture of double value of one year's profit of the benefice, and makes the living void.   *See* INDUCTION.

Insurance or Assurance, is an agreement or contract of indemnity, whereby a person, who is termed the insurer or underwriter, in consideration of a specified sum, denominated a premium, undertakes to secure another, who is called the assured, from certain risks or perils to which he is or may be exposed. This contract is termed a policy.   *Marine Insurance,* is the term used for the insurance on ships, goods, &c., and the freight and hire of ships ; and, incidental to this insurance, bottomry and respondentia are insurable, if expressed in the policy, unless by usage of the trade otherwise understood : *Fire Insurance.* Insurance against fire is a contract of indemnity by which the insurer, in consideration of a certain premium received by him, undertakes to indemnify the insured against all loss or damage he may sustain in his houses, stock, &c., by fire during a specified period. *Life Insurance,* is the term for the assuring the payment of a particular sum to another on the death of an individual, or to the executors or assignees of that individual on his own decease.

Interdict.—An ecclesiastical mode of censure. When a king is excommunicated all his subjects retaining allegiance are excommunicated also, and the clergy forbidden to perform any part of divine service or any clerical duties, except baptism and the office of confession. This severe censure has been long disused.

International Copyright.—The benefit of international copyright was secured to authors in certain cases by 1 & 2 Vict. c. 59 (July 31, 1838) which was extended by 15 Vict. c. 12 (May 28, 1852). A treaty on the subject was concluded with France in 1851, one was signed with the United States, Feb. 18, 1853, and with Hamburg in 1854.

Interpleader is the trying a point incidentally happening before the principal cause can be determined ; and occurs where two or more persons claim the thing in dispute, of a third party in whose hands it is, but who claims no interest, and desires to be relieved by way of indemnity at the hands of a Court of Law or Equity, which will adjudge to whom the thing belongs. (*See* 1 & 2 Wm. IV. c. 58 ; 1 & 2 Vict. c. 45, and 19 & 20 Vict. c. 108.)

Ireland, Union of. *See* Union of.

Jetsam.—Goods, &c., which having been cast overboard in a storm, or after shipwreck are thrown upon the shore.

Jewish Disabilities Bill.—Mr. Robert Grant's bill

for releasing the Jews from their civil disabilities was rejected by the Lords, August 1, 1833 ; another introduced by Lord John Russell, after passing the Commons, May 4, 1848, met with a similar fate, May 25. A third received the sanction of the Lower House, July 3, 1851, but was also thrown out by the Lords, July 17. A similar bill passed the Commons, April 15, 1853, and was again rejected, April 29 ; and after having been again approved by the Commons, was defeated by the Lords, July 10, 1857. By 21 & 22 Vict. c. 49 (July 22, 1858), the House of Commons was empowered to modify the oaths in such a manner that they might be taken by Jews ; and by 23 & 24 Vict. c. 63 (August 6, 1860), the words "upon the faith of a Christian" were expunged permanently in the case of Jewish members.

Joint Stock Companies' Act. — This statute by which Joint Stock Companies are now regulated was passed in 1862, and came into force November 2nd of the same year. By this Act no company consisting of more than ten persons can carry on the business of banking unless registered as a company under the Act, or formed in pursuance of some other Act or letters patent : and no company of more than twenty persons can be formed for carrying on any business that has gain for its object unless registered under this Act, or some other Act or letters patent, except it is a company for working mines, subject to the jurisdiction of the Stannaries. The Act is divided into nine parts. (*See* 25 & 26 Vict. c. 89.)

Judge.—One appointed by the Queen's letters patent, to determine any cause or question in a Court of judicature. He is continued in his office during good behaviour, notwithstanding any demise of the Crown, and his full salary is secured him during the continuance of his commission. It is treason "to kill the Chancellor, &c., or the King's justices of the one bench or the other, &c., justices in assize and all other justices assigned to hear and determine being in their places doing their offices," 25 Edw. III. c. 2. The Barons of the Exchequer are not within the protection of this Act. The following summary, showing when the different officers and Courts were instituted, may be useful to the historical reader :—

	A.D.	A.D.
Chief Justiciars	1067 to 1272.
Chancellors	1068 to 1215.
Vice-Chancellors, &c.	1190 to 1213.
Chancellors and Keepers	1216 to 1272.

Court of Chancery.

	A.D.	A.D.
Chancellors and Keepers	1272 to 1625.
Lord Keepers	1625 to 1648.
Lord Commissioners	1648 to 1660.
Lord Chancellors and Keepers	1660 to 1813.
Lord Chancellors	1813 to 1864.
Vice-Chancellors	1813 to 1864.
Masters of the Rolls	1286 to 1864.

Court of King's Bench.

	A.D.	A.D.
Chief Justices	1272 to 1864.
Puisne Judges	1272 to 1864.

Court of Common Pleas.

	A.D.	A.D.
Chief Justices	1272 to 1864.
Puisne Judges	1272 to 1864.

Court of Exchequer.

	A.D.	A.D.
Chief Barons	1307 to 1864.
Barons	1272 to 1864.

Judge Advocate General.—An officer appointed to attend all general military courts martial, either personally or by a deputy. His duties are to advise the Court on points of law, custom and form ; to administer the oaths to the members of the Court and to the witnesses, to make a minute of the proceedings, and so far to assist the prisoner if necessary as to elicit as full a statement as possible of the facts material to the defence. . All proceedings of general courts martial, either at home or abroad, are sent to the Judge Advocate General by the officiating Judge Advocate, to be laid before the Crown.

Judgment, in law, is the sentence pronounced by the Court upon the matter contained in the record. Judgments are of four sorts. First, where the facts are confessed by the parties, and the law determined by the Court; as in case of judgment upon demurrer: secondly, where the law is admitted by the parties, and the facts disputed; as in the case of judgment on verdict: thirdly, where both the fact and the law arising thereon are admitted by the defendant; which is the case of judgments by confession or default: or, lastly, where the plaintiff is convinced that either fact, or law, or both, are insufficient to support his action, and therefore abandons or withdraws his prosecution; which is the case in judgments upon a nonsuit or retraxit. Judgment, in criminal cases, is the next stage of prosecution, after trial and conviction are past. (*See* 1 & 2 Vict. c. 110; 18 & 19 Vict. c. 15; 23 & 24 Vict. c. 115.)

Judicial Committee of the Privy Council, was instituted by 3 & 4 Will. IV. c. 41 (August 14, 1833). It consists of the President of the Council, the Lord Chancellor, the Chief Justices and Chief Baron, the Master of the Rolls, and other judges to whom are referred all those appeals brought before the Sovereign. It sits as a Court, hears the appeal, and makes a report to the Sovereign, who thereupon gives judgment. Though styled a Committee, it is a Court of record, and has full power to punish contempts, and award costs.

Jury.—A certain number of men sworn to inquire of, and try a matter of fact, and declare the truth, upon such evidence as shall be delivered them in a cause; and they are sworn judges upon evidence in matter of fact. When a case, civil or criminal, is ready for trial, the jury is called and sworn. The jurors contained in the panel are either special or common jurors. Special juries are used when the causes are of too great

nicety for the discretion of ordinary juries. By 6 Geo. IV.
c. 50, s. 31, every man described in the jurors' book as an
esquire, or persons of higher degree, or as banker or merchant,
is qualified and liable to serve on special juries ; and his name
is to be inserted in a separate list to be subjoined to the jurors'
book, such list to be called "the Special Jurors' List." A
common jury is one returned by the sheriff, according to the
directions of the 6 Geo. IV. c. 50, ss. 15 to 26, which appoints
that the sheriff or officer shall return one and the same panel
for every cause to be tried at the same assizes, containing not
less than forty-eight, nor more than seventy-two jurors ; and
(s. 26) that their names being written on a card, shall be put
into a box or glass ; and when each cause is called, twelve of
these persons, whose names shall be first drawn out of the box,
shall be sworn upon the jury, unless absent, challenged, or excused ; or unless a previous view of the messuages, lands, or
place in question, shall have been thought necessary by the
Court ; in which case it is provided by s. 23 of the same Act,
that six or more of the jurors returned, to be agreed on by the
parties, or named by a judge or other proper officer of the
Court, shall be appointed by special writ of *habeas corpora*, or
distringas, to have the matters in question shown to them by
two persons named in the writ ; and then (s. 24) such of the
jury as have had the view, or so many of them as appear shall
be sworn on the inquest previous to any other jurors.

The first section of the above statute, defines the qualification
of jurors in England in the superior Courts, assizes, and sessions
of the peace ; and allows persons in Wales, being there qualified
to the extent of three-fifths of the qualification required in
England, to serve on juries in Wales : viz., every man between
twenty-one and sixty years of age (if not expressly excepted)
who shall have £10 per annum above reprises in lands or tenements, freehold, copyhold, customary, or of ancient demesne ;
or in rents issuing out of such lands, tenements, and rents

taken together in fee simple, fee tail, or for the life of himself
or any other; or £20 in land or tenements held by lease for
twenty-one years or longer, absolutely, or for any term determinable on life; or who, being a householder, shall be rated
or assessed to the poor rates (or to the inhabited house-duty) in
Middlesex upon a value of not less than £30, and in any other
county not less than £20; or who shall occupy a house not
containing less than fifteen windows. All such persons are
declared to be qualified, and liable to serve on juries, for the
trial of all such issues in the Courts of record in Westminster,
and in the superior Courts, both civil and criminal, and in all
Courts of assize, *nisi prius, oyer*, and *terminer*, and gaol delivery;
such assizes being respectively triable in the county in which
every man so qualified shall reside; and on grand juries in
Courts of session of the peace; and on petty juries for the trial
of all issues joined in such Courts of session of the peace, and
triable in the county, riding, or division, where the person so
qualified resides. Section 2. The following persons are exempted :—Peers, judges of the Courts of Westminster, &c.,
clergymen, Roman catholic priests, protestant dissenters, and
preachers duly registered, &c., and not following any secular
occupation, except that of schoolmaster; practising serjeants,
barristers, doctors, and advocates of the civil law, attorneys,
solicitors, and proctors; officers of all Courts of Justice, coroners, gaolers, physicians, and licentiates; surgeons of the Royal
Colleges of London, Edinburgh, and Dublin; apothecaries;
officers in the navy or army on full pay, licensed pilots, &c.;
the Queen's household servants; officers of custom and excise,
sheriff's officers, high constables, and parish clerks. All these
are absolutely freed and exempted from being returned, and
from serving upon any juries or inquests whatever, and are not
to be inserted in the lists required by the Act. Proviso is also
made for all persons exempted by any prescription, charter,
grant, or writ.

In criminal cases a prisoner may peremptorily challenge (*i. e.*, object to), without assigning any reason, to the number of twenty, and in treason to the number of thirty-five. Foreigners are tried by a jury of half foreigners, except in cases of treason. In cases strictly criminal, the prosecutor cannot withdraw a juror, or postpone the indictment because he is not prepared with his evidence ; for, after the jury are once sworn they can only be discharged by giving a verdict. In criminal cases the jury consider the evidence, and deliver their verdict, as in civil cases, but they cannot return a privy verdict ; the practice is for the judges to adjourn while the jury are withdrawn, and return to receive the verdict in open court.

Justices in Eyre, or Itinerant Justices, the judicial representatives of the royal authority, were regularly established by the Parliament held at Northampton, Jan. 26, 1176. They received a delegated power from the *aula regia*, and made their circuit round the kingdom once in seven years. By the 12th article of Magna Charta, in 1215, they were ordered to be sent into the country once a year.

Justices of the Peace are Judge's appointed by the Queen's Commission to be justices in certain limits, generally within the counties wherein they are resident. There are many persons who are justices by virtue of their offices, as the mayors and aldermen of cities or towns and liberties, and the chancellor or keeper. The Judges of the Queen's Bench are justices by prescription. The 18 Geo. II. c. 20, enacts that every justice of the peace acting for a county must have an estate of the clear yearly value of £100, with reserved rents of the value of £300 per annum. No attorney or solicitor can be a justice of the peace during such time as he practises as an attorney or solicitor (6 & 7 Vict. c. 73). Various statutes have been passed defining the jurisdiction of justices of the peace.

Justifiable Homicide. *See* MURDER.

Keeping the Peace, Security for.—An obligation to

the Crown taken in some court, by which a person acknowledges himself to be indebted to the Crown in a certain sum,
with condition to be void and of none effect if he shall appear in
court on such a day, and in the meantime shall keep the peace,
either generally to all the Queen's people, or particularly towards
the person who begs the security ; or with condition to keep the
peace not dependent on any appearance in court.   If this obligation is broken, the person and his sureties forfeit the sums in
which they are respectively bound.

Kidnapping.—The forcible abduction of a man, woman,
or child from their own country and sending them into another.
It is an offence punished by fine and imprisonment.   By the Act
24 & 25 Vict. c. 110, any one who shall decoy or take away any
child under the age of fourteen, with the intent to deprive such
child of its parents or guardians, is guilty of felony, and liable to
penal servitude for any term not exceeding seven years, and not
less than three years ; or imprisonment with hard labour for
two years.   Those harbouring any such child, knowing the same
to have been decoyed or taken away, are also liable to the same
penalty.

Kindred.—Persons of kin, or related to each other by
descent through the father or mother.   There are two degrees
of either kindred, the one in the right or direct line ascending
or descending, and the other in the collateral line.   The line
descending is from the father to the son, and so on to his
children in the male and female line ; and if no son, then to the
daughter and to her children in the male and female line *ad
infinitum.*   The line ascending is directly upwards, as from the
son to the father or mother ; and if neither father nor mother,
to the grandfather or grandmother ; and if no grandfather or
grandmother, to the great-grandfather or great-grandmother ;
if neither great-grandfather nor great-grandmother, to the father
of the great-grandfather or the mother of the great-grandmother ;
and if neither of them, then to the great-grandfather's grand-

father, or the great-grandmother's grandmother ; and if none
of them, to the great-grandfather's great-grandfather, or great-
grandmother's great-grandmother ; and so on *ad infinitum*.
The collateral line is either descending by the brother and his
children downwards, or by the uncle upwards, and downwards
to the nephew and his children ; and, if none of them, to the
niece and her children ; if neither nephew nor niece, nor any of
their children, then to the grandson or grand-daughter of the
nephew ; and, if neither of them, to the grandson or grand-
daughter of the niece : and if none of them, then to the great-
grandson or great-grand-daughter of the nephew and of the
niece ; and so *ad infinitum*, the collateral line being between
brothers and sisters, and to uncles and aunts, and the rest of
the kindred, upwards and downwards, across and amongst
themselves. If there are no kindred in the right descending
line, the inheritance of lands goes to the ascending line.
The right of representation of kindred (for the purposes of
distribution of personalty) in the descending line reaches
beyond the great-grandchildren of the same parents ; but in
the collateral line it is not by law allowed to reach beyond
brothers' and sisters' children. In the direct or right ascending
line, the father or mother is always in the first degree of
kindred.

King.—The supreme executive power of these kingdoms is
by law vested in a single person, the King, or Queen, for it
matters not to which sex the Crown descends, according to hereditary right. This power, however, may be defeated or qualified
by the supreme legislative authority of this kingdom, viz., the
King and both Houses of Parliament, or by the latter alone, if
the throne be declared vacant, or necessity dictate the alteration
of the course of succession.

King's Bench. *See* QUEEN'S BENCH.

Knight Marshal.—An officer in the royal household
who has jurisdiction over offences committed within the house-

hold and verge, and of all contracts made therein, a member of the household being one of the parties.

Knights of the Bath. *See* BATH.

Knights of the Garter. *See* GARTER.

Knights of the Shire.—Members of Parliament representing counties or shires in contradistinction to citizens or burgesses. They were so called because formerly it was necessary that they all should be knights; but at present any one, not being an alien, may be chosen to occupy the office. The money qualification is abolished by 21 Vict. c. 26.

Lancaster (Duchy of).—The dukedom of Lancaster was created by Edward III., in favour of Henry Plantagenet, March 6, 1351, and was bestowed upon his son, John of Gaunt, Nov. 13, 1362. It was made a county palatine. The duke was to have *jura regalia*, and power to pardon treasons or outlawries, and make justices of the peace and justices of assize within the county. The lordship of Ripon was annexed to it by 37 Hen. VIII. c. 16 (1645); and the revenue having declined, other lands were annexed to it by 2 & 3 Phil. & Mary, c. 20 (1555). The courts of the duchy of Lancaster were instituted by Edward III. in 1376. The management of the revenues was entrusted to them. Henry Bolingbroke was duke of Lancaster on his accession to the crown as Henry IV., Sept. 30, 1399. In the first year of his reign he procured an act of parliament, ordering that the duchy of Lancaster, &c., should remain to him and his heirs for ever. It was declared forfeited to the Crown in 1461, and was vested in Edward IV. and his heirs, kings of England, for ever.

Land Tax.—A tax assessed upon land made perpetual, but subject to redemption or purchase by the act 38 Geo. III. c. 60. It is levied under the authority of the land-tax commissioners of every county. This is a landlord's tax, payable by the tenant, who may deduct it from the rent of the *current* year, otherwise it cannot be recovered back from the landlord at any future time. Various statutes have been passed for the better regulation of land-tax and its redemption in the reigns of Geo. III. & IV., Will. IV., and her present Majesty.

Land-Waiter.—An officer of the Custom House, whose duty is, upon landing any merchandise, to examine, taste, weigh, measure them, &c., and to take an account thereof. In some ports they also execute the office of a coast-waiter. They are likewise occasionally styled *searchers*, and are to attend and join with the patent searcher in the execution of all cockets for the shipping of goods to be exported to foreign parts; and in cases where drawbacks on bounties are to be paid to the merchant on the exportation of any goods, they, as well as the patent searchers, are to certify the shipping thereof on the debentures.

Larceny.—The legal term for stealing or theft. The law defines a stealing or larceny to be the taking and carrying away with a felonious intent (*i.e.* with the intention of unlawful appropriation) the goods of another. It is distinguished as simple and compound; simple, when the stealing is unaccompanied with aggravating circumstances; compound, when the theft is committed upon the person, or consists in stealing from a dwelling-house. Stealing under particular circumstances is a crime of another denomination; for instance, taking from the person in a violent manner is *robbery*, and stealing in a dwelling-house, after having broken therein, is *burglary*. The intent is the material ingredient in this offence. The taking must be actual or constructive: actual, where the offender takes the goods away without the owner's consent; constructive, where the owner, although he has parted with the possession of the goods, has not divested himself of the right of such possession, or where a fraud has been practised with an intent to steal them. Violations of trust, where the possession of the goods have been previously obtained without any fraudulent intention, are not larcenies. Embezzlements by clerks or servants are larcenies, if the money or goods were actually received by the clerk or servant by virtue of his employment. Larceny cannot be committed of animals that are wild by nature and at large, as deer in a chase or forest, hares, rabbits in a warren, or wild fowls, rooks for instance; but deer in an enclosed part of a forest or park, fish in a trunk, or pheasants in a mew, as well as swans marked, and all valuable domestic animals, are subjects of larceny. Dogs, birds, pigeons, not kept inclosed, and other animals kept for pleasure, not being subjects of larceny, are protected by summary proceedings before justices, who may inflict fine, imprisonment, and whipping.

The punishment of larceny is penal servitude for from three to fourteen years, or imprisonment not exceeding two years (with or without hard labour, and with or without solitary confinement, for the whole or any part of the imprisonment), and, if a male, to be once, twice, or thrice whipped, in addition to the imprisonment, if the Court shall think fit. If the defendant be previously under sentence of penal servitude or imprisonment for another crime, the Court may award the penal servitude or imprisonment for every subsequent felony, to commence at the expiration of the penal servitude or imprisonment to which the prisoner was previously sentenced. (*See* 24 & 25 Vict. c. 96.)

Law Offices.—I give a brief list of the most important law offices, with their hours of attendance and respective addresses. (For the various government offices, see them under their several headings.)

Accountant-General's Office, Chancery Lane. Hours 11 to 3.

Acknowledgments of Deeds by Married Women, Office of, Lancaster Place, Waterloo Bridge. Hours 11 to 5; out of Term, 11 to 3.

Admiralty Court Office, Godliman Street, St. Paul's. Hours 10 to 4.

Appeals Registry Office, Godliman Street, St. Paul's. Hours 10 to 4.

Archdeacon of London's Office, Great Knightrider Street, St. Paul's. Hours 10 to 4.

Archdeacon of Middlesex's Office, Godliman Street, St. Paul's. Hours 10 to 4.

Archdeacon of Surrey's Office, Bennet's Hill. Hours 10 to 4.

Arches Court Registry Office, Godliman Street. Hours 10 to 4.

Attorney-General's Office, Stone Buildings, Lincoln's Inn. Hours 10 to 5 ; in Vacation, 11 to 3.

Attorneys and Solicitors Registrar's Office, Chancery Lane. Hours 10 to 4.

Chancery Registrar's Office, Southampton Buildings. Hours 9 to 3 ; and 4 to 6 in Term.

Chancery Inrolment Office, Chancery Lane. Hours 10 to 4 ; Vacation, 11 to 1.

City Remembrancer's Office, Guildhall Yard. Hours 9½ to 5.

City Solicitor's Office,   ,,   ,,   ,,

Commissioners for Affidavits in Chancery, 10, Southampton Buildings. Hours 10 to 4.

Common Pleas, Serjeants' Inn, Chancery Lane. Hours 11 to 5 ; Vacation, 11 to 3 ; Long Vacation, 11 to 2.

Crown Office, King's Bench Walk, Temple. Hours 11 to 5; Vacation, 11 to 3 ; Long Vacation, 11 to 2.

Examiner's Office, Rolls Yard, Chancery Lane. Hours 10 to 4, in Term.

Exchequer of Pleas Office, Stone Buildings, Lincoln's Inn. Hours 11 to 5 ; Vacation, 11 to 3 ; and Long Vacation, 11 to 2. In Rule Department the same hours.

Great Seal Patent Office, Cursitor Street. Hours 10 to 4.

Lunacy Office, Masters of, Lincoln's Inn Fields. Hours 10 to 4.

Nisi Prius Office, Judges' Chambers, Rolls Garden. Hours 11 to 5 ; Vacation, 11 to 2.

Petty Bag Office, Rolls Yard. Hours 10 to 4; Long Vacation, 11 to 1.

Queen's Bench Office, Temple. Hours 11 to 5. In Rule Office, 11 to 3.

Queen's Remembrancer's Office, Chancery Lane. Hours 11 to 4.

Record and Writ Clerk's Office, Chancery Lane. Hours 10 to 4 ; Long Vacation, 11 to 1.

Registrar's Office, Chancery Lane. Hours 10 to 3 ; Vacation, 11 to 1.

Secretary's (Lord Chancellor's) Office, Chancery Lane. Hours 11 to 4 ; Vacation, 11 to 1.

Secretary's (Master of the Rolls) Office, Chancery Lane. Hours 10 to 3 ; Vacation, 11 to 1.

Solicitor-General's Office, 2, Essex Court, Temple.

Taxing Masters in Chancery Office, Staple Inn, Holborn. Hours 10 to 4 ; Vacation, 11 to 1.

Last Court.—A court held by the twenty-four jurats in the marshes of Kent, and summoned by the bailiffs, whereby orders are made to levy taxes, &c., for the preservation of the said marshes.

Law Terms. *See* TERMS.

Lease.—A demise, or letting of lands, tenements, or hereditaments, unto another for life, term of years, or at will, for a rent reserved. A lease is either written, called an indenture, deed-poll, or lease in writing ; or by word of mouth, called lease parole. All estates, interests of freehold, or terms for years in lands, &c., not put in writing and signed by the parties, shall have no greater effect than as estates at will ; unless it be of leases not exceeding three years from the making ; wherein the rent reserved shall be two-thirds of the value of the things demised. Leases exceeding three years must be made in writing : and if the substance of a lease be put in writing, and signed by the parties, though it be not sealed, it shall have the effect of a lease for years, &c. An assignment differs from a lease only in this : that by a lease one grants an interest less than his own, reserving to himself a reversion ; in assignments he parts with the whole property, and the assignee stands to all intents and purposes in the place of the assignor. By 4 & 5 Vict. c. 21, every instrument purporting to be a release of a freehold estate, and expressed to be made in pursuance of that Act, shall be as effectual as if a bargain and sale or lease for a year had been executed, although such bargain and sale or lease for a year shall not in fact have been executed. The stamp on such bargain and sale or lease for a year is now abolished. (*See* Vict. 8 & 9, c. 106 ; 22 & 23, c. 35 ; and 23 & 24, c. 38.)

Lease and Release.—A conveyance of the inheritance in land, the lease giving first the possession, and the release, the right and interest. This mode or form of conveyance, which is almost universally adopted, was originally framed to avoid the necessity of a bargain and sale enrolled, which is quite as applicable to the purpose, and has the advantages of being registered at full length, thereby preventing the consequences of loss or accident to the writing. A feoffment is also a deed answering the same purpose, as an absolute conveyance ; but, though not en-rolled, a species of publicity is necessary for the effectuating this conveyance, for corporeal and formal possession must be given in the presence of witnesses, and this cause operates against the frequent adoption of this conveyance. Corporations, however, for technical reasons, cannot convey their lands by lease and release, and therefore they must take by a feoffment, or bargain and sale enrolled, when they purchase land.

Legacy.—A gift of personalty by will. There are four kinds of legacies. *General.*—When it is not a bequest of any particular thing or money as distinguished from all others of the same kind. *Specific.*—When it is a bequest of a particular thing or sum of money as distinguished from all others of the same kind. *Demonstrative.*—When it is in its nature a general legacy, but there is a particular fund pointed out to satisfy it ; and *Cumulative.*—When a testator, by the same testamentary instrument, or by different ones, has be-queathed more ·than one legacy to the same person, and the question arises whether he intended the second legacy to be in addition to the first, or substitutional for it. A year from the death of the testator is, generally speaking, the period fixed for the payment of a legacy, upon the presump-tion that by such time the property has been got in and is making interest ; this will be the case, though the fund out of which it is to be paid is making interest, the Court having adopted the year as a rule of convenience : there are, however, cases in which interest will be allowed from the death of the tes-tator. No legacy can be recovered in any court after twenty years next after a present right to receive it accrued to some persons capable of giving a discharge or release for the same, unless some principal or interest be paid thereon, or an acknow-ledgment in writing, signed by the party liable to pay, or his agent, and then only within twenty years after the last of such payments or acknowledgment; and the recovery of interest is in like manner limited to the last six years. The legacy duty was first imposed by 36 Geo. III. c. 52. All gifts by will were ordered to be deemed legacies by 8 & 9 Vict. c. 76, s. 4. The law of legacies was amended, and the legacy duty was extended to real property, by 16 & 17 Vict. c. 51.

Legal Tender. *See* TENDER.

Letter of Attorney.—A writing, authorising another person, who in such case is called the " attorney " of the party, appointing him to do any lawful act in the stead of another; as to receive debts or dividends, sue a third person, transfer stock, &c. It is either general or special: *i.e.*, general, in respect of the conduct of all a person's affairs, as where he leaves the country; special, in respect of any one or more named matters, as to receive money. This instrument gives the "attorney" authority to act in his name, exactly as the party giving it would himself do, until revocation. Letters of attorney which authorise the receipt of money payable, and are intended to operate as assignments thereof, are irrevocable, and will enable the " attorney " or assignee to receive the money for his own use. By 24 & 25 Vict. c. 96, any banker, merchant, broker, or other agent entrusted with a power of attorney for the sale or transfer of any share or interest in any public stock or fund, converting to his own use, or the use of any person other than the person by whom he shall have been so entrusted, the share or interest in the stock or fund to which such power of attorney relates, is guilty of a misdemeanor, punishable with penal servitude for any term not exceeding seven nor less than three years, or imprisonment for two years.

Letters of Marque.—Permission by a government in time of war to a ship belonging to private individuals, called a privateer, to seize and plunder the ships of the enemy.

Letter-Missive.—A letter from the Queen to a dean

and chapter containing the name of the person whom she gives them leave to elect (*congé d'élire*) as bishop. Also the letter addressed to a peer by the Chancellor, when a bill is filed against him in Chancery, requiring him to appear ; the writ of *subpœna* not being considered in its form sufficiently respectful.

Letters Patent.—Writings of the Queen, sealed with the great seal, by which a person or public company is enabled to do acts or enjoy privileges which could not be done or enjoyed without such authority. Peers are sometimes created by letters patent ; and by letters patent aliens are made denizens, and especially new inventions are protected.

Letters of Safe Conduct.—By the law of nations no subject of a country at war with us can travel upon the high seas, nor come within the realm, nor send his goods from one place to another without danger of being seized by our subjects, unless he have letters of safe conduct, which formerly were granted under the great seal and enrolled in Chancery. At the present time passports under the Sovereign's sign-manual, or licences from our ambassadors abroad, are more usually obtained, and are of equal validity.

Libel.—All contumelious matter that tends to degrade a man in the opinion of his neighbours, or to make him ridiculous, when conveyed in writing or the like, is a libel and punished by the law. I give briefly a few instances which come under the head of this subject. Words spoken of another tending to exclude him from society are actionable ; as, for instance, to charge him with having any particular disease. Also action may be sustained for words spoken of a man, which may hurt his trade or livelihood. An action will lie (without proving special damage) for all words spoken of another, which impute to him the commission of some crime punishable by law, such as high treason, murder, or other felony, forgery, perjury, subornation of perjury, or other misdemeanor ; or even an offence punishable merely by the custom of some particular place, if the words be uttered there. But words imputing to a man an act, which (however immoral) is not punishable criminally by law, cannot be made the subject of an action, without proof of special damage. Every written calumny is actionable, and punishable, although it do not impute any indictable offence, but merely tend to disgrace or ridicule, or bring into contempt the party calumniated, even by imputing hypocrisy and want of proper feeling, and still more if it impute fornication, swindling, or any other deviation from moral rectitude or principle. Writings, vilifying the characters of persons deceased, are libels, and may properly be made the subject of an indictment or information, on the prosecution of the relatives of the deceased. So with respect to writings which tend to degrade or revile persons in high office, in foreign countries, when they have a tendency to interrupt the pacific relations between the two countries. Also writings reflecting upon public or corporate bodies, if such writings have a manifest tendency to stir up public hatred against them, are libels. It is not an excuse in law to repeat in writing what has been previously spoken or written by others ; and in cases of verbal slander, it seems no excuse to repeat what another has said, though the party at the time of speaking the words names the person who told him what he relates. By 8 & 9 Vict. c. 85, it is enacted that any one threatening to publish a libel with intent to extort money shall be liable to imprisonment for a term not exceeding three years. The law of libel has been greatly mitigated with regard to publishers and editors of newspapers by statute 6 & 7 Vict. c. 96.

License.—A written permission given to do some lawful act. A license is necessary to found a church, to erect a park, to marry without publication of banns, &c., also to carry on various trades, and to practise any profession.

Lien.—A right in one man to retain that which is in his possession belonging to another until certain demands of the person in possession are satisfied. It is in fact a kind of pledge.

Limitation.—A certain time assigned by the statute law within which a civil action must be brought ; for felonies are punishable at any lapse of time, though in many statutes concerning penal offences, a time is limited for the bringing action thereupon, varying from three months to two years.

I mention a few of the periods fixed by the principal "Statutes of Limitation : "

Action, account of	within 6	years.
Advowson, recovery of. . . .	„ 60	„
Annuity, action of	„ 20	„
Appeal from a Court of Equity to the House of Lords	„ 2	„
Assault or false imprisonment . .	„ 4	„
Award, action of debt upon, where the submission was not by specialty .	„ 6	„
But if on specialty	„ 20	„
Bond or specialty	„ 20	„
Copyright, infringement of . . .	„ 1	„
Debt, if not on specialty . . .	„ 6	„
Ejectment	„ 20	„
Legacies	„ 20	„
Libels.	„ 6	„
Murder, within a year and a day after the act.		
Trespass	within 6	„

Limited Liability.—The liabilities of members of Joint Stock Companies, with a capital divided into shares of not less than £10 each, for the debts of their company, were limited upon certain conditions by 18 & 19 Vict. c. 133. It was amended by 19 & 20 Vict. c. 47 ; 20 & 21 Vict. c. 14 ; by 21 & 22 Vict. c. 60 ; and by 25 & 26 Vict. c. 89. By this last Act the liability of members is limited to such amount as they shall undertake to contribute to the assets of the company in case of winding up.

Lord Lieutenants of Counties, are officers, who upon any invasion or rebellion, have power to raise the militia and volunteers, and to give commissions to colonels and other officers, to arm and form them into regiments, troops, and companies.   Under the lord lieutenants are deputy-lieutenants, who have the same power; these are chosen by the lords lieutenants out of the principal gentlemen of each county, and presented to the Queen for her approbation.

Lord Privy Seal.—This office was before the 30 Hen. VIII. usually conferred on an ecclesiastic; but since then it has been generally occupied by temporal peers above the degrees of barons.   This officer is appointed by letters patent, and is a member of the Cabinet.   The Lord Privy Seal receiving a warrant from the Signet Office issues the Privy Seal, which is an authority to the Lord Chancellor to pass the Great Seal where the occasion requires it.   The Privy Seals for money begin in the Treasury.

Lords Justices of Appeal (COURT OF CHANCERY). —By 14 & 15 Vict. c. 83, passed August 7, 1851, power was given to the Queen to appoint two barristers, of not less than fifteen years' standing, to be judges of the Court of Appeal in Chancery, and, with the Lord Chancellor, to form such Court of Appeal.   They were to be styled Lords Justices, and the power exercised by the Lord Chancellor in the Court of Chancery was from October 1, 1851, transferred to this new Court.

Lord Steward of the Household.—This officer has the supreme control of the royal household, and is one of great dignity.   By 3 Hen. VII. c. 14 (1486), the Lord Steward was empowered to hold a Court for the trial of treasons committed by members of the royal household, and by 33 Hen. VIII. c. 12 (1541), this jurisdiction was extended to all cases of quarrelling and striking within the palace.   This authority was abolished by 12 & 13 Vict. c. 101 (August 1, 1849).

Lottery.—A distribution of prizes by chance. The first lottery in England was proposed in 1567 and 1568, and was drawn at the west door of St. Paul's Cathedral, day and night, from January 11 to May 6, 1569. The profit was devoted to the repair of harbours. Another was drawn for the benefit of the Virginian Company in 1612. Lotteries were suspended in 1620, on the ground of their immoral tendency. A lottery was, however, permitted in 1680, to aid a project for supplying the metropolis with water. Charles II. used them after the restoration in 1660, to reward his adherents. A loan of £1,000,000 was raised by government on the sale of tickets in 1694; another of £3,000,000 in 1746; and another of £1,000,000 in 1747. For a short period in the reign of Queen Anne they were prohibited. In 1778 an Act requiring an annual licence, at a cost of £50, to be taken out, reduced the number of offices from 400 to 51; and they were altogether abolished by 6 Geo. IV. c. 60 (1826); the last public lottery having been drawn October 18, 1826. An Act imposing a penalty of £50 for advertising them (6 & 7 Will. IV. c. 66), was passed August 13, 1836. In the case of Art Unions the legislature has legalised the distribution by lottery of works of Art.

Lunatics. *See* IDIOTS AND LUNATICS.

Magna Carta.—In the reign of King John the feudal tenures and forest laws were so rigorously enforced, and the liberties of the nation so seriously infringed upon, that a rebellion ensued among the barons against the absolute power of the sovereign. The result was the passing of the famous Magna Carta, the bulwark of our constitution, and the first step in advance towards that freedom from any arbitrary and unjust acts of a sovereign which we now so fully enjoy. The clauses contained in this Great Charter secured important liberties and privileges to every order of men in the nation—to the clergy, the barons, and the people. I give briefly its chief enactments :—

That freedom of elections be granted to the clergy, and the necessity of a royal *congé d'élire* and confirmation be superseded; that permission be accorded to every man to depart the kingdom at pleasure; that fines levied on the clergy be proportional to their lay estates, and not to their ecclesiastical benefices; that heirs on their majority shall possess their estates without paying any relief; that the king shall not sell his wardship, and shall only levy reasonable profits on the estate; that the king shall not claim the wardship of a minor who holds lands by military tenure of a baron; that no scutages (except in the three general feudal cases) shall be imposed but by the great council of the kingdom; that all prelates, earls, and great barons shall be called to this council, each by a particular writ, and the lesser barons by a general summons of the sheriff; that the king shall not seize any baron's land for a debt due to the Crown if his goods and chattels are sufficient to discharge the debt; that no vassal shall sell so much of his land as to incapacitate him from serving his master; that all privileges granted to the barons against the king shall be extended to their vassals; that one weight and measure shall be established throughout the kingdom; that merchants shall transact business without being exposed to any arbitrary tolls or impositions; they and all freemen to leave the kingdom and return to it at pleasure; that London, and all cities and burghs, shall preserve their ancient liberties, immunities, and free customs; that the goods of every freeman shall be disposed of by his will; that the king's courts of justice shall be stationary, and shall no longer follow his person; *they shall be open to every one, and justice shall no longer be sold, refused, or delayed by them;* that circuits shall be held every year, and no person shall be tried on rumour or suspicion alone, but by the evidence of lawful witnesses; that no freeman shall be imprisoned or dispossessed of his goods but by the legal judgment of his peers, or by the law of the land; that every freeman shall be fined in proportion to his fault, and no fine shall be levied on him to his utter ruin ; even a villain or rustic shall not by any fine be bereaved of his implements of husbandry.

No fewer than thirty-eight solemn ratifications of this Charter are recorded ; of which six were made by Henry III., three by Edward I., fifteen by Edward III., six by Richard II., six by Henry IV., one by Henry V., and one by Henry VI. The Charter received a few alterations upon its successive confirmations in the first, second, and ninth years of Henry III.'s reign, the last of which is in our statute book and has never received any alteration. The most important change in the Charter, as confirmed by Henry III., was the omission of the clause which prohibited the levying of aids or scutages without the consent of parliament. But though this clause was omitted, it continned to be observed during the reign of Henry, for we find the barons constantly refusing him the aids or subsidies which his prodigality was demanding. But he still retained the right of levying money upon towns under the name of tillage, and also claimed the right of levying other contributions, such as upon the export of wool. But a final stop was put to all these exactions by the celebrated statute passed in the 25th year of the reign of Edward I., entitled *Confirmatio Chartarum.* This statute not only confirmed the Great Charter, but gave, to use the words of Hallam, "the same security to private property which Magna Charta had given to personal liberty." In it the king solemnly declared that " for no business from thenceforth we shall take such manner of aids, tacks, nor prises, but by the common consent of the realm, and for the common profit thereof, saving the ancient aids and prises due and accustomed." Thus was the great principle of parliamentary taxation explicitly acknowledged eighty years after the first enactment of the Great Charter.

Maids of Honour. *See* HONOUR, MAIDS OF.

Majesty.—The title of majesty, at first applied amongst

the Romans to the dictators, the consuls, and the senate, as the
representatives of the power of the people, was appropriated by
the Emperor Tiberius (A.D. 14–37). It was also adopted by the
German emperors, and was introduced into France by Henry II.
about A.D. 1547, though Louis XI. was the first to assume it
permanently and officially. Francis I. saluted Henry VIII. with
this title at their interview in 1520, and he was the first English monarch to whom it was applied.

Malt.—A duty on malt was first imposed during the reign
of Charles I., and has formed a regular branch of the revenue
since 1697. It was made perpetual by 3 Geo. IV. c. 18 (April
3, 1822), and the law was amended by 11 Geo. IV. c. 17 (May
29, 1830). New regulations were imposed by 1 Vict. c. 49
(July 12, 1837), and subsequent Acts. An Act was passed
in 1865, allowing the excise duty to be charged according
to the weight of the grain used. The question of the repeal
of the malt-tax has frequently been debated in the House
of Commons. The tax was introduced into Scotland in 1713,
and into Ireland in 1783.

Man, Isle of.—This island was governed by a succession
of Norwegian kings, A.D. 1092 till A.D. 1264. In 1266 it was
invaded by Alexander III., king of Scotland, and was under
the dominion of the Scotch until 1290, when the inhabitants
claimed the protection of Edward I., who immediately took
possession of it. It was recovered by the Scots, under Robert
Bruce, in 1332, and re-conquered by the Earl of Shaftesbury in
1340. Henry IV. granted it to Sir John Stanley in 1403.
James I. bestowed it upon William, sixth earl of Derby, in 1610.
It fell, in 1736, by inheritance, to James, second Duke of Athol,
who sold it for £70,000 to the British government, in 1765. A
further sum of £133,000 was paid to the Athol family in discharge of revenue, in January, 1829. The whole island and
all its dependencies, except the landed property of the Athol
family and some other rights belonging to them, are inalienably

vested in the Crown, and subjected to the regulations of the British excise and customs.

Mandamus.—Is a high writ issuing in the Queen's name out of the Court of Queen's Bench, and directed to any person, corporation (public or incorporated by Act of Parliament), or inferior court of judicature, commanding them to do some particular thing therein specified, as appertaining to their public office and duty. This writ is remedial, and generally is used for the purpose of compelling the admission or restoration to an office; for the production of books and writings; to compel inferior courts to do particular acts, the delay or refusal of which may tend to interrupt the course of law and justice; to compel lords of manors to permit inspection of court rolls, churchwardens to deliver up books to their successors in office, and an infinite number of other purposes, which, though apparently injuring an individual, yet, as matters of public consideration, should be summarily remedied, even though an indictment might lie; for an indictment cannot compel a party to do a particular act, but can only be the means of inflicting a punishment for non-performance. By 11 & 12 Vict. c. 44, the court may grant a rule ordering justices to do an act instead of a mandamus; and by 19 & 20 Vict. c. 108, no mandamus shall issue to a judge or officer of a County Court for refusing to do any act relating to the duties of his office, but application must be made to a superior court or judge for a rule or summons to show cause why such an act should not be done.

Manslaughter, the unlawful killing of another, without malice either express or implied. This act may be either voluntary, upon a sudden heat; or involuntary, but in the commission of some unlawful act. Both are felony and punished by penal servitude for life, or for a term not less than three years, or by imprisonment for any term not exceeding two years, or by fine.

Marchioness.—A dignity in woman answering to that of

Marquis in a man, conferred by creation or by marriage with a Marquis.

Maritime Law.—The royal navy of England has always been its greatest defence and ornament ; and accordingly it has been assiduously cultivated from earliest ages. To so great a perfection had our naval reputation arrived at in the twelfth century, that the code of maritime laws, which are called the laws of Oleron, and are received by all nations in Europe as the ground of all their marine constitutions, was confessedly compiled by our King Richard the First at the Isle of Oleron on the coast of France, then part of the possessions of the crown of England. The present condition of our marine is in great measure owing to the salutary provisions of the statutes called the navigation acts ; whereby the constant increase of English shipping and seamen was not only enconraged, but rendered unavoidably necessary. By the statute 5 Richard II. c. 3, in order to augment the navy of England, then greatly diminished, it was ordained, that none of the king's liege people should ship any merchandise out of or into the realm, but only in ships of the king's ligeance, on pain of forfeiture. In the next year, by statute 6 Richard II. c. 8, this wise provision was enervated, by only obliging the merchants to give English ships (if able and sufficient) the preference. But the most beneficial statute for the trade and commerce of these kingdoms is that navigation act, the rudiments of which were first framed in 1650, with a narrow partial view ; being intended to mortify our own sugar islands, which were disaffected to the Parliament, and still held out for Charles II., by stopping the gainful trade which they then carried on with the Dutch, and at the same time to clip the wings of our opulent and aspiring neighbours. This prohibited all ships of foreign nations from trading with any English plantations, without license from the council of state. In 1651, the prohibition was extended also to the mother-country : and no goods were suffered to be imported into England, or any of its dependencies, in any other than English bottoms ; or in the ships of that European nation of which the merchandize imported was the genuine growth or manufacture. At the Restoration, the former provisions were continued, by statute 12 Charles II. c. 18, with this very material improvement, that the master and three-fourths of the mariners shall also be English subjects. Many other acts of a similar exclusive tenor were passed till the statute 16 & 17 Vict. c. 104, threw the entire trade open to vessels of all nations with very satisfactory results as regards commerce and private enterprise. Many laws have been made for the supply of the royal navy with seamen ; for their regulation when on board ; and to confer privileges and rewards on them during and after their service.

Marquis, a title of honour, next in dignity to that of duke. His office was to guard the frontiers and limits of the kingdom, which were called the marches, from the Teutonic word marche, a "limit:" especially the marches of Wales and Scotland, while they continued hostile to England. The persons who had command there were called lords marchers, or marquesses ; whose authority was abolished by statute 27 Henry VIII. c. 27, though the title had long before been made a mere design of honour, Robert Vere, Earl of Oxford, being created Marquis of Dublin by Richard II. in the eighth year of his reign. A marquis is created by patent ; his title is most honourable ; and his coronet has pearls and strawberry leaves intermixed round, of equal height. His sons are by courtesy styled lords and his daughters ladies.

Married Women. *See* HUSBAND AND WIFE.

Martial Law.—That rule of action which is imposed by the military power. It has no place in the institutions of this country ; and cannot be proclaimed within this kingdom, as it would appear, by the Petition of Rights.

Master of the Horse is reckoned the third great

officer of the court, and is an office of great honour and antiquity, and always (when not put in commission) filled by noblemen of the highest rank and abilities.   He has the management
and disposal of all the Queen's stables and bred horses.   He
has authority over the equerries and pages, coachmen, footmen,
grooms, riders of the great horse, farriers and smiths.   He
appoints all the other tradesmen who work for the Queen's
stables ; and by his warrant to the avenor, makes them give an
oath to be true and faithful.   In short, he is entrusted with all
the lands and revenues appropriated for the Queen's breed of
horses, the expenses of the stable, and of the coaches, litters, &c.
He alone has the privilege of making use of any of the Queen's
horses, pages, footmen, &c.; and at any solemn cavalcade he
rides next the Queen, and leads a horse of state.

Master of the Rolls.—A law officer of the Crown who
ranks next to the Lord Chancellor.   He is judge of the Equity
Court, and has the custody of the Rolls and grants which pass
the great seal and the records of the Chancery.   All orders and
decrees made by him are deemed valid, subject nevertheless to
be discharged or altered by the Lord Chancellor, and cannot be
enrolled till the same are signed by the Lord Chancellor.   He
is specially directed to hear motions, pleas, and demurrers as
well as causes generally.   The Master of the Rolls is a patentee
officer and privy councillor.

Mayor.—The chief governor or magistrate of a city or
town corporate ; as the lord mayor of London, the lord mayor
of Dublin, the lord mayor of York, the mayor of Southampton,
&c.   King Richard I., anno 1189, changed the bailiffs of London
into a mayor.   Mayors of corporations are justices of peace.
The powers and duties of a mayor, or other head officer of a
corporation, depend in general on the provisions of the charters,
or prescriptive usages of the corporation, or the express provisions of the Act of Parliament regulating municipal corporations.   Where the mayor's presence is necessary at a corporate

assembly, his departure before a business regularly begun be concluded, will not invalidate that particular business ; but the assembly cannot proceed to anything else. And on the death of the mayor, or during the vacation of the office, the corporation can do no corporate act but that of choosing a new mayor.

Mesne Process.—Such process as issues pending the suit upon some collateral interlocutory matter, as to summon juries, witnesses, and the like ; distinguished from the original process which is the writ. Mesne process is also sometimes put in contradistinction to final process, or process of execution ; and then it signifies all such process as intervenes between the beginning and end of a suit.

Metropolitan.—A term applied to the prelate who resides in the capital city of each province, the clergy and the other bishops of the province being subject to his authority. The establishment of metropolitans originated at the end of the third century, and was confirmed by the council of Nicæa. The first metropolitan or archbishop of Canterbury was Augustine, created by King Ethelbert, on his conversion to Christianity, in 598. Paulinus, the first metropolitan of York, was appointed by Pope Gregory in 622. Patrick Graham, made bishop of St. Andrews in 1466, was the first metropolitan in Scotland.

Military Offices.—These offices are those of the Commander-in-Chief, Adjutant-General, Quartermaster-General, and Judge Advocate-General. They are all under the immediate control of the Commander-in-Chief, and under his direction govern all movements of troops, grant commissions, and make the necessary staff and other appointments. In all matters relating to pay and allowances these departments are controlled by the Secretary of State for War. Hours, 10 to 4. Whitehall and Westminster.

Militia.—The national force, denominated the Fyrd, which existed in this country in the Anglo-Saxon period, was improved and extended by Alfred. Henry II. issued an ordinance commanding all persons to provide themselves with arms in 1181. By 13 Edw. I. c. 5 (1285), the scale of arms for different ranks was revised. Hallam, with reference to the changes that occurred in the system of national defence, remarks, "The feudal military tenures had superseded that earlier system of public defence which called upon every man, and especially every landholder, to protect his country. The relations of a vassal came in place of those of a subject and a citizen. This was the revolution of the ninth century. In the twelfth and thirteenth another innovation rather more gradually prevailed, and marks the third period in the military history of Europe. Mercenary troops were substituted for the feudal militia." The first commission of array for the defence of the kingdom, of which any record remains, was issued in 1323, and the last in 1557. The modern system was introduced by 13 Charles II. c. 6 (1661), by which the sole right of commanding the militia by sea or land was vested in the crown. Further provisions were made by 13 & 14 Charles II. c. 3 (1662), and by 15 Charles II. c. 4 (1663); and the various regulations already in force were amended by 1 Geo. I. c. 14 (1714). Measures were taken for the better ordering of the militia by 30 Geo. II. c. 25 (1757), which was explained and amended by 31 Geo. II. c. 26 (1758). All the laws in force were consolidated 2 Geo. III. c. 20 (1762). Protestant dissenting ministers and schoolmasters were exempted from service in the militia by 19 Geo. III. c. 44 (1779). The militia laws were amended and consolidated by 26 Geo. III. c. 107 (1786). The supplementary militia act, 37 Geo. III. c. 3 (Nov. 11, 1796), provided for an augmentation of the militia, and the laws relating to the subject were again amended by 42 Geo. III. c. 90 (June 26, 1802). The acts of the Irish parliament respecting the militia in Ireland were amended and consolidated by 49 Geo. III. c. 120 (June 19, 1809). Police constables are exempted from serving in the militia by 2 & 3 Vict. c. 93 (Aug. 27, 1839). The militia laws were again amended by 15 & 16 Vict. c. 50; by 16 & 17 Vict. c. 133; by 17 & 18 Vict. c. 13; 20 & 21 Vict. c. 82, and 26 & 27 Vict. c. 37.

Ministry.—A collective noun for the heads of departments in the state. The ministry, or executive government, consists of the First Lord of the Treasury, the Lord Chancellor, the Lord President of the Council, the Lord Privy Seal, the Chancellor of the Exchequer, the Secretaries of State for the Home, Foreign, Colonial, War, and India Offices—all of whom are in the cabinet; also of the following, many of whom are not necessarily but usually in the cabinet :—the Chief Commissioners of Woods and Forests and of Works and Public Buildings, the Chancellor of the Duchy of Lancaster, the First Lord of the Admiralty, the President of the Board of Trade, the Paymaster-General of the Forces, the Master of the Mint, the Judge Advocate-General, the Postmaster-General, the Master-General of the Ordnance, and the Chief Secretary for Ireland. It sometimes happens that a statesman who holds no office is a member of the cabinet. The First Lord of the Treasury is at the head of the government and appoints his colleagues. In addition to the abovementioned officers there are the Law Officers of the Crown, the Under Secretaries of various departments, the Lord Lieutenant and Lord Chancellor and Law Officers of Ireland and Scotland, and the great officers of Her Majesty's Household.

Misdemeanor, in law, signifies a crime. Every crime is a misdemeanor; yet the law has made a distinction between crimes of a higher and a lower nature; the latter being denominated misdemeanors, the former felonies, &c. "A crime, or misdemeanor, is an act committed or omitted, in violation of a public law, either forbidding or commanding it. This general definition comprehends both crimes and misdemeanors; which, properly speaking, are mere synonymous terms; though, in common usage, the word crime is made to denote such offences as are of a deeper and more atrocious dye; while smaller faults and omissions of less consequence are comprised under the gentler name of misdemeanors only."

Misprisions are, in the acceptation of our law, generally understood to be all such high offences as are under the degree of capital, but nearly bordering thereon. Misprisions are generally divided into two sorts : *negative,* which consist in the concealment of something which ought to be revealed ; and *positive,* which consist in the commission of something which ought not to be done.

1. Of the first, or negative kind, is what is called *misprision of treason,* which consists in the bare knowledge and concealment of treason, without any degree of assent thereto : for any assent makes the party a principal traitor. But it is now enacted by the statute 1 & 2 Phil. & Mary, c. 10, that a bare concealment of treason shall be only held a misprision. This concealment becomes criminal, if the party apprised of the treason does not, as soon as conveniently may be, reveal it to some judge of assize or justice of the peace. Misprision of felony is also the concealment of a felony which a man knows, but never assented to ; for, if he assented, this makes him either principal or accessory.

2. Misprisions, which are merely positive, are generally denominated *contempt* or *high misdemeanors;* of which the principal is the *mal-administration* of such high officers as are in public trust and employment. This is usually punished by the method of parliamentary impeachment ; wherein such penalties, short of death, are inflicted, as to the wisdom of the House of Peers shall seem proper ; consisting usually of banishment, imprisonment, fines, or perpetual disability. Hither also may be referred the offence of embezzling the public money, called among the Romans *peculatus;* which the Julian law punished with death in a magistrate, and with deportation, or banish-

ment, in a private person. With us it is not a capital crime, but punishable by fine and imprisonment.

Mortgage.—A pledging or pawning of freehold or leasehold or other property of a nature not susceptible of personal delivery. The form of a mortgage of land is, by a conveyance of the inheritance or estate to another, on condition that if the borrower do not by a certain day repay the money, the lender may enter and enjoy the land, or, in technical language, *that the lender's estate shall be absolute in the premises;* equity, however, intervenes and compels the lender or mortgagee to account to the borrower or mortgagor for the true value; and if the mortgagee is in possession by virtue of an ejectment brought at law, equity will make him render an account of the profits received; and this account may be opened at any time during twenty years, in favour of heirs, infants, and other parties entitled. This rule also extends to cases where the conveyance has *apparently* been an absolute conveyance, but the transaction has been treated as a mortgage, by the payment and receipt of interest or other similar acts. The right which a mortgagor has to redeem his property is termed his *equity of redemption.*

Mortgages are either legal, which are enforceable at Common Law; or equitable, which can only be enforced in Chancery.

When a mortgagee wants to bar or deprive the mortgagor of his equitable rights, or rather have the mortgagor's equitable rights ascertained, he files a bill of foreclosure, *i. e.*, he prays to have a decree for the purpose of having the accounts taken, and that his mortgage-money be repaid, which is either done by the mortgagee's retaining the estate, if the value be swallowed up with principal, interest, and charges, or by a sale being made, and the surplus rendered to the mortgagor, or by the mortgagee's paying any sum (if the balance be but small) to the mortgagee in full, for an absolute right.

Mortmain.—Purchases made by corporate bodies are said to be purchased in *mortmain,* or *dead hand;* the reason for the title, according to Blackstone, being that such purchases were " usually made by ecclesiastical bodies, the members of which (being professed) were reckoned dead persons in law ; land, therefore, holden by them might, with great propriety, be said to be held *in mortua manu.*" In order to check the increasing importance of the Church, the giving of land in mortmain was prohibited by 9 Hen. III. c. 36 (1225), which was enforced by 7 Edw. I. st. 2 (1279), and extended to all guilds and corporations, lay or ecclesiastical, by 15 Richard II. c. 5 (1391). These prohibitions were repealed by 1 & 2 Phil. and Mary, c. 8 (1554). The King was empowered to grant licences to purchase in mortmain by 7 & 8 Will. III. c. 36 (1696). Gifts in mortmain by will were restrained by 9 Geo. II. c. 36 (1736), which took effect June 24, 1736. It was repealed, as far as it related to the Universities of Oxford and Cambridge, by 45 Geo. III. c. 101 (July 10, 1805).

Murder is homicide, or the slaying of another with malice aforethought, either express or implied. Malice is presumed from the very fact of killing or homicide; but the party charged may rebut that presumption, by proving that the homicide was justifiable or excusable, or that at most it amounted to manslaughter and not to murder. Malice and intent are the peculiar ingredients of murder ; and the indications of malice can only appear from the facts proved, though in many cases where no malice is expressly or openly indicated, the law will imply it. Murder is a felony punishable by death. (24 & 25 Vict. c. 100.)

Duel.—If two persons deliberately fight a duel and one of them be killed, the other and his second are guilty of murder, no matter how grievous the provocation, or by which party it was given : the second of the deceased also is deemed guilty of murder, as being present, aiding and abetting.

Fighting.—Persons who quarrel and afterwards fight, whereby one kills the other, are guilty of murder or manslaughter, according to the facts; for if there intervened between the quarrel and the fight a sufficient cooling time for passion to subside, and reason to interpose, the killing would be murder, otherwise not; for if the parties on the quarrel went out and fought in a field (this being deemed a continued act of passion), the killing in such a case would be manslaughter only.

Negligence.—Any act lawful in itself, but which by want of precaution in the performance occasions the death of another, may be deemed murder or manslaughter, according to the circumstances and the degree of caution used; if every reasonable caution was used, it will be homicide by misadventure, *i. e.*, excusable homicide.

Mutiny Act. — A statute annually passed to punish mutiny and desertion, and for the better payment of the army and their quarters. It was first passed in 1688. It regulates the dispersion of the soldiers among the innkeepers in the kingdom, and establishes a law martial for their government. This statute enacts that if any officer or soldier shall excite any mutiny, or shall desert, or enlist in any other regiment, or sleep on his post, or hold correspondence with the enemy, or strike or use violence to his superior officer, or disobey his commands, such offender shall suffer such punishment as a court-martial shall inflict, though it extend to death itself. *See* 26 & 27 Vict. c. 8.

National Debt.—The money owing by Government to some of the public, the interest of which is paid out of the taxes raised by the whole of the public.

National Debt Office.—The Commissioners for the reduction of the National Debt are, the Speaker of the House of Commons, the Chancellor of the Exchequer, the Master of the Rolls, the Governor and Deputy-Governor of the Bank of England, the Lord Chief Baron of the Exchequer, and the Accountant-General of the Court of Chancery. These are appointed *ex officio;* the permanent management of the department being exercised by a Comptroller-General and other officials. Hours 10 to 4. Old Jewry, Cheapside.

Naturalisation.—The act of investing aliens with the privileges of natural-born subjects. This can be effected by Act of Parliament, or by certificate of a Secretary of State. If an alien be naturalised by Act of Parliament, his son born previously may inherit. The certificate of a Secretary of State can be obtained by any alien coming to reside in any part of Great Britain or Ireland, with intention to settle therein, upon his taking the oath of allegiance and abjuration. He will then enjoy all the rights of a natural-born British subject, except the privilege of being a member of the Privy Council, or of either House of Parliament. For naturalisation in a British colony, *see* 10 & 11 Vict. c. 83.

Navigation Laws.—Foreign ships were prohibited from fishing and trading on the British coasts by 5 Eliz. c. 5 (1562). The Act of Navigation of the Republican Parliament, passed October 9, 1651, prohibited all importation into the British territories, except in ships owned and manned by English subjects, and these restrictions were confirmed by 12 Charles II. c. 18 (1660), which is sometimes styled the *Charta Maritima.* Several Acts of similar import were afterwards passed, which were consolidated and amended by 3 & 4 Will. IV. c. 54 (Aug. 28, 1833). Most of these restrictions were repealed by the Act to amend the laws in force for the encouragement of British shipping and navigation, 12 & 13 Vict. c. 29 (June 26, 1849), which came into operation Jan. 1, 1850. Steam navigation is regulated by 14 & 15 Vict. c. 79 (Aug. 7, 1851), which took effect Jan. 1, 1852. Further provisions were made by the Merchant Shipping Law Amendment Act, 16 & 17 Vict. c. 131 (Aug. 20, 1853). Foreign ships were admitted to the coasting trade by 17 & 18 Vict. c. 5 (March 23, 1854).

Ne Exeat Regno.—A writ to restrain a person from going out of the kingdom without the Queen's licence. It is directed to the sheriff to make the party find surety that he will not depart the realm; and, on his refusal, to commit him to prison.

It is, however, now used for private purposes; and is granted by the Chancellor, on the application of a creditor who fears that his debtor may leave the kingdom.

Nisi Prius, in law, a judicial writ which lies in cases where the jury being impannelled and returned before the justices of the bank, one of the parties requests to have such a writ for the ease of the country, in order that the trial may come before the justices in the same county on their coming thither. The purport of a writ of *nisi prius* is, that the sheriff is hereby commanded to bring to Westminster the men impannelled, at a certain day, before the justices, *"nisi prius justiciarii domini regis ad assisas capiendas venerint."*

Nonsuit.—A renunciation of a suit by the plaintiff, most commonly upon the discovery of some error or defect, when the matter is so far proceeded in that the jury is ready to deliver their verdict. Before the jury gave their verdict on a trial, it was formerly usual to call or demand the plaintiff, in order to answer the amercement, to which by the old law he was liable, in case he failed in his suit. And it is now usual to call him, whenever he is unable to make out his case, either by reason of his not adducing any evidence in support of it, or any evidence arising in the proper county.

Notary, is one who publicly attests deeds or writings, to make authentic in another country; but their principal business in London and elsewhere is to protest foreign bills of exchange, and inland bills and notes; which latter are, if protested, to be at the charge of the holders, if paid on the day of protest, as it is not imperative on holders of inland bills to cause them to be protested. Notaries are regulated by an Act, 41 Geo. III. c. 79, which imposes a seven years' apprenticeship to a notary, and an admission in the Civil Law Courts, under a penalty. Notaries are prohibited from permitting others to act in their names; and in London they must be free of the Scriveners' Company.

Nuisances, in law, are of two kinds.

Private, as when a man uses his own property so as to injure that of another. The proper form of remedy for an injury sustained by a private nuisance is an action on the case.

Public, which are classed amongst crimes and misdemeanors, and are annoyances to all the Queen's subjects. When they annoy private individuals only, they form the subject of a civil action. Public nuisances are:—The rendering of bridges, roads, rivers, &c., dangerous to pass; offensive trades and manufactures; disorderly inns, gaming-houses, &c.; all lotteries, except in the case of art-unions; making and selling fireworks in unlicensed places, &o., &e. In these cases the Courts of Equity will interfere by injunction.

Oath.—An affirmation or denial of anything before one or more persons who have authority to administer the same, for the discovery and advancement of truth and right, calling God to witness that the testimony is true; it is called a corporal oath, because the witness, when he swears, lays his right hand on the Holy Evangelists, or New Testament. All oaths must be lawful, allowed by the common law, or some statute: if they are administered by persons in a private capacity, or not duly authorised, they are void; and those administering them are guilty of a high contempt, for doing it without a warrant of law, and punishable by fine and imprisonment. If oath be made against oath in a cause, it is not apparent to the court which oath is true; and in such case the court will take that oath to be true which is to affirm a verdict, judgment, &c., as it would be absurd to set aside a verdict or judgment upon conflicting testimony. The 17 & 18 Vict. c. 125, allows any person called as a witness in civil proceedings, who shall be unwilling to be sworn from conscientious motives, to obtain from the court permission to make a solemn affirmation instead. This permission is now extended to criminal proceedings. There are many kinds of oaths in our laws, the principal of which will be found under their distinctive names.

Oblivion, Act of.—An Act passed in 1660, granting a general pardon and indemnity for state offences committed between 1637 and 1660, excepting certain persons mentioned by Charles II., and those who had embezzled the king's goods, and the Romish priests engaged in the Irish rebellion in 1641.

Offences.—An "offence" is the general term for an injury inflicted either against the public peace in the person or property of an individual, against the laws of religion or decency, or against those laws of constitution and state recognised and allowed for the preservation of society.

In 1861, six Acts were passed for the consolidation and amendment of the statute law regarding certain criminal offences. They are usually divided into the following classes :—

I. Offences against the person. These are homicide, assaults, rape, bigamy, child-stealing, concealing the birth of a child, attempts to murder, false imprisonment, &c.

II. Offences against property. These are larceny, fraud by agents and others, receiving stolen goods, sacrilege, burglary, injuries by fire, forgery, malicious injuries to all kinds of property, &c.

III. Offences against the Sovereign and civil government. These are offences relating to the coin, embezzling the Queen's stores, serving foreign states, speaking against the Sovereign, contempt against the Crown's ecclesiastical supremacy, selling offices in the gift of the Crown, &c.

IV. Offences against religion. These are apostasy, heresy, blasphemy, reviling the ordinances of the Established Church, swearing, witchcraft, simony, profanation of the Lord's day, disturbing public worship, &c.

V. Offences against the law of nations. These are, piracy on the high seas, violation of safe conducts, infringements of the rights of ambassadors, &c.

VI. Offences against public justice. These are, falsely certifying a record, intimidation, bribery, extortion, &c.

VII. Offences against the public peace. These are, unlawful assemblings, fighting, spreading false news, libel, going armed with dangerous weapons, riot, &c.

VIII. Offences against public trade. These are, smuggling, using false weights, monopoly, conspiracy, &c.

IX. Offences against the public health, police, or economy. These are, breach of the laws respecting quarantine or of the Vaccination Acts, selling unwholesome provisions, obstructing public highways, carrying on unwholesome occupations near to public highways, keeping gaming-houses, indecency, vagrancy, refusing to serve a public office, &c.

Of these various offences, some few are capital felonies ; some are simple felonies, punishable with penal servitude for life or lesser punishment ; and many (especially those which endanger the administration of public justice, public peace, trade, or policy) are mere misdemeanors, the punishment of which is in some cases allotted by particular statutes, or, where the offence is punishable " at common law," left to the discretion of the presiding judge.

Offerings, parsons' tithes, payable by custom to the parson or vicar of the parish, either occasionally, as at sacraments, marriages, christenings, churching of women, burials, &c., or at constant times, as at Easter or Christmas. The law enforces the payment of offerings according to the custom and place where they grow due. The four offering days are, Christmas, Easter, Whitsuntide, and the feast of the dedication of the parish church. It seems that 1s. is all that need be given, or less, according to the state in life of the parishioner.

Ordeal, Trial by.—Ordeals, or God's judgments, are of great antiquity, some writers being of opinion that the jealousy-offering mentioned in Numbers is a test of this kind. Blackstone says :—" The most ancient species of trial was that by ordeal ; which was peculiarly distinguished by the appellation of Judicium Dei, and sometimes Vulgaris Purgatio, to distinguish it from the canonical purgation, which was by the oath of the party." The trial by ordeal in England was of two sorts, either fire ordeal or water ordeal. Fire ordeal was performed, either by taking up in the hand a piece of red-hot iron, of one, two, or three pounds weight ; or else by walking barefoot and blindfold over nine red-hot ploughshares, laid lengthwise at unequal distances ; and if the party escaped being hurt, he was adjudged innocent ; but if it happened otherwise, as without collusion it usually did, he was then condemned as guilty. Water ordeal was performed, either by plunging the bare arm up to the elbow in boiling water, and escaping unhurt thereby ; or by casting the person suspected into a river or pond of cold water, and if he floated without any action of swimming, it was deemed an evidence of his guilt, but if he sank he was acquitted. There were several other species of ordeal in use in different countries. Notice of ordeals in England first occurs in the laws of Ina, who reigned in Wessex from A D. 628 to 727. This mode of punishment was formally abolished by Henry III. in 1218, when assize of battel, or trial by combat, for some time took its place.

Order of Discharge.—An order made under the Bankruptoy Act, 1861, by a Court of Bankrnptcy, the effect of which is to discharge a bankrupt from all debts, claims, or demands provable under the bankruptcy. It is analogous to a certificate of conformity under the previous law. Any time within thirty days after an order of discharge has been granted or refused by any commissioner or county court judge, application can be made to the Court of Appeal in Chancery, that such order of discharge may be granted or recalled and delivered up to be cancelled, and such court may order such application to be granted, on good cause shown.

Order of the Garter. *See* GARTER.

Ordinary, in common or canon law, means one who has ordinary or immediate jurisdiction in matters ecclesiastical, in any place. In this sense archdeacons are ordinaries, but the appellation is most frequently applied to the bishop of the diocese, who has of course the ordinary ecclesiastical jurisdiction, and the collation to benefices within such diocese. There are some chapels, chapters, abbeys, &c., exempted from the jurisdiction of the ordinary, The archbishop is ordinary of the whole province, to visit, and receive appeals from the inferior judicatures.

Ordination, the act of conferring holy orders, or of initiating a person into the priesthood by prayer and the laying on of hands. Ordination has always been esteemed the principal prerogative of bishops, and they still retain the function as a mark of spiritual sovereignty in their diocese. Without ordination, no person can receive any benefice, parsonage, vicarage, &c. A person must be twenty-three years of age before he can be ordained deacon, or have any share in the ministry; and full twenty-four before he can be ordained priest. A bishop, on the ordination of clergymen, is to examine them in the presence of the ministers, who, in the ordination of priests, but not of deacons, assist him at the imposition of hands; but this is only done as a mark of assent, not because it is thought necessary. In case any crime, as drunkenness, perjury, forgery, &c., be alleged against any one that is to be ordained, either priest or deacon, the bishop ought to desist from ordaining him. The person to be ordained is to bring a testimonial of his life and doctrine to the bishop, and both priests and deacons are required to subscribe the Thirty-nine Articles. The ordination of bishops is more properly and more commonly called consecration. As to ordination for or in the colonies, see 3 & 4 Vict. c. 33, and 15 & 16 Vict. c. 52.

Outlawry, the punishment of a person who, being called into law, and lawfully, according to the usual forms, sought, does contemptuously refuse to appear. The effect of being outlawed at the suit of another, in a civil cause, is the forfeiture of all the person's goods and chattels to the Queen, and the profits

of his land, while the outlawry remains in force. If in treason
or felony, all the lands or tenements which he has in fee or for
life, and all his goods and chattels, are also forfeited ; and besides, the law interprets his absence as a sufficient evidence of
guilt ; and without requiring farther proof, accounts the person
guilty of the fact, on which ensues corruption of blood, &c.
However, to avoid inhumanity, no man is entitled to kill him
wantonly or wilfully ; but in so doing he is guilty of murder,
unless it happens in endeavouring to apprehend him : for any-
body may arrest an outlaw, either of his own head, or by writ or
warrant, in order to bring him to execution. If after outlawry,
in civil cases, the defendant publicly appear, he is to be arrested
and committed till the outlawry be reversed : which reversal
may be had by the defendant's appearing in court, and any
plausible circumstance, however trifling, is in general sufficient to
reverse it ; it being considered only as a process to force appearance. The defendant must, however, pay full costs. Peers
and members of Parliament are exempt from outlawry, except
in criminal cases. Women, and infants under twelve years of
age, cannot be outlawed.

Overseers of the Poor.—Public officers created by the
43 Eliz. c. 2, to provide for the poor in every parish. Churchwardens, by this statute, are called " overseers of the poor," and
they join with the overseers in making a poor-rate. This statute requires that the overseers of parishes shall be four, three,
or two substantial householders ; and that they shall be nominated yearly in Easter week, or within one month after Easter.
The principal duties of the overseers are, to collect a poor-rate,
and to do various acts in relation thereto, as, to remove such
persons as the parish or place is not liable to support, and other
acts incidental to the management of the poor under the directions of the poor-law commissioners, or their assistant commissioner, or according to the provisions of any local Act for that
purpose ; also, to enter in the rate-books the names of the

owners or their proxies who wish to avail themselves of the privilege of voting for guardians ; they are to give publicity to the rules of commissioners ; and to account quarterly; and when going out of office ; and they are liable to various penalties if they refuse or neglect to pay the balance, or if they disobey the legal or reasonable orders of justices or guardians, or purloin the property of the parish.

Oyer and Terminer.—A commission directed to the judges and other gentlemen of the courts to which it is issued, by virtue whereof they have power to hear and determine treasons and all manner of felonies and trespasses.

Oyer and Terminer, Courts of.—Tribunals held before the Queen's commissioners, among whom usually are two judges of the superior courts of law at Westminster, twice in every year in every county of the kingdom, the metropolis and its vicinity excepted.

Pains and Penalties.—Acts of Parliament to attaint particular persons of treason or felony, or to inflict pains and penalties contrary to the common law to serve a special purpose. They are in fact new laws made *pro re natâ*.

Pardon.—The pardoning of crimes is the peculiar prerogative of the Sovereign. By 27 Henry VIII. c. 24, it is declared that " no other person hath power to remit or pardon any treason or felonies whatsoever ; but that the King hath the whole and sole power thereof united and knit to the imperial crown of this realm." The Queen may pardon all offences merely against the crown or the public ; excepting, that, to preserve the liberty of the subject, the committing any man to prison out of the realm is, by the Habeas Corpus Act, 31 Charles II. c. 2, made a *præmunire*, unpardonable even by the crown. Nor, can the Queen pardon, where private justice is principally concerned in the prosecution of offenders : *Non potest rex gratiam facere cum injuria et damno aliorum.* Therefore, in appeals of all kinds (which are the suit, not of the

Queen, but of the party injured), the prosecutor may release ; but the Queen cannot pardon. Neither can she pardon a common nuisance, while it remains unredressed, or so as to prevent an abatement of it : though afterwards she may remit the fine : because though the prosecution is vested in the Queen to avoid the multiplicity of suits, yet (during its continuance) this offence savours more of the nature of a private injury to each individual in the neighbourhood, than of a public wrong. Neither, lastly, can the Queen pardon an offence against a popular or penal statute, after information brought ; for thereby the informer hath acquired a private property in his part of the penalty. There is also a restriction of a peculiar nature, that affects the prerogative of pardoning, in case of parliamentary impeachments, viz., that the Queen's pardon cannot be pleaded to any such impeachment, so as to impede the inquiry, and stop the prosecution of great and notorious offenders (12 & 13 Will. III. c. 2). The effect of such pardon by the Queen is to make the offender a new man ; to acquit him of all corporal penalties and forfeitures annexed to that offence for which he obtains his pardon ; and not so much to restore his former, as to give him a new, credit and capacity. But nothing can restore or purify the blood when once corrupted, if the pardon be not allowed till after attainder, but the high and transcendent power of Parliament.

Parent and Child.—The power of a parent by the English law is merely sufficient to keep the child in order and obedience. He may lawfully correct his child, being under age, in a reasonable manner ; for this is for the benefit of his education. The consent or concurrence of the parent to the marriage of his child under age was also directed by our ancient law to be obtained ; but now it is absolutely necessary ; for without it the contract is void. A father has no other power over his son's estate, than as his trustee or guardian ; for though he may receive the profits during the child's minority, yet he must account for them when he comes of age. He may indeed have the benefit of his children's labour while they live with him, and are maintained by him ; but this is no more than he is entitled to from his apprentices or servants. The legal power of a father over the persons of his children ceases at the age of twenty-one ; for they are then enfranchised by arriving at years of discretion, when the empire of the father or other guardian gives place to the empire of reason. Yet, till that age arrives, this empire of the father continues even after his death ; for he may by his will appoint a guardian to his children. He may also delegate part of his parental authority, during his life, to the tutor or schoolmaster of his child ; who is then *in loco parentis*, and has such a portion of the power of the parent committed to his charge, *viz.*, that of restraint and correction, as may be necessary to answer the purposes for which he is employed. With respect to the mother, she has no legal power over the child in the father's lifetime, except under special order from the Lord Chancellor. After the father's death the mother is entitled to the custody of her child until the age of twenty-one, but she cannot appoint a guardian by will. The Divorce Court has power to make such orders as it may think fit with regard to the custody and education of the children of the parties to suits for judicial separation or dissolution of marriage. *See* 20 & 21 Vict. c. 85 ; and 22 & 23 Vict. c. 61.

Parish Clerk.—In every parish the parson, vicar, &c., has a parish-clerk under him, who is the lowest officer of the church. These were formerly clerks in orders, and their business at first was to officiate at the altar ; for which they had a competent maintenance by offerings ; but they are now laymen, and have certain fees with the parson on christenings, marriages, burials, &c., besides wages for their maintenance. The law looks upon them as officers for life ; and they are chosen by the minister of the parish, unless there is a custom for the parishioners or churchwardens to choose them ; in which case the canon cannot abrogate such custom; and when chosen it is to be signified, and they are to be sworn into their office by the archdeacon, for which the Court of Queen's Bench will grant a mandamus.

Parliament, Act of. *See* ACT OF PARLIAMENT.

Parliament.—The derivation of the word Parliament is of French origin, signifying an assembly that meets and confers together. But long before the introduction of the Norman language in England, all matters of importance were debated and settled in the great councils of the realm. These councils were called *micel synoth, micel gemote,* and more frequently *witena gemote.* They were also in Latin *commune concilium regni, curia magna,* and sometimes *communitas regni Angliæ.* Hence it appears that Parliaments, or general councils, are coeval with the kingdom itself. The Parliament as it now exists possesses the supreme and absolute authority of the State; but the sovereign alone has the exclusive power to convene it; and this he (or she) is bound to do every year (by the ancient statutes of the realm), *if need be,* a clause which many of our monarchs took so great an advantage of, till in the reign of Charles II. it was enacted that a new Parliament should be called within three years after the determination of the former. Its constituent parts are the three estates of the realm : the sovereign, sitting in his royal political capacity, the lords spiritual and temporal (forming one house), and the commons (forming another); and these parts combined contain the body politic of the kingdom, of which the crown is the head. Hence the balance of the constitution is admirably preserved, as every branch of our civil polity supports and is regulated by the rest. For the crown has the power of rejecting any measure, thus preventing any encroachments; whilst in the legislature the people are a check upon the nobility, and the nobility a check upon the people, by the mutual privilege of rejecting what the other has resolved. The spiritual lords consist of the two archbishops, twenty-six bishops, and the four lords spiritual from Ireland, who sit in Parliament by rotation. The lords temporal are the peers of the realm ; possessing their seats either by descent, as do all ancient peers, or by creation, as do all new-made ones, or by election, as do the sixteen peers who represent Scotland, and the twenty-eight peers who represent the nobility of Ireland. Thus the number of lords temporal is indefinite. The commons are all such men of property in the kingdom who have not seats in the House of Lords ; every one of whom has a voice in Parliament, either personally or by his representatives—representatives chosen by a number of separate districts where the voters are easily distinguished. The counties are represented by knights elected by the proprietors of lands ; and the cities and boroughs by citizens and burgesses chosen by the trading interest of the nation. Every member must have attained to his majority. The numerical strength of the House of Commons is 500 (English and Welsh) 53 (Scotch), and 105 (Irish), thus in all 658. Every member, though elected for a particular district, serves for the whole realm—not merely for the advantage of his constituents, but for the commonwealth. Such are the three essences of Parliament—each so necessary that the consent of all three is required to make a new law. Legislative authority without the king incurs the penalties of a *præmunire*. The jurisdiction of Parliament extends to all matters either ecclesiastical, civil, military, or criminal, and it is the ultimate court of appeal in this land.

A.D.

1205. The first writ on record is issued by John.

1244. The prelates and barons deliberate separately.

1254. A representative parliament, composed of two knights from every shire, is convened to grant an aid.

1258. The barons assemble at Oxford. This meeting is the first called a parliament.

A.D.

1265. The earliest writ extant is issued.

1295. Borough representation is regarded as commencing this year.

1311. Annual parliaments are ordered.

1322. Wales is represented in parliament.

1327. Jan. 7. King Edward II. is deposed by both houses of parliament.

1362. English is made the language of the law.

1399. Sept. 30. King Richard II. is deposed by parliament, and the House of Commons begins to assert its control over pecuniary grants.

1404. Oct. 6. The Unlearned Parliament, so called because lawyers were prohibited from attending, meets at Coventry.

1407. Nov. 9. The Lords and Commons are permitted to assemble and transact business in the sovereign's absence.

1413. May 25. Members of parliament are ordered to reside in the cities and boroughs they represent.

1430. Feb. 23. The Commons adopt the 40s. qualification for county electors.

1483. The statutes are first printed.

1542. Members of parliament are exempted from arrest.

1549. The eldest sons of peers are permitted to sit in parliament.

1640. Nov. 3. The Long Parliament assembles.

1649. Feb. 6. The House of Lords is abolished.

1653. April 20. Cromwell dissolves the Long Parliament.

1660. April 25. The House of Lords is restored, but only consists of peers temporal.

1661. Nov. 20. The bishops are permitted to resume their seats in the House of Lords.

1667. An attempt is made to unite the English and Scotch parliaments

A.D.

1677. Roman Catholics are excluded from sitting in either house, by 30 Charles II. st. 2.

1694. Triennial parliaments are ordered by 6 Will. & Mary, c. 2.

1707. May 1. The parliaments of England and Scotland are united by 5 Anne, c. 8. Oct. 23. The first parliament of Great Britain assembles.

1715. Septennial parliaments are ordered by 1 Geo. I. st. 2, c. 38.

1800. July 2. The Irish parliament is incorporated with that of Great Britain by 39 & 40 Geo. III. c. 67.

1801. Jan. 22. The united parliament of Great Britain and Ireland holds its first meeting.

1829. April 13. The Roman Catholic Emancipation Act (10 Geo. IV. c. 7) permits Roman Catholics to sit and vote in either house of parliament on swearing fidelity to the king and constitution.

1832. June 7. Passing of the Reform Bill.

1858. July 23. Jews are admitted to sit in both houses by 21 & 22 Vict. c. 49.

(See HOUSE OF COMMONS, HOUSE OF LORDS.)

Parliamentary Committee.—A committee of members of the House of Lords or of the House of Commons, appointed by either house to inquire into those matters which cannot conveniently occupy the attention of the whole house. Any subject brought under the consideration of either house may be referred to a committee. All private bills, such as bills for railways, canals, roads, &c., are referred to select committees of each house before receiving the sanction of that house. Their reports are not absolutely binding, but great weight is attached to them and their decisions are seldom reversed.

Partners and Partnership. — When two or more agree to come into any trade, bargain, or speculation, in the nature of a trading concern, in equal proportions or as agreed on, they are partners. A partnership, is a voluntary contract, by words, bare consent, or writing, by two or more persons, for joining together their money, goods, labour, skill, or all or either of them, upon an agreement that the gain or loss shall be divided in certain proportions amongst them. In general, all the partners appear ostensibly to the world, and constitute what is called the house or firm. It is, however, by no means uncommon for moneyed men to embark considerable sums in trade, without taking any part in the management of the concern or suffering their names to appear; such persons are called dormant or sleeping partners, and when discovered, are liable, in common with the rest, to the creditors of the firm. There are also special partnerships, formed for a single adventure, and the consequences and liabilities of these are confined to the transactions thence arising. Every person except a married woman can contract a partnership.

Patent Letters. *See* LETTERS PATENT.

Patent Office.—This office was established in 1852, and the Lord Chancellor, the Master of the Rolls, the Attorney-General, the Solicitor-General, the Lord Advocate and the Solicitor-General for Scotland, and the Solicitor-General for Ireland, were appointed Commissioners of Patents and Inventions. Hours, ten to four, Southampton Buildings, Chancery Lane.

Paymaster-General's Office.—In 1836 the Army and Navy Pay-offices were amalgamated under the title of the Paymaster-General's Office. The offices of Paymaster of Exchequer Bills and of Civil Services were subsequently merged into this department. The Paymaster-General, who is also Vice-President of the Board of Trade, quits office on a change of Government; the other officials have permanent appointments. Hours 10 to 4. Whitehall.

Peace, Commission of the.—A special commission under the Great Seal appointing justices of the peace. It is one of the authorities by virtue of which judges sit upon circuit.

Peculiars, Court of.—This Court is a branch of the Court of Arches, and has a jurisdiction over all those parishes dispersed throughout the province of Canterbury in the midst of other dioceses, which are exempt from the ordinary's jurisdiction, and subject to the metropolitan .only. All ecclesiastical causes arising within these peculiar jurisdictions are originally cognizable in this Court, from which an appeal lies to the Court of Arches.

Peers and Peerage.—The nobility of the realm, consisting of dukes, marquises, earls, viscounts, and barons, are called peers, or equals, because they enjoy an equality of right in all public proceedings. They are created either by writ, or by patent. The earliest peerage by writ is of the year 1265, when a writ of summons to parliament was issued by Henry III. The first peer created by patent was John de Beauchamp, who was made baron of Kidderminster by Richard II. October 10, 1387. Peers are exempt from arrest in civil, but not in criminal cases. In cases of treason and felony, they can only be tried by their fellow peers ; but in misdemeanors they are tried by an ordinary jury. Peeresses are tried by the same tribunals as peers, by 20 Hen. VI. c. 9 (1442). By 4 & 5 Vict. c. 22 (June 21, 1841), peers convicted of crimes were rendered liable to the same penalties as commoners. The elevation of Sir James Parke to the peerage for the term of his natural life, by the title of Lord Wensleydale, January 16, 1856, led to the appointment of a committee by the House of Lords to inquire into the legality of life-peerages. A report, deciding that such peerages could not entitle their holders to sit or vote in parliament, was presented February 25, in consequence of which Lord Wensleydale received a patent with the usual remainder to "the heirs male of his body lawfully begotten,' the following July. The peers of Scotland are regarded as forming part of the nobility of Great Britain. By the 23rd article of the Act of Union, 5 Anne, c. 8 (1706), sixteen of their number are permitted to sit in the House of Lords as representatives of the rest. As this Act limits the right of election of these representatives to the Scotch peers then existing, it follows that no new Scotch peerages can be created. The Irish peers also form part of the nobility of the realm ; and by the 4th article of the Irish Act of Union, 39 & 40 Geo. III. c. 67 (July 2, 1800), four of the Irish bishops and twenty-eight temporal peers are permitted to sit in the House of Lords. The same Act permits the sovereign to create one new Irish peerage whenever three of those existing become extinct ; and when the number is reduced to 100 noblemen, every vacancy may be immediately supplied.

Peeress.—A woman who is noble by descent, creation, or marriage. If a peeress, by descent or creation, marries a person under the degree of nobility, she still continues noble : but if she obtains that dignity only by marriage, she loses it on her afterwards marrying a commoner ; yet by the courtesy of England she generally retains the title of her nobility. A countess or baroness may not be arrested for debt or trespass ; for though, in respect of their sex, they cannot sit in parliament, they are nevertheless peers of the realm, and shall be tried by their peers, &c.

Penal Laws.—Severe laws enacted against the Roman Catholics of these realms, which remained unrepealed till the passing of the Roman Catholic Emancipation Bill (which see). By these laws Roman Catholics were excluded from parliament, from civil and military offices ; from serving on juries ; from burying their dead in any but Protestant churchyards ; from education, &c., &c.

Perjury.—The taking a false oath or making a false declaration before a magistrate in writing, or if a Quaker, Moravian, or Separatist, making a false affirmation knowingly, so that a thing material to the question before a competent and judicial authority be falsely and wittingly denied or intentionally concealed. Voluntary and corrupt perjury must be proved, for mistake or inadvertence, however reprehensible, will not subject a party to an indictment for this offence. The allegation of a falsehood as well as the suppression of a truth are equally perjuries, especially when a witness is sworn in open Court to tell *the truth, the whole truth, and nothing but the truth.* It seems that a conviction for perjury renders the party incapable of giving testimony again, notwithstanding the rule that a party who has undergone his punishment is restored to legal competence. Where perjury is committed on a trial in Court, the judge may commit the party, and order him to be prosecuted, and such prosecution is to be carried on without payment of fees. The soliciting or procuring perjury to be committed is punishable as perjury : but it must be proved that the perjury was committed. The punishment for perjury is annexed to offences of swearing to false affidavits, and making false written declarations before persons not strictly judicial, as registrars, &c. By 16 & 17 Vict., and 20 & 21 Vict., perjury is punished by penal servitude for not more than seven nor less than three years.

Petty-Bag Office.—An office belonging to the common law jurisdiction of the Court of Chancery for suits for and against solicitors and officers of that Court, and for process and proceedings by extents on statutes, recognizances, &c.

Petition of Right.—A petition presented to Charles I. in 1628, to limit the encroachments of the Crown upon the liberties of the people. It petitioned that no man be compelled to make or yield any gift, loan, benevolence, or tax, without common consent by Act of Parliament ; that none be called upon to make answer so to do ; that no freeman be imprisoned but by the law of the land, and not by the King's special command, without any charge ; that persons be not compelled to receive soldiers or sailors into their houses against the laws of the realm, and that the proceedings by martial law be revoked and annulled. This petition was finally acceded to by Charles.

Pirates.—Common sea rovers, without any fixed place of residence, who acknowledge no law, and support themselves by pillage and depredation on the high seas in ships or vessels. Many statutes, the earliest of which is in the reign of Hen. VIII., define what is piracy, but these are repealed, as far as relates to punishment of the offence, by 1 Vict. c. 88, which declares that the act of assaulting (on the occasion of committing piracy) with intent to murder, or stabbing, cutting, or wounding any person on board the vessel, in respect of which the piracy is committed, or doing any act whereby the life of such person shall be endangered, is a capital felony. The punishment of simple piracy is penal servitude for life, at the discretion of the Court, or for not less than fifteen years, or imprisonment not exceeding three years, with or without hard labour and solitary confinement. The offence of piracy is generally stated to consist in committing those acts of robbery and depredation upon the high seas which, if committed on land, would have there amounted to felony. It has been by various statutes more closely defined to be the boarding of a merchant vessel, though without carrying her off, or seizing any of her goods. The assisting or combining with known pirates is also deemed piracy, and such accessories are deemed principal pirates. Pirates are also those who, owing allegiance to the Crown of Great Britain, during war commit hostilities on the sea against her Majesty's subjects, by colour of any commission from the enemy, or adhere or give aid to the enemy upon the sea. 18 Geo. II. c. 30.

Pluralities.—The holding of more than one benefice with cure of souls was strictly prohibited by the Council of Lateran A.D. 1215, except in the case of men specially eminent for learning, who were sometimes permitted to enjoy more than one benefice, provided they were not more than thirty miles distant from each other, and agreed to reside in each of them for some reasonable time every year. The holding of pluralities in the Anglican Church was restrained by 21 Hen. VIII. c. 13 (1529), which was amended by 57 Geo. III. c. 99 (July 10, 1817). Both these statutes were repealed by 1 & 2 Vict. c. 106; and by 13 & 14 Vict. c. 98, it is enacted that no spiritual person shall hold any two benefices, except when their churches are within three miles of one another, and the annual value of one of them does not exceed £100; that no spiritual person holding a benefice, with a population of more than 3000, shall hold any other, having a population of more than 500, or *vice versâ*; and that no spiritual person holding more than one benefice shall take to hold therewith any other, or any cathedral preferment. The prohibitions respecting population and yearly value are subject to a provision enabling the Archbishop of Canterbury to grant a dispensation therefrom in certain cases, on recommendation of the bishop of the diocese. Provisions for the union of contiguous benefices were made by 18 & 19 Vict. c. 127.

Police.—The celebrated writer Fielding introduced, A.D. 1753, a system of paid police, who were placed under the orders of the acting magistrate at Bow Street. The Thames police was established in 1798. The new police force for the metropolis was established by 10 Geo. IV. c. 44 (June 19, 1829), and was to extend to twelve miles from Charing Cross. By 2 & 3 Vict. c. 47 (Aug. 17, 1839), this distance was extended to fifteen miles from Charing Cross; and the force was placed under the control of two commissioners. The City police, though similar in organisation, remains under the control of the corporation. By 19 Vict. c. 2 (Feb. 28, 1856), the metropolitan police was placed under the management of one commissioner and two assistant commissioners. The police for counties and boroughs is regulated by 19 & 20 Vict. c.

69 ; 22 & 23 Vict. c. 32 ; and 25 & 26 Vict. c. 101, and the police for Scotland is regulated by 20 & 21 Vict. c. 72.

Poll Tax or Capitation Tax.—A tax first levied in 1379 ; and again levied in 1513. In 1667 every subject was again assessed ; a duke £100, a marquis £80, a baronet £30, a knight £20, an esquire £10, and every single person 12*d*. It was abolished in 1690.

Poor-Laws.—By 23 Edw. III. c. 7 (1349), it was declared illegal to give anything to a beggar who was able to work. Poor people were ordered to abide in the place of their birth by 12 Rich. II. c. 7 (1388). Appropriators of benefices were ordered to distribute an annual sum to their poor parishioners by 15 Rich. II. c. 6 (1391). The first act enjoining the systematic maintenance of the aged and impotent poor was 27 Hen. VIII. c. 25 (1535). The present system of poor-laws was commenced by 43 Eliz. c. 2 (1601), which appointed overseers of the poor, authorised the erection of poor-houses, and taxed the householders in order to raise a poor-rate. This was followed by numerous statutes, which were consolidated and amended by the Poor-Law Amendment Act, 4 & 5 Will. IV. c. 76 (Aug. 14, 1834). This act instituted the "Poor-Law Commissioners," whose period of office was extended by subsequent acts to 1847, when they were superseded by the "Commissioners for administering the Laws for the Relief of the Poor in England," to consist of the Lord President of the Council, the Lord Privy Seal, the Secretary of State for the Home Department, and the Chancellor of the Exchequer, who were appointed by 10 & 11 Vict. c. 109 (July 23, 1847). Their name was changed to that of the "Poor-Law Board" by 12 & 13 Vict. c. 103 (Aug. 1, 1849). The removal of the poor is regulated by 9 & 10 Vict. c. 66, 11 & 12 Vict. c. 110, 25 & 26 Vict. c. 113, and 26 & 27 Vict. c. 89. The Union Relief Act was passed in 1862, to enable certain unions to obtain temporary aid through the suspension of cotton manufactures. Metropolitan

Houseless Poor Act, authorising guardians to receive destitute persons into workhouses, and the Metropolitan Board to reimburse them, passed 1864. Union Chargeability Act passed 1865. The duty of levying the poor-rate belongs to the churchwardens and overseers. The rate is raised prospectively for some given portion of the year, and upon a scale adapted to the probable exigencies of the parish. As an occupier, a man is ratable for all lands which he occupies in the parish, whether he is resident or not. Appeals against parochial assessments, by those who state that they are improperly assessed to the poor-rate, are heard at a special sessions held by the justices for every petty sessions division, and appointed by them, notice being affixed at or near to the church door twenty-eight days previously. An appeal is given from their decision to the quarter sessions, the appellant, within fourteen days after the decision, giving notice of appeal, and entering into a recognisance, with securities conditioned to try the same at the next sessions, and also giving seven clear days' notice previous to the session to the collector, overseers, or other persons making the rate. The office of the Poor Law Commissioners, who are assisted in their duties by a staff of inspectors and other officials, is in Whitehall. Hours 10 to 4.

Posse Comitatus.—The power of the county, which includes the aid and attendance of all persons of the degree or wealth of a knight, including all persons of lower quality, and men above fifteen, within the county; and this *posse* the sheriff may raise to the assistance of the justices, upon apprehension or happening of any riot or breach of the peace. Ecclesiastical persons, peers, and invalids are not compelled to attend. Justices may also raise the *posse*. Persons refusing to attend, when charged by the sheriff or a justice, are indictable for a misdemeanor.

Postmaster-General.—He who is at the head of the Post Office. He is usually one of the Ministry. Formerly there were two postmasters, but in 1822 one was abolished. In 1581 Sir Thomas Randolph was the first postmaster-general.

Post Office Savings Banks.—By 24 & 25 Vict. c. 14 (May 17, 1861), the postmaster-general was empowered to direct his officers at various places to receive cash deposits for remittance to the general office at London, to be repaid at $2\frac{1}{2}$ per cent. interest. No deposit may be of less value than one shilling, and all the existing acts relating to savings banks apply to the Post-office banks. In accordance with this act, Post-office savings banks were opened throughout Great Britain, Sept. 16, 1861.

Post Office.—Herodotus describes the Persian mode of forwarding communications by what they called relays, couriers being stationed along the road, one man and horse to every day's journey, B.C. 480. A somewhat similar course was pursued by the Romans in the time of Augustus, B.C. 31. Establishments of this kind existed in France under Charlemagne, Louis XI., and Charles V. In England royal messengers were employed, under the name of cokinus, nuncius, and garcio, for the conveyance of letters as early as A.D. 1252; Sir Bryan Tuke exercised supervision over these officials, holding a situation analogous to the modern postmaster-general, in 1533. An act was passed fixing the rate for post-horses at one penny per mile in 1548. Sir Thomas Randolph was the first postmaster of England, appointed by Queen Elizabeth in 1581. The letter-office of England and Scotland was established in 1635, and a weekly conveyance to all parts of the kingdom was set on foot by Edmund Prideaux in 1649, which was opposed by the common council of London; but parliament declared that the office was " in their sole power and at their disposal," March 21, 1649. The private undertakers, who performed the work for the public at a cheaper rate, continued to flourish, and expressed their determination, " by God's help," to go on; but John Manley, Esq., having farmed it for £10,000 per annum, the adventurers were forcibly put down in 1653; and an ordinance of the House of Commons, in 1657, set forth that government, holding the monopoly of posts, would be the best means to discover and prevent many dangerous and wicked designs against the commonwealth. Farmed to Daniel O'Neal for £21,500, the revenue was settled upon the Duke of York, the king's brother, in 1663. It was again farmed to Sir William Petty at £43,000 in 1674. The metropolitan penny post was established in 1683, the net revenue being £65,000 in 1685. A distinct postal system had been organised for Scotland in 1662, and Sir Robert Sinclair received a grant from King William III. of the whole revenue, with a salary of £300 a year to keep up the establishment, in 1698. The system was reorganised and consolidated by 9 Anne, c. 10. The cross-posts were farmed in 1720 to Mr. Allen, who cleared out of his contract £12,000 a year, for forty-two years. The net revenue was £96,339 in 1724. The privilege of franking was confirmed and regulated by parliament in 1764. Mr. Palmer's improvements were inaugurated Aug. 2, 1784. All previous post-office acts were repealed, their chief provisions being consolidated into one general statute by 1 Vict. cc. 32, 33, 34, 35, 36, and c. 76. The more recent statutes relating to the Post Office are 1 & 2 Vict. cc. 97 & 98; 2 & 3 Vict. c. 52; 3 & 4 Vict. c. 96; 7 & 8 Vict. c. 49 (as to Colonial posts); 10 & 11 Vict. c. 85; 11 & 12 cc. 88, 117; 12 & 13 Vict. c. 66 (enabling Colonial legislature to establish inland posts); 18 & 19 Vict. c. 27; 23 & 25 Vict. c. 65. The London district postage was reduced to one penny, Dec. 5, 1839, and the uniform rate of a penny came into operation Jan. 10, 1840. Hours 10 to 4. St. Martin's-le-Grand.

Poursuivant. *See* HERALD.

Power of Attorney. *See* LETTERS OF.

Poyning's Law, or Statute of Drogheda.—An Act of Parliament made in Ireland in 1495, by which all general statutes before then made in England were declared of force in Ireland. This Act was so called because Sir Edward Poyning was Lieutenant in Ireland when it came into operation.

Præmunire, from *præmuniri*, a corrupt form of *præmoneri*, to be forewarned, is the name of a writ issued for the prosecution of persons charged with certain offences, and it is also applied to the offences for which the writ is issued, which were originally such as related to the dominion of the Papacy in this country. Persons convicted under writs of præmunire are placed out of the pale of the royal protection, their possessions are forfeited to the Crown, and they themselves are committed to prison during the sovereign's pleasure. The original meaning of the offence is introducing a foreign power into this land, and enacting an *imperium in imperio* by paying that obedience to papal process which constitutionally belonged to the sovereign alone long before the Reformation. The first statute of præmunire is 27 Edw. III. s. 1, c. 1 (1353); but the most important is 16 Rich. II. c. 5 (1392), which prohibits the purchase of papal bulls from Rome, and declares the English Crown independent of the temporal sovereignty of the Pope. The killing of a person attainted in a præmunire was first declared unlawful by 5 Eliz. c. 1, s. 21 (1562). By 13 Chas. II. c. 1 (1661), the assertion that parliament possesses legislative authority, independent of the royal sanction, is declared a præmunire, and by the Habeas Corpus Act, 31 Chas. II. c. 2, s. 12 (1679), the illegal confinement of English subjects in foreign prisons submits the offender to the same penalties. By 7 & 8 Wm. III. c. 24, all· officers of Courts practising without having taken the proper oaths are guilty of præmunire. By 6 Anne, c. 83, if the Assembly of Peers in Scotland, convened to elect their sixteen representatives in the British parliament, treat of any other matter except of the election, they incur the penalties of præmunire. The punishment of the offence is, that from the conviction the defendant is out of the Crown's protection, and his lands and tenements, goods and chattels, are forfeited to the Crown ; and that his body shall remain in prison during the royal pleasure. It is not lawful, however, to kill any person attainted in a præmunire.

Precedence.—Degrees of superiority amongst the nobility, who are all peers, *i.e.*, equal, as being of the greater nobility ; and amongst the commoners, of whose lesser nobility the law takes no notice, they being all peers, *i.e.*, equals, in the eye of the law. Many of the following degrees are established by ancient usage, some by letters patent or statute :—

TABLE OF PRECEDENCE.

The Queen's children and grand-children.
————— brethren.
————— uncles.
————— nephews.
Archbishop of Canterbury.
Lord Chancellor or Keeper, if a Baron.
Archbishop of York.
Lord Treasurer,
Lord Pres. of the Council } if Barons.
Lord Privy Seal,
Lord Great Chamberlain.
 But see private act 1 G. I. c. 3.
Lord High Constable.
Lord Marshal.
Lord Admiral.
Lord Steward of the Household.
Lord Chamberlain of the Household.
{ Above all peers of their own degree.
Dukes.
Marquises.
Dukes' eldest sons.
Earls.
Marquises' eldest sons.
Dukes' younger sons.
Viscounts.
Earls' eldest sons.

Marquises' younger sons.
Secretary of State, if a Bishop.
Bishop of London.
————— Durham.
————— Winchester.
Bishops.
Secretary of State, if a Baron.
Barons.
Speaker of the House of Commons.
Lords Commissioners of the Great Seal.
Viscounts' eldest sons.
Earls' younger sons.
Barons' eldest sons.
Knights of the Garter.
Privy Councillors.
Chancellor of the Exchequer.
Chancellor of the Duchy of Lancaster.
Chief Justice of the King's Bench.
Master of the Rolls.
Chief Justice of the Common Pleas.
Chief Baron of the Exchequer.
Judges, and Barons of the Coif.
Knights Bannerets, Royal.
Viscounts' younger sons.
Barons' younger sons.
Baronets.
Knights Bannerets.
Knights of the Bath.

Knights Bachelors.
Baronets' eldest sons.
Knights' eldest sons.
Baronets' younger sons.
Knights' younger sons.
Colonels.
Serjeants-at-Law.
Doctors :—With whom, it is said, rank Barristers-at-Law.
Esquires (of whom Companions of the Bath rank first.)
Gentlemen.
Yeomen.

Tradesmen.
Artificers.
Labourers.

Married women and widows are entitled to the same rank among each other, as their husbands would respectively have borne between themselves ; except such rank is merely professional or official :—and unmarried women to the same rank as their eldest brothers would bear among men, during the lives of their fathers.

Prerogative Court.—A Court formerly held by each of the Archbishops of England and Ireland for the purpose of trying the validity of wills, registering them, and granting probate. This Court ceased to exist on the transference of the jurisdiction of the spiritual Courts in matters testamentary to the Crown by statute 20 & 21 Vict. c. 77. (*See* PROBATE, COURT OF.)

President of the Council, Lord. — The fourth great officer of state. He is appointed by letters patent, and has to attend the royal person, to manage the debates in council, to propose matters from the Queen at the council table, and to report to Her Majesty the resolutions taken thereon.

Press, The.—There is no censorship over the press, but the author, printer, and publisher of a libel are liable to an action for damages at the suit of the party injured ; or to an indictment, or, in certain cases, to a criminal information. For laws relating to the press see 39 Geo. III. c. 79, amended by 51 Geo. III. c. 65, and 2 & 3 Vict. c. 12.

Preventive Service.—The body of armed police officers engaged in watching the coasts for the purpose of preventing smuggling and other illegal acts.

Primogeniture.—In the times of the patriarchs the firstborn son always inherited his father's position as head of his family. The Roman law did not acknowledge the principle of primogeniture, and it was not recognised in France until the time of the Capets. It was established in England by the Normans, and takes effect almost in all cases, except where its operation is hindered by the customs of gavelkind and borough-English.

Privy Council, Judicial Committee. *See* JUDICIAL, &c.

Privy Council.—A great council of state held by the sovereign with her councillors, to concert matters for the public service, and for the honour and safety of the realm. The sovereign's will is the sole constituent of a privy councillor; and it also regulates their number, which in ancient times was about twelve. Afterwards it increased to so large a number, that it was found inconvenient for secrecy and despatch; and therefore Charles II. in 1679, limited it to thirty; whereof fifteen were principal officers of state, and to be councillors *ex officio;* and the other fifteen were composed of ten lords and five commoners of the King's choosing. Since that time, however, the number has been much augmented, and now continues indefinite.

Privy Councillors.—Advisers of the sovereign. They are made by the royal nomination, without patent or grant. After taking the necessary oaths they become immediately privy councillors during the life of the sovereign who chooses them, but subject to removal at the royal discretion. Any natural-born subject of England is capable of being a member of the privy council. The duty of a privy councillor appears from the oath of office, which consists of seven articles. 1. To advise the sovereign according to the best of his cunning and discretion. 2. To advise for the sovereign's honour and good of the public, without partiality, through affection, love, need, doubt, or dread. 3. To keep the sovereign's counsel secret. 4. To avoid corruption. 5. To help and strengthen the execution of what shall be there resolved.   6. To withstand all persons who would attempt the contrary.   And, lastly, in general, 7. To observe, keep, and do all that a good and true councillor ought to do to his sovereign lord.

Privy Seal.—The Privy Seal is a seal of the sovereign under which charters, pardons, &c., signed by the sovereign, pass before they come to the Great Seal, and also for some documents of less consequence, such as discharges of recognisances, &c.

Privy Seal, Lord. *See* LORD PRIVY SEAL.

Prize Court.—An international tribunal existing only by virtue of a special commission during war, until litigations incident to war have been brought to a conclusion.   In the Court are decided questions relating to captures, prize, and booty, and also questions upon the law of nations.   It is frequently confounded with the Court of Admiralty, but there is no connection between the two.

Probate Court.—The grant of letters of administration of the effects of persons dying intestate, and of probate of wills, which were formerly the prerogative of the Ecclesiastical Courts, have been recently vested (1857) in a newly established Court called the Court of Probate.   The functions of this Court are confined entirely to deciding upon the authenticity of wills, and upon the proper persons to whom administration is to be committed when no will exists.   The practice of the Court of Probate has been thrown open to the whole legal profession.   The Court is presided over by a single judge, who sits at Westminster.   An appeal lies from his decision direct to the House of Lords.   The rules of evidence in the Court of Probate are the same as those in Courts of law and equity, while its proceedings are assimilated to those of the Courts of common law.

A central registry of wills and administrations is established in London, and district registries are established in forty of the principal towns of England. These towns are*:—Bangor, Birmingham, Blandford, Bodmin, Bristol, Bury St. Edmunds, Canterbury, Carlisle, Carmarthen, Chester, Chichester, Derby, Durham, Exeter, Gloucester, Hereford, Ipswich, Lancaster, Leicester, Lewes, Lichfield, Lincoln, Liverpool, Llandaff, Manchester, Newcastle, Northampton, Nottingham, Norwich, Oxford, Peterborough, St. Asaph, Salisbury, Shrewsbury, Taunton, Wakefield, Wells, Winchester, Worcester, and York. Original wills proved in the country are preserved in the district registries, but copies of them are transmitted to the office in London, so that the metropolitan registry is the most convenient office to search for any will whatever.

Proctors.—Are those who, in the Ecclesiastical and Admiralty Courts, discharge duties similar to those of solicitors and attornies in other Courts. From the jurisdiction of the Ecclesiastical Courts having been mainly abolished, the 20 & 21 Vict. c. 77 and 85, award Proctors compensation, and admit them to practice not only in the Probate and Divorce Courts, but also in the Courts of equity and common law.

Prohibition.—A writ which issues from the Queen's Bench, and Courts of Chancery, Exchequer, and Common Pleas, to prohibit inferior Courts, either ecclesiastical or temporal, as Courts of request, &c., from taking cognizance of suits that do not belong to them, or are not comprehended within their jurisdiction. It is doubtful whether a prohibition will lie to the Court for Divorce and Matrimonial Causes.

Prolocutor of the Convocation House, an officer chosen by ecclesiastical persons publicly assembled in convocation by virtue of the Sovereign's writ; at every Parliament there are two prolocutors, one of the Upper House of Convocation, the other of the Lower House, the latter of whom is chosen by the Lower House, and presented to the Bishops of the

---

* Latest edition of Bond's "Handy Book for verifying Dates."

Upper House as their prolocutor, that is, the person by whom the Lower House of Convocation intends to deliver its resolutions to the Upper House, and have its own House especially ordered and governed ; his office is to cause the clerk to call the names of such as are of that House, when he sees cause, to read all things propounded, gather suffrages, &c.

Prorogation.—The continuance of the Parliament from one session to another. It never extends beyond eighty days, but fresh prorogations may take place from time to time by proclamation.

Protector.—The person who, upon the settling or limiting of an estate in tail, is actually in possession of a prior estate of freehold or for lives : his consent is requisite, if the tenant in tail wishes to alien. If the tenant in tail is in possession, he may alien by deed enrolled. A power is also given by the Act for abolishing fines and recoveries, for a settler to appoint three protectors in lieu of the protector by operation of law, who may be perpetuated as they may happen to die or relinquish their protectorship. The number is not to exceed three, and aliens are incapable. The person who would be at law, protector, as having a prior estate for life, may also be protector with those appointed, unless otherwise directed. The protectorship appointments are to be enrolled in chancery.

Provisors, Statutes against.—Were passed in the reign of Edward III., and enact that the Court of Rome shall not present or collate to any bishopric or living in England ; and that whoever disturbs any patron in the presentation to a living by virtue of a papal provision, be fined and imprisoned ; and the same punishment is awarded to such as cite the King or any of his subjects to answer in the Court of Rome. These statutes were confirmed by Richard II. (*See* Præmunire.)

Public Records.—*See* Records, Public.

Quakers.—The name of members of a religious society, more properly termed Friends. An act of indulgence to the

Quakers, that their solemn affirmation should be accepted instead of an oath, was passed in 1696, and in 1828 their affirmation was allowed in civil and criminal trials. By 23 Vict. c. 18 (May 15, 1860), marriages solemnized according to the usage of Quakers, where only one of the parties is a Quaker, are declared valid.

Quarantine.—A regulation by which all communication with individuals, ships, or goods, arriving from places infected with the plague, or other contagious disease, or supposed to be peculiarly liable to such infection, is interdicted for a certain definite period. The term is derived from the Italian *quaranta*, forty ; it being generally supposed that, if no infectious disease break out within forty days, or six weeks, no danger need be apprehended from the free admission of the individual under quarantine. During this period, too, all the goods, clothes, &c., that might be supposed capable of retaining the infection, are subject to a process of purification. The period of quarantine varies, as respects ships coming from the same place, according to the nature of their bills of health. These are documents, or certificates, signed by the consul or other competent authority in the place which the ship has left, describing its state of health at the time of her clearing out. A clean bill imports that, at the time of her sailing, no infectious disorder was known to exist : a suspected, or, as it is more commonly called, a touched bill, imports that rumours were afloat of an infectious disorder, but that it had not actually appeared. A foul bill, or the absence of clean bills, imports that the place was infected when the vessel sailed. The existing quarantine regulations are embodied in the Act 6 Geo. 4, c. 78, and the different orders in council issued under its authority. These orders specify what vessels are liable to perform quarantine, the places at which it is to be performed, and the various formalities and regulations to be complied with. The publication in the *Gazette* of any order in council with respect to quarantine is deemed sufficient notice to all concerned, and no excuse of ignorance is admitted for any infringement of the regulations. To obviate, as far as possible, any foundation for such plea, it is ordered that vessels clearing out for any port or place, with respect to which there shall be at the time any order in council subjecting vessels from it to quarantine, are to be furnished with an abstract of the quarantine regulations; and are to furnish themselves with quarantine signal flags and lanterns, and with materials and instruments for fumigating and immersing goods.[*]

Quare impedit.—The name of a writ and suit which can be brought only in the Court of Common Pleas, and lies to recover a presentation when the patron's right is disturbed, or to try a disputed title to an advowson.

Quarter Sessions.—*See* GENERAL QUARTER, &c.

Queen.—The Queen of England is either—queen-regent; queen-regnant, or sovereign holding the crown in her own right; or queen-consort, the wife of the reigning king. The widow of a deceased king is queen-dowager. The queen-regent, in all respects, has the powers and authorities of a king. The queen-consort is, by the law, deemed a single woman, for the purpose of purchasing property, or enjoying her own revenues, and of devising them by will. She has many exemptions; but, unless expressly exempted, is upon the same footing as other subjects, being the king's subject, not his equal.

Queen's Advocate.—*See* ADVOCATE, QUEEN'S.

Queen Anne's Bounty.—*See* BOUNTY, QUEEN ANNE'S.

Queen Consort.—The wife of the reigning king. She is a public person exempt and distinct from the king, for she can purchase lands, make leases, &c., without the concurrence of her husband. She has separate courts and offices distinct from the king; and her attorney and solicitor-general are entitled to a place within the bar of the King's Courts, together with the king's counsel. She pays no toll, nor is she liable to

---

[*] McCulloch's Commercial Dictionary.

any fine in any court. With regard to the security of her life and person, she is placed on the same footing with the king.

Queen Dowager.—The widow of a deceased king. She possesses most of the privileges enjoyed by her as queen consort. No man can marry her without special licence from the Crown, on pain of forfeiting his lands and goods. If she marry a subject she does not lose her regal dignity, as dowager peeresses (if commoners by birth) do their peerages when they marry commoners.

Queen's or King's Bench, Court of, is so called, because the king used formerly to sit there in person. During the reign of a queen it is called the Queen's Bench. This Court consists of a chief justice and four puisne judges, though in practice seldom more than four sit on the bench, and they are by their office the sovereign conservators of the peace, and supreme coroners of the land. The jurisdiction of this Court is very high, and claims precedence of the Court of Chancery. It keeps all inferior jurisdictions within the bounds of their authority, and may either remove their proceedings to be determined here, or prohibit their progress below. It superintends all civil corporations in the kingdom. It commands magistrates and others to do what their duty requires, in every case where no particular remedy is appointed. It protects the liberty of the subject, by liberating persons unjustly imprisoned or restrained of their liberty, by *habeas corpus* or bail. It takes cognisance both of criminal and civil causes, the former in the Crown side or Crown office, the latter in the plea side of the Court. On the Crown side it exercises jurisdiction over all criminal cases, from high treason to breach of the peace ; and on the plea side over all actions between subject and subject, with the exception of real actions and suits concerning the revenue. Error lies from this Court to the Exchequer Chamber.

Queen's Counsel.—Are barristers who have been called within the bar and selected to be the Queen's counsel. They must not be employed against the Crown without special licence, which is, however, never refused.

Queen's or King's Evidence.—An accomplice to whom a hope is held out, that if he will fairly disclose the truth as a witness on the trial, and bring the other offenders to justice, he shall escape punishment.

Quo warranto.—A writ formerly proceeding from the Queen's Bench against him who claims or usurps any office, franchise or liberty, to inquire "by what authority" he supports his claim in order to determine the right. A more expeditious mode of proceeding is now adopted. An information by the Attorney General can be filed in the nature of a *quo warranto*, in which the person usurping is considered as an offender, and punishable by fine.

Railways.—Several statutes have been passed for the general regulation of railroads. The conveyance of mails by railroad was regulated by 1 & 2 Vict. c. 98 (Aug. 14, 1838). Companies were compelled to provide proper gates and gate-keepers at places where railroads and public highways cross by 2 & 3 Vict. c. 45 (Aug. 17, 1839), and railways were placed under the supervision of the Board of Trade by 3 & 4 Vict. c. 97 (Aug. 10, 1840). The phraseology of railway bills was much simplified by the Railway Clauses Consolidation Act, 8 & 9 Vict. c. 20 (May 8, 1845), and the gauge was regulated by 9 & 10 Vict. c. 57 (Aug. 18, 1846). The jurisdiction of the Board of Trade was transferred to a body of railway commissioners by 9 & 10 Vict. c. 105 (Aug. 28, 1846). This Act. was repealed by 14 & 15 Vict. c. 64 (Aug. 7, 1851), which restored the authority of the board. Malicious acts upon railways are punished by 14 & 15 Vict. c. 19 (July 3, 1851), and further measures for the regulation of the railroad system were made by 17 & 18 Vict. c. 31 (July 10, 1854). See also 21 & 22 Vict. c. 95 ; 22 & 23 Vict. c. 59 ; 23 & 24 Vict. c. 41 ; 24 & 25 Vict. c. 97 ; and 26 & 27 Vict. c. 92.

Ranger, a sworn officer of the forests and parks, appointed by the queen's letters patent ; whose business is to walk through his charge, to drive back the deer out of the purlieus, &c., and to present all trespasses within his jurisdiction at the next forest-court.

Rank.—*See* TABLE OF PRECEDENCE.

Rape.—The ancient Jewish laws punished this crime with death when the woman was betrothed to another man ; and in other cases compelled the ravisher to marry her, and pay a fine of 50 shekels to her father. The Roman codes made it in every case a capital offence ; and it was treated with the same severity by the laws of the Goths and the Anglo-Saxons. William the Conqueror commuted the penalty to mutilation and blinding, and by 3 Edw. I. c. 13 (1275), it was reduced to a mere misdemeanour, punished by two years' imprisonment and a fine, unless the offender were prosecuted within forty days after the commission of the crime. In consequence of the inefficacy of this law, rape was made a capital felony by 13 Edw. I. c. 34 (1285) ; and by 18 Eliz. c. 8 (1576), persons convicted of this crime were deprived of benefit of clergy. The laws on the subject were consolidated by 9 Geo. IV. c. 31 (June 27, 1828), which made the carnal abuse of a girl under ten years of age a capital felony, and of females of greater age a misdemeanour, punishable by imprisonment at the pleasure of the Court. Transportation for life was substituted for the capital penalty by 4 & 5 Vict. c. 56 (June 22, 1841). By 24 & 25 Vict. c. 100, whoever shall be convicted of rape shall be guilty of felony, and shall be kept in penal servitude for life, or for not less than three years, or to be imprisoned for any term not exceeding two years with or without hard labour.

Reading in.—The title of a person admitted to a benefice will be void if, within two months after actual possession, he does not read in the church of the benefice upon some Sunday the morning and evening service, and the thirty-nine articles, and declare his assent thereto. He must also within three months of his admission read publicly before his congregation, in the time of divine service, a declaration by him subscribed before the ordinary of conformity to the liturgy, together with the certificate of the ordinary of its having been so subscribed.

Receipt.—Is an acquittance for a sum of money. It cannot be demanded by law. By 16 & 17 Vict. c. 59, a penny stamp duty is imposed on a receipt given for the payment of money amounting to two pounds or upwards, except receipts given for money deposited in any bank. Receipts not stamped or improperly stamped cannot be given in evidence, nor can they be re-stamped to render them valid as evidence of payment.

Receiving Stolen Goods, knowing the same to have been stolen, is felony punishable by penal servitude for not more than fourteen years or not less than three ; or to be imprisoned for two years with or without hard labour, or with or without whipping. If viewed as a misdemeanour, the receiving stolen goods is punished by penal servitude for not less than three or not more than seven years, or imprisonment not exceeding two years, with or without hard labour.

Record, Trial by.—A species of trial which is used only in one particular instance, and that is where a matter of record is pleaded in any action, as a fine, a judgment, or the like ; and the opposite party pleads, *nul tiel record*, that there is no such matter of record existing. Upon this, issue is tendered and joined in the following form, " and this he prays may be inquired of by the record, and the other doth the like ;" and hereupon the party pleading the record has a day given him to bring it in, and proclamation is made in court for him to " bring forth the record by him in pleading alleged, or else he shall be condemned ;" and on his failure, his antagonist shall have judgment to recover. The trial, therefore, of this issue, is merely by the record : for, as Sir Edward Coke observes, a record or enrolment is a monument of so high a nature, and importeth in itself such absolute verity, that if it be pleaded that there is no such record, it shall not receive any trial by witness, jury, or otherwise, but only by itself. Thus titles of nobility, as whether earl or not earl, baron or not baron, shall be tried by the Sovereign's writ or patent only, which is matter of record. Also in case of an alien, whether alien friend or enemy, shall be tried by the league or treaty between his Sovereign and ours; for every league or treaty is of record. And also, whether a manor be held in ancient demesne, or nor, shall be tried by the record of Domesday.

Recorder, a person whom the mayor and other magistrates of a city or corporation associate to them, for their better direction in matters of justice and proceedings in law ; on which account he is generally a counsellor, or other person well skilled in the law. The recorder of London is chosen by the lord mayor and aldermen ; and as he is held to be the mouth of the city, delivers the judgment of the courts therein, and records and certifies the city customs, &c.

Records, Public.—Records in the legal sense are contemporaneous statements of the proceedings in those higher courts of law which are distinguished as courts of record, written upon rolls of parchment. Examined copies of the contents of public documents are received as evidence in courts of law. The greater part of records are kept as rolls written on skins of parchment and vellum, averaging from nine to fourteen inches wide, and about three feet in length. "Our stores of public records," says Nicolson, "are justly reckoned to excel in age, beauty, correctness, and authority whatever the choicest archives abroad can boast of the like sort." A very important step was taken by the Legislature at the commencement of her Majesty's reign to provide for the better custody and preservation of the public records by passing the Act 1 & 2 Vict. c. 49. By this statute the Master of the Rolls is made the guardian of the national archives, having power to appoint a deputy, and, in conjunction with the Treasury, to do all that may be necessary in the execution of the service. Under Lord Romilly, the present Master of the Rolls, and Mr. Hardy, the Deputy Keeper of the Public Records, greater facilities have been adopted for the free use of the records by the public than before existed. I give briefly a list of the most important of our national archives, arranged under their respective courts :—

CHANCERY :

    Almain Rolls, 18 Edw. I. to 15 Edw. III.

    Answers. *See* "Bills," &c.

    Answers, Replications, and Decrees. *See* "Charitable Uses."

    Bill Books, 1673 to 1800.

    Bills, Answers, and Depositions, 1452 to 1800.

    Brevia Regia, 9 Chas. I. to 24 Geo. III.

    Cardinal's Bundles (accounts of Wolsey's possessions), Hen. VIII.

    Chancery Proceedings. *See* "Bills, Answers," &c.

    Charitable Uses, Answers, Replications, and Decrees of Commissioners of, 43 Eliz., &c.

    Chartæ Antiquæ, Saxon period to Hen. III.

    Charter Rolls, John to Hen. VIII.

    Close Rolls, 1204–5 to 1864.

    Commissions, Inquisitions, and Decrees. *See* "Charitable Uses."

    Confirmation Rolls, before Rich. III., *see* "Patent and Charter Rolls ;" 1 Rich. III. to 12 Jas. I., *see* "Confirmation Rolls ;" 12 Jas. I. &c., *see* "Patent Rolls."

    Coronation Rolls, 1 Edw. II. to Victoria (imperfect series).

    Court Rolls, 17 Edw. I. to 1687.

    Decrees. *See* "Charitable Uses."

    Decrees, Enrolments of, Hen. VIII. to present time.

    Decrees and Orders, Entries of, Reg. Lib. A., 36 Hen. VIII. to 1700.

        ,,   Index to same, 2 Edw. VI. to 1700.

        ,,   Entries of, Lib. Reg. B., 38 Hen. VIII. to 1700.

        ,,   Index to same, 1 Edw. VI. to 1700.

    Deeds Enrolled. See "*Close Rolls.*"

        ,,   Index "Indentures," Eliz. to 1864 ; also "Close Roll Calendars," Hen. III. to 1848.

    Denization, Letters Patent of. *See* "Patent Rolls."

    Disentailing Assurances, 1834 to 1863, *see* "Close Rolls ;" before 1834, *see* "Recoveries, Common Pleas."

Dispensation Rolls, 37 Eliz. to 1740.

Escheats, John to Chas. II.

Exchange Rolls, 6 Rich. II. to 12 Hen. VI.

Fine Rolls, 6 John to 23 Chas. I.

French Rolls, 26 Hen. III. to 20 Chas. I.

Forest Rolls, John to Chas. I.

Forfeited Estates, pursuant to stat. 1, Geo. I.

Gascon, French and Norman Rolls, John to Hen. VI.

Household Books, 20 Hen. VIII. to 3 Edw. VI.

Hundred Rolls, Edw. I. to Edw. II.

Inquisitions, *ad quod damnum*, 1 Edw. II. to 39 Hen. VIII.

Inquisitions, *post mortem. See* "Escheats."

Irish Rolls, 1 to 50 Edw. III.

Letters Royal, &c. Various dates.

Liberate Rolls, 2 John to 14 Hen. VI.

Lunacy Commissions, &c., Chas. I. to 1783.

Memorials of Annuity Deeds, before 1813, *see* "Close Rolls;" 1813—
1854, after 1854, *see* "Common Pleas Register of Judgments."

Misæ Roll, 11 John.

Naturalization Certificates of Aug. 6, 1844, to present time, *see* "Close
Rolls."

Norman Rolls, 2 John to 10 Hen. 21.

Oblata Rolls, 1 to 9 John.

Orders and Decrees. *See* "Decrees."

Pardon Rolls, 22 Edw. I. to 2 Jas. I.

Parliament Rolls, 5 Edw. II. to Vict.

Parliamentary Pawns (abstracts of writs of summons and writs of
election for a new Parliament), 21 Hen. VIII. to 1818.

Patent Rolls, 3 John to 1858.

Privy Seals and Signet Bills, Edw. I. to 1841.

Prayer Book, known as the sealed copy of the "Book of Common
Prayer," pursuant to statute 14, Chas. II.

Recognizance Rolls, Hen. VIII. to 1863.

Royal Letters Patent, &c., Rich. I to Edw. I.

Scotch Rolls, 19 Edw. I to 7 Hen. VIII.

Specification Rolls :—

    Specifications enrolled on Close Rolls, Anne to 1848.

    Specification and Surrender Rolls, Anne to 1848, Petty Bag.

            „   „   „   Rolls Chapel.

    Specification Rolls, 1849 to 1852. *See* "Close Rolls."

         „   1852, &c. *See* "Patent Office."

Staple Rolls, Edw. III. to Hen. VI.

Subsidy Rolls, 1 Edw. III. to 18 Eliz.

Surrenders. *See* Specifications.

Vascon Rolls, 26 Hen. III. to 7 Edw. IV.
Welsh Rolls, 5 to 23 Edw. I.

COURT OF QUEEN'S BENCH—PLEA SIDE :
Affidavits, General, 1733 to 1842.
Attornies, Roll or Book of, 1729 to 1842.
Attornies' Oath Roll, 1750 to 1842.
Coram Rege Rolls. See *"Judgment Rolls."*
Declarations, 1781 to 1842.
    ,,   in Ejectment, 1728 to 1842.
Deeds enrolled. *See* "Judgment Rolls."
    ,,   Index. *See* "Doggett Rolls," and "Doggett Books
             (Special Remembrances)" to 1839 Trin. ;
             1839 to 1842, *see* "Day-book of Judgments."
Doggett Books of Judgments, 1390 to 1655. *See* "Doggett Rolls ;"
    1656 to 1839 Trinity, (cease) ; entries continued in "Judgment
    Day-books."
Doggett Rolls, 1390 to 1655. *See* "Doggett Books."
Essoin Rolls, 3 Hen. VII. to 40 Geo. III.
Judgments, Issues, &c. Entry Books of, 1699 to 1842.
Judgment, or Plea Rolls, before 1702. *See* "Coram Rege," Crown
    side, 1702 to 1842.
Plea Rolls. See *"Judgment Rolls."*
Prayer Book, 14 Car. II. (known as the sealed copy of the "Book of
    Common Prayer,") pursuant to stat. 14, Chas. II.
Precipes, for the issue of Writs, 1783 to 1842.
Remembrances (Special). Indexes to Deeds, *see* also "Doggett ·
    Rolls."
Rules, Entry Books of, 1603 to 1842.
Special Remembrances. *See* "Doggett Rolls and Books."
Warrants of Attorney, 1802 to 1842.
Writs Judicial, 1629 to 1842.
   ;, Special, Original, 1629 to 1842.
Writs of Outlawry, 1785 to 1843.

COURT OF QUEEN'S BENCH—CROWN SIDE :
Affidavits, General, in support of motions, 1716 to 1842.
Agarde's Indexes to Assize Rolls, Coram Rege, De Banco, &c., Hen.
    III. to Hen. VI.
Assize Rolls. See *"Coram Rege."*
Baga de Secretis, 17 Edw. IV. to Geo. III.
Controlment Rolls, 1 Edw. III. to 1842.
Convicts' Returns, 1785 to 1819 ; after this at the Home Office.
Coram Rege, De Banco, and Assize Rolls, 5 Rich. I. to 1701-2.

At this time the Plea Rolls were separated from the Crown Rolls.
Plea Rolls continued.   *See* Plea side.

Coram Rege, now called Crown Rolls, 1701-2 to 1842.

Gaol Delivery Rolls, 4 Edw. I. to 38 Hen. VI.

Indictments, 1675 to 1842.

Judgment Rolls.   See " *Coram Rege*" and " *Crown Rolls*."

Placita de Quo Warranto, &c., 8 John to 6-7 Eliz.   See also " *Crown Rolls*" and " *Controlment Rolls*."

Plea Rolls.   See " *Coram Rege*."

Rules, Entries of, 1589 to 1842.

Court of Common Pleas :

Acknowledgment of Deeds by Married Women, Certificates of, 1834 to 1852.

Affidavits, General, 1704 to 1849.

Appearance Books, 1735 to 1849.

Attornies' Admissions, 1775 to 1814, afterwards at Common Pleas Office
Attornies' Oath Roll, 1789 to 1849.

Banco, Placita de, &c., before Edw. I.   *See also* " Coram Rege," &c., (Queen's Bench), Hen. III. to 1849.

Common Rolls, or Judgment Rolls, Pleas of Land.   *See* Banco, Placita de.

Declarations in Ejectment, 1704 to 1842.

Deeds Enrolled, before East., 25 Eliz., *see* "Common Rolls"; East. 25 Eliz. to Hil. 1834, *see* "Recovery Rolls and Pleas of Land"; East. 1834 to Mich. 1837, *see* "Pleas of Land"; Hil. 1838 to Mich. 1849, *see* "Common Rolls."

Ditto, Index.   Deed Index, 1555 to 1835.

Doggett Rolls, 1 Hen. VIII. to 1849.

Error, Proceedings in, 1835 to 1856.

Exigents.   *See* "Outlawries."

Fines, Feet of, Hen. II. to 1834, Hil., abolished.   *See further*, "Acknowledgments of Deeds by Married Women."

Judgment Rolls.   *See* "Banco, Placita de," &c.

King's Silver Books, Eliz. to 4 Will. IV.

Outlawries, Writs of, 1820 to 1838 ; after 1838, *see* "Writs filed," 1839 to 1849.

     ,,   Index, 1821 to 1837, called "Exigents" ; 1838 to 1848, "Outlawries."

Outlawry Books, 1752 to 1848.

Pleas of Land.   *See* "Doggett Rolls," "Remembrance Rolls," and " Recovery Index."

Posteas, Eliz. to 1852.

Prayer Book, 14 Chas. II. 1662 (known as the sealed copy of the " Book of Common Prayer,") pursuant to stat. 14, Chas. II.

Recovery Rolls, 25 Eliz. to 1834, abolished ; continued under the name
of " Disentailing Assurances," enrolled in Chancery Close Rolls.
Registers of Judgments, 1838 to 1849.
Remembrance Rolls, 6 Hen. VIII. to 1770.
(Rules, &c. for Judgments and Pleas of Land).
Remembrance Rolls, 1770 to 1849.
(Rules, &c. for Judgments.)
Remembrance Rolls, 1770 to 1850.
(For Pleas of Land only.)
Writs filed, 1800 to 1849.
Writs of Covenant, 1 Edw. III. to 6 Will. IV.

Fines and Recoveries for Wales, to 1830. *See* Welsh Records in the
Public Record Office.
   ,, 1830 to 1834. *See* "Common Pleas
Office."

EXCHEQUER, COURT OF :
Accounts, Public, Enrolments of, Eliz. to 1859.
(Queen's Remembrancer.)
Affidavits, Original, 1572 to 1842.
(Queen's Remembrancer.)
Affidavits of Service, 1832 to 1853.
(Exchequer of Pleas.)
Affidavits of Debt, 1772 to 1838.
(Exchequer of Pleas.)
Affidavits, General, 1830 to 1842.
(Exchequer of Pleas.)
Appearance Books, 1576 to 1850.
(Exchequer of Pleas.)
Attornies' Oath Roll, 1830 to 1842.
(Exchequer of Pleas.)
Bills and Answers, &c., Eliz., to 1841. (In 1841, abolished.) For
further proceedings, *see* " Chancery."
(Queen's Remembrancer.)
Bills and Writs, 3 Edw. III., 1845. (Bills cease after 4 Wm. 4.)
(Exchequer of Pleas).
Chancellor's Rolls, 9 Hen. II. ; 3 & 4 Will. IV.
(Lord Treasurer's, Remembrancer's, and Pipe Offices.)
Chartæ Antiquæ—Various.
(Augmentations).
Charters and Deeds—Various.
(Augmentations).
Colleges and Chantries, Certificates of, (Hen. VIII, to Edw. VI.).
(Augmentations.)

Court or Manor Rolls, Edw. I. to Chas. I.
> (*Augmentations.*)

Decrees and Orders, Original and ⎫
,,   ,,   Entry Books ⎬ 1580 to 1841.
> (*Queen's Remembrancer.*)

Deeds Enrolled in Exchequer of Pleas. See "*Plea*" or "*Judgment Rolls.*"

Deeds Enrolled. See "*Memoranda Rolls.*"
> (*Queen's Remembrancer.*)

Deeds Enrolled. See "*Memoranda Rolls.*"
> (*Lord Treasurer's Remembrancer.*) They cease in 1833.

Depositions taken by Commission ⎫
,,   ,,   before the Barons ⎬ Eliz. to 1841.
> (*Queen's Remembrancer.*)

Doggett Books, 1 Eliz. to 1839 Trin. (cease).
> (*Exchequer of Pleas.*)

Escheator's Accounts, Enrolments of, 33 Edw. I. to 22 Jas. I.
> (*Lord Treasurer's, Remembrancer's, and Pipe Offices.*)

Estreats, 5 Edw. VI. to 5 Will. IV.
> (*Lord Treasurer's, Remembrancer's, and Pipe Offices.*)

Exannual Rolls, Edw. I. to 4 Geo. III.
> (*Lord Treasurer's, Remembrancer's, and Pipe Offices.*)

Extents and Inquisitions, 1685 to 1842.
> (*Queen's Remembrancer.*)

Fee Farm Rents, reserved upon grants from the Crown. Particular for the sale of, and counterparts of Deeds, Commonwealth.
> (*Augmentations.*)

Foreign Accounts, Enrolments of, Hen. III. to Chas. II.
> (*Lord Treasurer's, Remembrancer's, and Pipe Offices.*)

Grants, particulars for, Hen. VIII. to Jas. I.
> (*Augmentations.*)

Judgment Rolls or Plea Rolls, 53 Hen. III. to 1842.
> (*Exchequer of Pleas.*)

Judgment or Plea Rolls before the Justices of the Jews, 3 Hen. III. to 14 Edw. I.
> (*Exchequer of Pleas.*)

Land and Assessed Tax Accounts, Entries of, 1689 to 1842; before 1689, *see* "Subsidies."
> (*Lord Treasurer's and Pipe Offices, Augmentations and Queen's Remembrancer.*)

Leases, Conventual—Various. Before 27 Hen. VIII.

Leases, Crown, Particulars for and Counterparts and Enrolments of, Hen. VIII. to 1831.
> (*Augmentations.*)

Memoranda Rolls, 1 Hen. III. to 1842.

(*Queen's Remembrancer.*)

Memoranda Rolls, 1 Hen. III. to 3 & 4 Will. IV.

(*Lord Treasurer's, Remembrancer's, and Pipe Offices.*)

Ministers' Accounts of the Issues and Profits of Lands in the hands of the Crown, Hen. III. to 38 Hen. VIII.

(*Exchequer and Court of General Surveyors.*)

Ministers' Accounts of the issues and profits of Monastic Lands in the hands of the Crown, 27 Hen. VIII. to 38 Hen. VIII.

(*Augmentations.*) After this date the Court of Augmentations was abolished, and the New Court established.

Ministers' Accounts of the issues and profits of lands in the hands of the Crown, 1 Edw. VI. to 1 Mary.

(*New Court of Augmentations.*)

Ministers' Accounts of the issues and profits of lands in the hands of the Crown, Mary to Chas. II.

(*Exchequer.*)

Minute Books, 1657 to 1830.

(*Exchequer of Pleas.*)

Minute Books, Common (Orders), 1616 to 1821, afterwards at Exchequer Office.

(*Queen's Remembrancer.*)

Minute Books (Decrees), 1695 to 1841 (cease).

(*Exchequer Chamber.*)

Minute Books, 3 Jas. II. to 35 Geo. III.

(*Lord Treasurer's, Remembrancer's, and Pipe Offices.*)

Order Books, 3 Edw. VI. to 1830, afterwards Judgment Day-books.

(*Exchequer of Pleas.*)

Order Books, 35 Chas. II. to 3 & 4 Will. IV. (cease).

(*Lord Treasurer's, Remembrancer's, and Pipe Offices.*)

Originalia Rolls, Hen. III. to 3 & 4 Will. IV.

(*Lord Treasurer's, Remembrancer's, and Pipe Offices,* 1833 *to* 1842, *Exchequer.*)

Outlawries, Chas. I. to Will. IV.

(*Queen's Remembrancer.*)

Particulars for the sale of the Estates of Chas. I., the Queen and Prince, *tempore* Commonwealth.

(*Lord Treasurer's, Remembrancer's, and Pipe Offices.*)

Pipe Rolls, 31 Hen. I., 2 & 3 Hen. II. to 3 & 4 Will. IV. (cease).

(*Lord Treasurer's, Remembrancer's, and Pipe Offices.*)

Plea Rolls, *see* "Judgment Rolls."

(*Exchequer of Pleas.*)

Purchase and Exchange Deeds, Hen. VIII. to Edw. VI.

(*Augmentations.*)

Recusant Rolls, 34 Eliz. to Will. and Mary.
   (*Lord Treasurer's, Remembrancer's, and Pipe Offices.*)
Reports and Certificates, 1648 to 1841.
   (*Queen's Remembrancer.*)
Rule Books, or Records of Rules, 1811 to 1842.
   (*Exchequer of Pleas.*)
Sheriffs Accounts, Hen. VI. to 1660.
   (*Lord Treasurer's Remembrancer's and Pipe Offices.*)
Special Pleas, Eliz. to 1842.
   (*Queen's Remembrancer.*)
Surveys, Parliamentary, of the King's lands, *tempore* Commonwealth.
Wardrobe and Household Accounts, 42 Hen. III. to 56 Geo. III.
   (*Lord Treasurer's, Remembrancer's, and Pipe Offices.*)
Warrants of Attorney and Cognovits, 1803 to 1842.
   (*Exchequer of Pleas.*)
Writs and Posteas, Will. & Mary to Will. IV.
   (*Queen's Remembrancer.*)

RECORDS OF THE EXCHEQUER—FIRST FRUITS AND TENTHS :
   Bishops Certificates of Institutions to Livings, called Bishops' Returns, 1556 to 1841.
   Composition Books, Entries concerning Payments of First Fruits and Tenths, 1536 to 1838.
   Valor Ecclesiasticus, 1535.

*** The Public Record Office also contains numerous records of the Offices of the Exchequer of Receipt or Pell Office ; of the Treasury of the Receipt of the Exchequer ; of the Courts of Admiralty; Requests; Star Chamber ; and Wards and Liveries ; of the Admiralty, Audit, Treasury, Home, Foreign, Colonial, and War Offices ; and also the records of the various Welsh courts, the jurisdiction of which courts ceased in 1830, when their duties were transferred to the English courts, and the records themselves subsequently removed to the Public Record Office, London.

Recoveries and Fines, were proceedings by which persons were enabled to bar estates tail, and, with the concurrence of their wives, to bar them of dower, and to exclude remaindermen. As all men's titles to their real estates must, for a few years, depend upon the law of fines and recoveries, it may be useful to notice, in the words of the commissioners of real property, their intent and operation, and to show briefly how their abolition by a late act is beneficial; which act, to check the alienation by a tenant in tail with remainder, has introduced a "protector," without whose consent this alienation cannot be effected—a measure which may have the operation of confining improvident alienations of entailed property within a narrower compass :—

" A fine in its origin was an amicable composition, by leave of the king or his justices, of an actual suit, whereby the lands were acknowledged to be the right of one of the parties; and, at common law, all persons were barred by it who did not claim within a year and a day. The safe title acquired by this process led, it is supposed, to the practice of transferring lands, by means of a fictitious suit of the same nature as the real suit above alluded to. This is the origin of the fines of the present day, which, subject to certain modifications made from time to time by statutes, have been in use for centuries. The statutes 1 Rich. III. c. 7, and 4 Hen. VII. c. 24, have declared, that a fine proclaimed in four successive terms, the first proclamation being made in the term in which the fine is engrossed, shall operate as a bar by non-claim, at the end of five years after the last proclamation; but with a certain limited extension of time in cases of infancy, coverture, lunacy, and absence beyond seas; and by the latter statute, and the statute of 32 Hen. VIII. c. 36, the further effect of barring estates tail was given to fines levied with proclamations. The three principal uses to which fines are applied are to bar estates tail, and enable a tenant in tail to acquire or pass a base (or conditional) fee, determinable on the failure of the issue in tail, to gain a title by non-claim, and to pass the estates and bar the rights of married women. A common recovery is a judgment in a fictitious suit, in the nature of a real action, brought by the demandant against the tenant of the freehold, who vouches some person to warrant the lands, and judgment is given for the demandant to recover them against the tenant in consequence of the person vouched, or the person last vouched, if there should be more than one vouchee making default to the title to the lands, which title he is supposed to have warranted. In a recovery, the regular process of a real action is pursued throughout, and no compromise takes place as in a fine. The principal use of a recovery is to enable a tenant in tail to bar not only his estate tail, but also all remainders, reversions, conditions, collateral limitations, and charges, not prior to the estate tail, and acquire or pass a fee-simple, or an estate commensurate with the estate of the settler; but a reversion vested in the crown cannot, as it is generally understood, be barred by a recovery. Although it is not usual to suffer a recovery, except when it is necessary to bar entails and remainders over, yet, when resorted to for those purposes, it is not unfrequently made use of, at the same time, to convey, release, bar, or extinguish the estates, rights, powers, and interests of married women and others."

Fines and recoveries, the report stated, had other effects; viz., to operate to bar or shut out persons who had contingent or expectant interests, and sometimes expectant heirs; and they also extinguished contingent remainders, and a variety of other floating interests and claims. The artificial devices which these fictitious proceedings gave rise to, and the expense with which they were attended, independent of the inconvenience, viz., that they could only be transacted at particular times of the year, rendered it necessary that the legislature should provide a certain remedy; and, while it restrained the improvident power of alienation which the eldest son of a tenant in tail or fee-simple has during the life of his father, should facilitate the conveyance of land for prudent and legitimate purposes. Therefore the statute 3 & 4 Will. IV. c. 74, abolishes fines and feigned recoveries; enables tenants in tail to make an effectual alienation by any deed to be inrolled in chancery, by which a tenant in fee can convey; creates a protector to the estate, by requiring that the owner of a beneficial and prior. estate for life should first give his concurrence; provides new methods for barring estates tail and expectant interests, and enables married women to dispose of their lands and money subject to be invested in lands with the concurrence of their husbands, independent of many other subsidiary provisions. This act extends to freehold as well as copyhold estates, and money subjected to be invested in lands, which, in equity, is equivalent to a real estate.

Reform Bills.—Mr. Pitt's bill for reform in parliament was lost by a majority of 20, May 7, 1782. His proposal was again defeated by a majority of 144, May 7, 1783, and of 74, April 18, 1785. Sir Francis Burdett's plan was negatived by a majority of 59, June 15, 1809; and Mr. Daniel O'Connell's project for introducing universal suffrage, triennial parliaments, and the ballot, was rejected by 306 votes, May 28, 1830. The first reform bill introduced by government was that of the Grey administration, which was brought before the House of Commons, March 1, 1831. The first division took place March 22, when a majority of one declared in favour of the second reading. On the question of a committee, General Gascoigne proposed as an amendment, "that the number of representatives for England and Wales ought not to be diminished," which was carried by a majority of eight, April 19. The bill was relinquished in consequence, and parliament dissolved April 22. A new parliament assembled June 14, and the bill was again introduced June 24. The motion for its second reading passed by a majority of 136, July 6; and a majority of 109 declared in favour of the third reading, Sept. 21; but the bill was rejected in the Lords on the question of its second reading by a majority of 41, Oct. 7. A new bill was introduced by Lord John Russell Dec. 12, and passed its first reading without a division. The motion for its second reading was carried by a majority of 162 (the number of assentients being just double that of the dissentients), Dec. 17 ; and it was read a third time by a majority of 116, March 22, 1832. This bill was read a first time in the Lords, March 26 ; and the second reading was carried by a majority of nine, April 13. The bill was consequently carried into a committee of the Lords, where an amendment by Lord Lyndhurst for considering the question of enfranchisement before that of disfranchisement was carried against government by a majority of 35, May 7. The ministry resigned May 9, but resumed their offices May 18, having obtained powers to create a sufficient number of new peers to secure them a majority in the Lords. The bill passed the Lords' committee May 30, and was read for the third time by a majority of 84, June 4. It received the royal assent June 7, and appears in the statute-book as the " Act to amend the Representation of the People in England and Wales, 2 & 3 Will. IV. c. 45 (June 7, 1832). Its main principles were, that boroughs having a less population than 2000 should cease to return members, and that those having a less population than 4000 should cease to return more than one member. It created between forty and fifty new boroughs, including the four metropolitan ones of Marylebone, Finsbury, the Tower Hamlets, and Lambeth, each of the last returning two members. It extended the county and borough franchises. In the counties the old 40s. freeholders were retained, and three new classes introduced : 1, copyholders of £10 per annum ; 2, leaseholders of the value of £10 for a term of sixty years, or of £50 for twenty years ; and 3, occupying tenants paying an annual rent of £50. In boroughs the franchise was given to all £10 resident householders, subject to certain conditions.

Lord John Russell received leave to introduce another Reform Bill Feb. 13, 1854 ; which, in consequence of the Russian war, was withdrawn April 11. Mr. Disraeli introduced a bill Feb. 28, 1859, which was thrown out on the second reading by a majority of 39, March 31. Lord John Russell introduced another measure March 1, 1860, which was withdrawn June 11. The Reform Bill of Mr. Gladstone was thrown out, 1866.

Regency Bills.—A measure of this kind was passed, appointing the Princess Dowager of Wales regent, on the death of Frederick, Prince of Wales, should the crown descend to a minor, A.D. 1751. During the first illness of George III. he himself proposed one, the name of his mother being included, April, 1765. The Premier moved three resolutions in the House of Commons, when George III. was a second time attacked by his malady, to consider what steps should be taken to provide for the government, Dec. 10, 1788. The decision of the Legislature as to what powers should be invested in the Regent, was submitted to the Prince of Wales, Dec. 30, 1788, and a Bill, which passed the Commons, after a warm discussion, was introduced Feb. 3, 1789, and reached the second reading in the Lords, Feb. 19, 1789, after which it was abandoned, owing to the recovery of his Majesty. It was, however, revived and passed Feb. 5, 1811, and the Prince of Wales exercised the regency till the death of his father. In Dec. 23, 1830, the administration of the government, in the event of the crown descending to the Princess Alexandrina Victoria, while under eighteen years of age, was provided for. And in Aug. 4, 1840, a Bill was passed appointing the Prince Consort regent in case of the demise of the Queen until her next lineal successor should attain the age of eighteen. This Act, however, restrained him from giving the royal assent to any bill for varying the course of succession to the Crown as established by 12 & 13 Will. III. c. 2, or for altering the Act of Uniformity, 13 & 14 Car. II. c. 4, relative to the services and ceremonies of the Church of England. And it further provided, that if after becoming guardian and regent he should profess, or marry a person who professed, the Popish religion, or should cease to reside in the United Kingdom, all the authorities so vested in him should determine.

Registrars.—Officers in the Chancery who enter all decrees and orders made by the Chancellor, Vice-Chancellor, or Master of the Rolls; they are experienced barristers. Similar officers are appointed in other courts of equity; and in other courts, where no such officer is appointed by name, the burden of the office lies on the chief clerk. Registrars are also functionaries in the Courts of Probate and Bankruptcy.

Registrar-General's Office. *See* GENERAL REGISTER OFFICE.

Registrar-General.—An officer appointed by the Crown to whom the general superintendence of the whole system of registration of births, deaths, and marriages is entrusted.

Registry of Ships.—A ship is a personal chattel, and is acquired by building, purchase, mortgage, or capture; the evidence of the owner's title being a certificate of registry from the collector and controller of the customs at the port where registered, or similar functionaries in other parts of the world, being British possessions. As no vessel can be entitled to the privileges of a British registered ship until registry, and as forfeiture accrues in case a ship exercises any such privileges before registry, all merchant and trading vessels are registered under the provisions of the 17 & 18 Vict. c. 104. The registry of vessels takes place at the port to which they belong, unless the Commissioners of Customs think fit to permit a registry at another port. A vessel is deemed to belong to that port at or near to which those owners or that managing owner resides who subscribes the declaration required by the Act before registry be made; and a new registry is required if the managing owner change his residence to another port.

Remainder, is an estate limited in lands, tenements, or rents, to be enjoyed after the expiration of another intervening, or, as it is technically termed, "particular" estate. An estate in remainder is an estate limited to take effect, and be enjoyed, after another estate is determined. As if a man, seised in fee-simple, grants land to one for twenty years, and, after the determination of the said term, then to another and his heirs for ever ; here the former is tenant for years, remainder to the latter in fee. In the first place, an estate for years is created or carved out of the fee, and given to the former, and the residue and remainder of it is given to the latter. Both their interests are, in fact, only one estate ; the present term of years, and the remainder afterwards, when added together, being equal only to one estate in fee. Remainders are either vested or contingent. Vested remainders, or remainders executed, are those by which a present interest passes to the party, though to be enjoyed in future, and by which the estate is invariably fixed to remain to a determinate person after the particular estate is spent. It is not the uncertainty of ever taking effect in possession that makes a remainder contingent, for to that every remainder for life or in tail is and must be liable, as the remainder-man may die, or die without issue, before the death of the tenant for life. The present capacity of taking effect in possession, if the possession were to become vacant, and not the certainty that the possession will become vacant before the estate limited in remainder determines, universally distinguishes a vested remainder from one that is contingent.

Remembrancer.—An officer of the Exchequer who reminds the Lord Treasurer and the justices of the Court of such things as are to be called on and dealt in for the benefit of the Crown. A remembrancer is also an officer of corporations, &c.

Rent.—In law, a sum of money or other consideration issuing yearly out of lands or tenements. There are several kinds of rents, such as rent service, rent charge, fee farm rent, rent seck, rents of assize, chief rents, quit rents, rack rents, &c. All kinds of rents are now recoverable by distress.

Replevin, in law, a remedy granted on a distress, by which the first possessor has his goods restored to him again, on his giving security to the sheriff that he will pursue his action against the party distraining, and return the goods or cattle if the taking them shall be adjudged lawful. In a replevin the person distrained becomes plaintiff, and the person distraining is called the defendant or avowant, and his justification an avowry.

Reserve Forces.—By 22 & 23 Vict. c. 40 (Aug. 13, 1859), the Admiralty was empowered to raise a body of men, not exceeding 30,000, to be called the Royal Naval Volunteers; and by 22 & 23 Vict. c. 42 (Aug. 13, 1859), the Sovereign was empowered to raise and keep up in the United Kingdom a reserve force of soldiers not exceeding 20,000 men.

Returning Officer.—The official who conducts a parliamentary election. He is the sheriff in counties and the mayor in boroughs.

Reversion, in the law of England, has two significations; the one of which is an estate left, which continues during a particular estate in being; and the other is the returning of the land, &c., after the particular estate is ended; and it is further said to be an interest in lands, when the possession of it fails, or where the estate which was for a time parted with, returns to the granters, or their heirs. But, according to the usual definition of a reversion, it is the residue of an estate left in the granter, after a particular estate granted away ceases, continuing in the granter of such an estate. The difference between a remainder and a reversion consists in this, that the remainder may belong to any man except the granter, whereas the reversion returns to him who conveyed the lands, &c.

Revising Barristers' Courts.—Courts held in the autumn throughout the country to revise the list of voters for members of Parliament. An appeal lies to the Court of Common Pleas.

Riot Act.—Means for the suppression of riots were provided by 17 Rich. II. c. 8 (1393), by 13 Hen. IV. c. 7 (1411), by 2 Hen. V. st. 1, c. 8 (1414), and by 3 & 4 Edw. VI. c. 5 (1548). The last-mentioned act made it high treason for an assemblage of twelve or more persons to refuse to disperse upon proclamation. The act usually known as the Riot Act is I Geo. I. st. 2, c. 5 (1714). It enacts that if any twelve persons are assembled for the disturbance of the peace, and refuse to disperse upon command from the proper authority, such refusal shall be visited as felony; also if they pull down any church, chapel, meeting-house, &c., to be felony. The latter clause has been repealed, and the punishment for the former, instead of being capital, is penal servitude or imprisonment for three years, by 7 Will. IV. and 1 Vict. c. 91.

Robes, Master of the.—An officer of the household who has the ordering of the sovereign's robes. He has several officers under him, as grooms, pages, &c., at St. James's, Windsor Castle, Hampton Court, &c. There are also a mistress of the robes, and two keepers of the robes.

Roman Catholic Relief Bill. *See* Catholic, &c.

Salvage Money.—A reward allowed by the civil and statute law for the saving of ships or goods from the danger of the sea, pirates, or enemies. Where any ship is in danger of being stranded, or driven on shore, justices of the peace are to command the constables to assemble as many persons as are necessary to preserve it; and on its being preserved by their means, the persons assisting therein shall, in thirty days after, be paid a reasonable reward for their salvage; otherwise the ship or goods shall remain in the custody of the officers of the customs as a security for the same.

Sanctuary.—The custom of setting apart places where criminals were safe from legal penalties is of great antiquity, and was sanctioned by the Levitical appointment of cities of refuge. The right of sanctuary is said to have been introduced into this country by King Lucius about A.D. 181, and it was expressly recognised by the code of Ina, which was promulgated in 693. Alfred the Great in 887 allowed criminals to obtain safety for three days by fleeing to a church; and in 1067

William the Conqueror made express laws on the subject. Sanctuary was understood to be merely a temporary privilege, and by 21 Hen. VIII. c. 2 (1529), felons or murderers availing themselves of it were compelled to be branded with the letter A on the right thumb, in token that they abjured the realm. The privilege of sanctuary was taken away from all persons guilty of high treason by 26 Hen. VIII. c. 13 (1534), and from pirates by 27 Hen. VIII. c. 4 (1535). By 27 Hen. VIII. c. 19 (1535) all persons in sanctuary were compelled to wear badges and were prohibited from wearing weapons, and from going abroad before sunrise or after sunset. By 32 Henry VIII. c. 12 (1540), many sanctuaries were abolished, and the only places permitted to retain the privilege were cathedrals, parish churches, and hospitals, together with Wells, Westminster, Manchester, Northampton, Norwich, York, Derby, and Lancaster. The same statute abolished the privilege of sanctuary in cases of wilful murder, rape, burglary, highway robbery, and arson. Westchester was substituted for Manchester as a sanctuary city by 33 Hen. VIII. c. 15 (1541). These Acts were all repealed by 1 James I. c. 26, s. 34 (1604), and the abolition of sanctuary was again enforced by 21 James I. c. 28, s. 7 (1623). In the case of debtors, however, it continued to exist in a modified form until it was finally removed by 8 & 9 Will. III. c. 27 (1697). The London sanctuaries were the Minories ; Salisbury Court, Whitefriars ; Ram Alley and Mitre Court, in Fleet Street ; Fulwood's Rents, Holborn ; Baldwin's Gardens, Gray's-Inn Lane ; the Savoy ; Montague Close, Deadman's Place ; and the Mint, in Southwark. Owing to the laxity of the authorities, the Mint retained some of its privileges as a sanctuary until the reign of George I.

Scan. Mag.—*Scandalum magnatum* (libelling of great men), a criminal proceeding against those who speak scandalous or derogatory words, of peers, judges, "great men of the realm," and some high officers, now seldom resorted to. It is founded upon an ancient statute against "devisers of false news and horrible lies of prelates, dukes, earls, barons, &c.," and compels the offender to produce his authority; and in default punishes him at the discretion of the council. *Scan. Mag.*, or scandalising peers, &c., is very often committed; but the punishment or remedy seems unconstitutional; and though words which would not support an action in the case of a commoner, are punishable as *scan. mag.* in the case of a peer, the proceeding is in disuse. A peeress is not within the statute, or any women noble by birth. Words imputing corruption to a judge, are *scan. mag.;* but punishment by information or indictment is the more usual course.

Schism Bill.—An Act passed in the reign of Queen Anne restraining dissenters from educating their own children, and forbidding all tutors and schoolmasters to be present at any conventicle or dissenting place of worship. Repealed in 1718.

Scire Facias (that you cause to know).—A writ which lies to enforce the execution of judgments, patents, or matters of record, or to vacate, or annul them. A judgment upon which execution has not issued within a year and a day, is revived by this writ. A recognisance, which is matter of record, is enforced by this process; and a patent is repealed by its operation. The writ calls upon the party to make known to the Court why such and such thing should not be done, and calling upon him to show sufficient cause to the contrary.

Scotland, Union of. *See* UNION OF, &c.

Sculpture.—By the stat. 54 Geo. III., called the Copyright Act, every person who shall make any new and original sculpture or model, or copy, or cast of the human figure, or of any bust or part of the human figure, clothed in drapery or otherwise, or of any animal or part of any animal combined with the human figure or otherwise, or any subject being matter of invention in sculpture, or of any alto or basso rilievo, or any cast from nature, of man or animals, whether separate or com-

bined, &c., shall have the sole right and property of the whole
of such new and original sculpture, &c., for fourteen years,
putting their name and date thereon. Persons (not having
purchased the property in the original) making, importing, or
selling pirated copies or casts of such sculptures, are made liable
to damages in an action on the case. An additional term of
fourteen years is given to the proprietor, if living, and not
having assigned his property.

Seaman.—A British seaman must be a natural born
subject or be naturalized ; or (being a foreigner) have served on
board of Her Majesty's ships of war, in time of war, for three
years. The Queen, however, may declare during war that
foreigners who have served two years during such war be
deemed British seamen. *See* 17 & 18 Vict. c. 104.

Secretaries of State, cabinet ministers attending the
sovereign, for the receipt and despatch of letters, grants,
petitions, and many of the most important affairs of the
kingdom, both foreign and domestic. There are five principal
secretaries, one for the home department, another for foreign
affairs, a third for the colonies, a fourth for war, and a fifth for
India. These have under their management the most considerable affairs of the nation, and are obliged to a constant
attendance on the sovereign. They receive and despatch
whatever comes to their hands, be it for the Crown, the church,
the army, private grants, pardons, dispensations, &c., as likewise petitions to the Crown, which, when read, are returned to
the secretaries for answer ; all which they despatch according
to the sovereign's command and direction. Each of them has
two under-secretaries, and one or more chief clerks, besides a
number of other clerks and officers wholly depending on them.
The Secretaries of State are allowed power to commit persons
for treason and other offences against the State in order to
bring them to their trial. They have the custody of the
signet, and the direction of the signet office and the paper

office. Ireland is under the direction of a chief secretary to the Lord-Lieutenant, who has under him a resident under-secretary.

Sedition.—All contempts against the sovereign and the government, riotous assemblies for political purposes, and all offences against the Crown not amounting to treason, or not capital, may be classed under this head.

Septennial Elections.—By 1 Geo. I. c. 38, it is enacted that our parliament must die a natural death at the end of every seventh year, if not previously dissolved by the royal prerogative. In 1734 and 1837, attempts for the repeal of this Act were made, but both were negatived by a large majority.

Sequestration, is setting aside the thing in contro-versy from the possession of both the parties that contend for it. In which sense it is either voluntary, as when done by the consent of the parties ; or necessary, as where it is done by the judge, of his own authority, whether the parties will or not. Sequestration is also used for the act of gathering the fruits of a benefice void, to the use of the next incumbent. Some-times a benefice is kept under sequestration for many years, when it is of so small value that no clergyman fit to serve the cure will be at the charge of taking it by institution ; in which case the sequestration is committed either to the curate alone or to the curate and churchwardens jointly. Sometimes the profits of a living in controversy, either by the consent of the parties or the judge's authority, are sequestered and placed for safety in a third hand, till the suit is determined, a minister being appointed by the judge to serve the cure, and allowed a certain salary out of the profits. Sometimes the profits of a living are sequestered for neglect of duty, for dilapidations, or for satisfying the debts of the incumbent.

Serjeant-at-Law, or of the Coif, is the highest degree taken in the common law, as that of Doctor is of the civil law. The monopoly enjoyed by the Serjeants in the Court of Common Pleas during term time has been abolished, and the Court thrown open to the bar generally, 9 & 10 Vict. c. 54.

Serjeants-at-Arms.—Officers attending the sovereign's person to arrest individuals of distinction giving offence, &c. Two of these attend in the Houses of Parliament, and each has a deputy. The office of the Serjeant-at-Arms in the House of Commons is to keep the doors and execute such commands touching the apprehension and taking into custody of any offender as the House shall command him. There are also Serjeants-at-arms attending the Court of Chancery, the Lord Treasurer of England, and the Lord Mayor of London,—the latter, however, only on extraordinary occasions.

Serjeant, Common.—An officer in the city of London, who attends the Lord Mayor and Court of Aldermen on Court days, and is in council with them on all occasions, within and without the precincts or liberties of the city. He is to take care of orphans' estates, either by taking account of them, or to sign their indentures, before their passing the Lord Mayor and Court of Aldermen.

Sessions of the Peace.—There are three different kinds of sessions holden by justices of the peace :—1. General sessions, which may be held at any time of the year, for the general execution of the authority of the justices ; 2. The general quarter sessions, holden at four stated times in the year, pursuant to statute ; 3. A special or petty sessions, which is holden upon particular occasions or settled times, as every market day, and is rather a voluntary arrangement of the justices to decide matters which should belong to the jurisdiction of two justices, a single justice having previously granted a summons compelling the party summoned to appear before the petty sessions. In most corporate towns there are quarter sessions, &c. ; and the Queen is empowered to grant a court of quarter sessions to those municipal corporations who shall petition for the same under particular circumstances.

Settlement, Act of.—The death of the Duke of Glouoester (July 29, 1700), son and last surviving child of the Princess Anne, afterwards queen, rendered a new settlement of the Crown necessary, it being unprovided for after the death of William III. and of Anne. Accordingly, a measure was introduced during the session of 1701, to supply matters of great importance, omitted in the Bill of Rights. This statute (12 & 13 Will. III. c. 2) provided that in case of default of issue of William III. and also of the Princess Anne respectively, the crown should devolve upon the next Protestant in succession, Sophia, married to the elector of Hanover, and the heirs of her body, being Protestants. It was further enacted, that the occupant of the throne "shall join in communion with the Church of England as by law established;" that if a foreigner succeeded, the nation should not be required to defend any foreign dominions without the consent of parliament; that the sovereign should not leave the country without permission of parliament; that all matters cognizable in the privy council should be transacted there, and all resolutions taken thereupon signed by such of the privy council as should consent to them; that only those born of English parents should be eligible to a seat at the privy council, in either house of parliament, or to hold any office or receive any grant under the Crown; that no person serving under, or receiving a pension from the Crown, should be capable of serving as a member of the House of Commons; that the judges should hold upon good behaviour, and not be removed except upon the address of both houses of parliament; and that no pardon under the great seal of England should be pleaded to an impeachment by the Commons (June 12, 1701). The provision against the sovereign quitting the kingdom without consent of parliament was repealed in 1715 (1 Geo. I. stat. 2, c. 51). The provision respecting matters to be transacted in the privy council was repealed by 4 Anne, c. 8 (1705), and the general disqualification of pensioners and placemen having been found inconvenient, was repealed by 4 Anne, c. 8, which statute was re-enacted by 6 Anne, c. 7, at the union between England and Scotland. Section 25 of 6 Anne, c. 7, decreed that the holders of certain offices, therein specified, and of all new offices or places of profit under the Crown, created at any time since Oct. 25, 1705, should not be allowed to sit in the House of Commons ; and section 26 provided that any member accepting any office of profit from the Crown should vacate his seat, being eligible to stand again. So numerous are the special disqualifications, that they have to be collected from at least 116 statutes.

Sewers, Court of Commissioners of.—This is a temporary tribunal erected by virtue of a Commission under the Great Seal. Its jurisdiction is to overlook the repairs of the banks and walls of the sea-coast and navigable rivers ; and to cleanse such rivers and their various communicating streams. Its authority is confined to such county or particular district as the Commission shall expressly name. The Commissioners are a Court of Record, and may make any order for the conservation of sewers within their commission. By the Land Drainage Act, 1861, 24 and 25 Vict. c. 133, the Queen is empowered to direct Commissions of Sewers into all parts of England, and to give them jurisdiction over such areas as may be thought most expedient for draining purposes. This Court is subject to the discretionary consideration of the Court of Queen's Bench.

Sheriff.—A conservator of the peace, appointed by the sovereign for the purpose of executing process, and preserving the peace, and assisting justices and others therein. He is, during his office, which is for a year, the first man in the county, and superior to any nobleman : he sits, or is entitled to sit, on the bench with the justices of assize. Barristers and attorneys, militia officers, and prisoners for debt, are exempted from being chosen sheriffs. No man who has served as sheriff for one year can be compelled to serve again within three years after, if there be other sufficient person in the county. The duties of a sheriff are very numerous : he executes all writs directed to him ; also all precepts, warrants from justices of the peace, upon extraordinary occasions, to apprehend felons, traitors, and notorious delinquents ; he executes all sentences of the law ; and, in many instances, acts in a judicial capacity, as by executing writs of trial for debts under £20, administering justice in the county court, &c. All fines due to the sovereign are receivable by him, and he is accountable for them. He is the returning officer for his county, and has various duties to discharge in reference to elections of members of Parliament. The gaol of the county is under his government ; the houses of correction being under that of the justices. The under-sheriff performs most of the duties of the office. The under-sheriff is not to be an attorney or sheriff's officer, or continue in his office above a year.

Ship Money.—An imposition formerly levied on port towns and other places for fitting out ships, revived by Charles I., and abolished in the same reign.

Simony, is the corrupt presentation of any one to an ecclesiastical benefice for money, gift, or reward. It is so called from the resemblance it is said to bear to the sin of Simon Magus, though the purchasing of holy orders seems to approach nearer to his offence. It was by the canon law a very grievous crime ; and is so much the more odious, because, as Sir Edward Coke observes, it is ever accompanied with perjury ; for the presentee is sworn to have committed no simony. However, it was not an offence punishable in a criminal way at the common law ; it being thought sufficient to leave the clerk to ecclesiastical censures. But as these did not affect the simoniacal patron, nor were efficacious enough to repel the notorious practice of the thing, divers acts of parliament have been made to restrain it by means of civil forfeitures. The statute 31 Eliz. c. 6, enacts, that if any patron, for money or any other corrupt consideration or promise, directly or indirectly given, shall present, admit, institute, induct, install, or collate any person to an ecclesiastical benefice or dignity, both the giver and taker shall forfeit two years' value of the benefice or dignity; one moiety to the king, and the other to any one who will sue for the same. If persons also corruptly resign or exchange their benefices, both the giver and taker shall in like manner forfeit double the value of the money or other corrupt consideration. And persons who shall corruptly ordain or license any minister, or procure him to be ordained or licensed (which is the true idea of simony), shall incur a like forfeiture of forty pounds; and the minister himself of ten pounds, besides an incapacity to hold any ecclesiastical preferment for seven years afterwards. Corrupt elections and resignations in colleges, hospitals, and other eleemosynary corporations, are also punished, by the same statute, with forfeiture of the double value, vacating the place or office, and a devolution of the right of election, for that turn, to the Crown. The sale of an advowson however (whether the living be full or not) is not simoniacal, unless connected with a corrupt contract or design as to the next presentation, though if an advowson be granted during the vacancy of the benefice, the presentation on that vacancy can in no case pass by the grant.

Six Articles, or Bloody Statute.—The name given to an act (31 Hen. VIII. c. 14) passed June 28, 1539. It was enacted for "abolishing diversity of opinions in certain articles concerning the Christian religion." The six articles enforced were transubstantiation, communion in one kind, celibacy of the clergy, vows of chastity, private masses, and auricular confession. All persons denying the first were to be punished as heretics, and those who denied any of the remaining five as felons. This statute was repealed in 1558.

Smoke Nuisance.—An act of parliament, 16 and 17 Vict. c. 128, was passed August 20, 1853, to abate the nuisance arising from the smoke of furnaces in the metropolis, and from steam-vessels above London Bridge. It was amended by 19 and 20 Vict. c. 107 (July 29, 1856), which came into operation Jan. 1, 1858.

Solicitor-General.—A law officer of the Crown, appointed by patent, and holding office during the continuance of the ministry of which he is a member. He is usually knighted, and is a member of the House of Commons. He has the care of managing the sovereign's affairs, and has fees for pleading besides other fees. He ranks after the Attorney-General.

Speaker of the House of Commons.—This important officer of the Crown is chosen by the House of Commons from amongst its own members, subject to the approval of the Sovereign, and holds his office till the dissolution of the parliament in which he was elected. His duties are, to read to the Sovereign petitions or addresses from the Commons, and to deliver in the royal presence such speeches as are usually made on behalf of the Commons ; to manage, in the name of the House, where counsel, witnesses, or prisoners are at the bar ; to reprimand persons who have incurred the displeasure of the House ; to issue warrants of committal or release for breaches of privilege ; to communicate in writing with any parties, when so instructed by the House ; to exercise vigilance in reference to private bills, especially with a view to protect property in general, or the rights of individuals, from undue encroachment or injury ; to express the thanks or approbation of the Commons to distinguished personages ; to control and regulate the subordinate officers of the House ; to entertain the members at dinner, in due succession and at stated periods ; to adjourn the House at four o'clock if forty members be not present ; to appoint tellers on divisions. The Speaker must abstain from debating, unless in committee of the whole House. As chair-

man of the House, his duties are the same as those of any
other president of a deliberative assembly.   When Parliament is
about to be prorogued, it is customary for the Speaker to address
the Sovereign, in the House of Lords, a speech recapitulating
the proceedings of the session.   Should a member persevere in
breaches of order, the Speaker may "name" him, as it is
called, a course uniformly followed by the censure of the House.
In extreme cases the Speaker may order members or others
into custody, until the pleasure of the House be signified.   On
divisions, when the numbers happen to be equal, he gives the
casting vote, but he never otherwise votes.   At the end of his
official labours he is generally rewarded by a peerage, and a
pension of £4000 for two lives.   He is a member of the Privy
Council, and entitled to rank after barons.

Speaker of the House of Lords.—The Lord Chancellor, by virtue of his office, becomes, on the delivery of
the seal to him by the Sovereign, Speaker of the House of
Lords.   He is usually, but not necessarily a peer.   There has
always been a Deputy-Speaker, and formerly there were two
or more, but since the year 1815 there has been only one.
The chairman in committees generally fills this office.   In the
absence of the Lord Chancellor and of the Deputy-Speaker, it
is competent to the House to appoint any noble lord to take the
woolsack.   The Speaker is the organ or mouthpiece of the
House, and it therefore is his duty to represent their lordships
in their collective capacity, when holding intercourse with other
public bodies or with individuals.   He has not a casting vote
upon divisions, for should the numbers prove equal, the non-
contents prevail.   The Deputy-Speaker of the Lords is appointed
by the Crown.

Special Jury.   *See* JURY.

Specification.—A description of a patent directed to be
enrolled in Chancery, within a specified time, the object of
which is to put the public in full possession of the inventor's

secret, so that any person may be in a condition to avail himself of it when the period of exclusive privilege has expired.

Spiritual Courts. *See* ECCLESIASTICAL COURTS.

Stamp Duties.—By 22 & 23 Charles II. c. 9 (1670), certain duties were imposed on deeds enrolled, Crown grants and law proceedings, but they were not denoted by stamps. Stamp duties, properly so called, were introduced into this country from Holland, and were first imposed by 5 Will. & Mary, c. 21 (1694). By 6 & 7 Will. III. c 6 (1694), they were granted on marriages, births, and burials, and by 8 Anne, c. 9 (1709), on premiums with apprentices. Newspapers were first taxed by 10 Anne, c. 19 (1711). Stamp duties were introduced into Ireland in 1774. Bills of exchange and notes were subjected to the stamp laws by 22 Geo. III. c. 33 (1782), and patent medicines by 23 Geo. III. c. 62 (1783). All the stamp duties were repealed by 44 Geo. III. c. 98 (July 28, 1804), which was amended by 48 Geo. III. c. 149 (July 4, 1808). Both these statutes were repealed by the general stamp act, 55 Geo. III. c. 184 (July 11, 1815). By 7 & 8 Geo. IV. c. 55 (July 2, 1827), the stamp offices of Great Britain and Ireland were consolidated, and by 4 & 5 Will. IV.c. 60 (Aug. 13, 1834), the boards of stamps and taxes were united. The stamp laws were amended by 13 & 14 Vict. c. 97 (Aug. 14, 1850); 16 & 17 Vict. c. 59 (Aug. 4, 1853); 16 & 17 Vict. c. 63 (Aug. 4, 1853); 17 & 18 Vict. c. 83 (Aug. 9, 1854); 23 & 24 Vict. c. 111 (Aug. 28, 1860); and by 24 & 25 Vict. cc. 21 & 92.

Stannary Courts.—Courts established for the administration of justice among the tinners of Cornwall and Devonshire, who are to be sued only in these courts, except in cases of murder or maiming. They are presided over by the vice-warden of the Stannaries. Appeal lies first to the lord-warden, then to the judicial committee.

Star Chamber, Court of.—A court of great antiquity, originally composed of all the members of the King's ordinary council. Its jurisdiction embraced both civil and criminal cases. The title was derived from the *camera stellata*, or Star Chamber in the Palace at Westminster, where it held its sittings. It appears to have gradually declined till its revival by Henry VII., when it continued to exercise its tremendous power until abolished by the Long Parliament. The judges were the Lord Chancellor or Lord Keeper as President, the Treasurer, the Privy Seal, and the President of the Council; and with these were associated the members of the Council and such peers as chose to be present. Under James I. and Charles I. only those peers being members of the Privy Council were summoned, and the bishops ceased also to attend. The jurisdiction of the Star Chamber extended legally over riots, perjury, misbehaviour of sheriffs, and other notorious misdemeanors, contrary to the laws of the land. Yet this was afterwards, as Lord Clarendon informs us, stretched "to the asserting of all proclamations and orders of state; to the vindicating of illegal commissions and grants of monopolies; holding for honourable that which pleased, and for just that which profited; and becoming both a court of law to determine civil rights, and a court of revenue to enrich the treasury; the council-table by proclamations enjoining to the people that which was not enjoined by the laws, and prohibiting that which was not prohibited; and the Star Chamber, which consisted of the same persons in different rooms, censuring the breach and disobedience to those proclamations by very great fines, imprisonments, and corporal severities; so that any disrespect to any acts of state, or to the persons of statesmen, was in no time more penal, and the foundations of right never more in danger to be destroyed." · For which reasons it was finally abolished by statute 16 Car. I. c. 10, to the general joy of the whole nation.

Statutes of Limitations. *See* LIMITATIONS.

Subpœna.—A writ commanding attendance in a Court under a penalty.

Subsidy.—An aid or tax granted to the Crown, for the pressing occasions of the kingdom, to be levied on every subject of ability, according to the value of his lands or goods.

Succession Duty.—By 16 & 17 Vict. c. 51 (Aug. 4, 1853), real property was made subject to the legacy duty, paid on succession to every kind of property. This act was to be taken to have come into operation May 19, 1853.

Supply, Committee of.—All bills which relate to the public income or expenditure must originate with the House of Commons, and all bills authorising expenditure of the public money are based upon resolutions moved in a Committee of Supply, which is always a committee of the whole House. The practice with regard to these bills is as follows :—In the course of the session estimates are submitted to a Committee of Supply, and resolutions moved therein granting to the Crown the sums requisite for defraying the expenses attendant on the various branches of the public service. Those resolutions having been considered and disposed of, such amongst them as may be affirmed are reported to the House, reconsidered, and adopted, or rejected. Under authority of those to which the House agree, the Lords of the Treasury issue the requisite funds for carrying on the service of the country. At the end of the session the supply resolutions are consolidated in the Appropriation Bill, which is sent up to the Lords, and after being there considered and agreed to, receives the Royal Assent and becomes law. The Lords may reject this or any other money-bill, but it would be considered an invasion of the privileges of the Commons if their Lordships were substantially to modify measures of this class. The Commons, however, do not object to consider any verbal emendations which may be made by the other House.

Supremacy, Act of.—In 1534, by 26 Hen. VIII. c. 1, the King was declared "the only supreme head in earth of the Church of England," and he formerly assumed that title on the 15th of January. All beneficed ecclesiastics, and all laymen holding office under the Crown, were obliged by this Act to take the oath abjuring the spiritual as well as the temporal jurisdiction of the Pope. In 1554, by 1 & 2 Phil. & Mary, c. 8, s. 12, this law was repealed, but it was restored by 1 Eliz. c. 1, in 1559. The denial of the King's supremacy was declared treasonable in 1547, by 1 Edw. VI. c. 12, s. 7. An oath of supremacy is taken by all public officers, &c., whereby they swear to uphold the supreme power of the kingdom in the person of the reigning sovereign. *See* 21 & 22 Vict. c. 48, and 22 Vict. c. 16.

Sweinmote, Court of, one of the forest-courts, which is to be holden before the verderors as judges, by the steward, thrice in every year, the sweins or freeholders within the forest composing the jury. The principal jurisdiction of this Court is first to inquire into the oppressions and grievances committed by the officers of the forest; and secondly, to receive and try presentments certified from the Court of attachments, against offenders in vert and venison. And this Court may not only inquire but convict also, which conviction shall be certified to the Court of Justice-seat under the seals of the jury; for this Court cannot proceed to judgment.

Tail, or Fee-tail.—A conveyance of lands (not copyhold, unless by special custom of the manor,) to a man and the heirs of his body, or the heirs of the bodies of him and his wife: the first is called tail general, the latter tail special. The estate, provided the entail be not barred, reverts to the donor or reversioner, if the donee die without leaving descendants answering to the condition annexed to the estate upon its creation, unless there be a limitation over to a third person on default of such descendants, when it vests in such third person or remainderman. This estate is a freehold in law, and the tenant or party entitled, although his interest is but for life, may commit waste and cut timber; and as to dower, curtesy, or the like, it is subject to the same incidents as freehold. As limitations of estates, in this manner, are constantly made for perpetuating the possession of landed property, either by will or settlement, it has been the object of the legislature, for many years, to facilitate their alienation, and to render them subject to the debts and contracts of the possessor : this is completely effected with regard to bankrupt tenants in tail ; and with respect to other persons entitled, they can, where the limitation does not extend beyond their own issue, bar the entail, and either dispose of the land, or resettle it. This process was effected by fictitious suits, termed "fines and recoveries," now superseded by an ordinary conveyance enrolled, and, if married women are parties, acknowledged before a judge, or two commissioners to administer oaths in Chancery, with the consent of the person called the "protector," if he is not in possession, or has not the prior estate ; but those in immediate expectancy cannot bar such their interests or expectancies ; for instance, an eldest son of a tenant in tail cannot sell his interest during his father's life, who is the tenant in tail ; nor can the father himself do it, if a kind of trustee, called a "protector," has been appointed, whose consent must be obtained before any alienation can be perfected. Leases made by tenants in tail, which do not tend to the prejudice of the issue in tail, being for three lives, or twenty-one years, and reserving the usual rents, are good, but will not bar the reversioners or remainder-men, although they will the issue ; such leases not being granted to take effect at a future time. And if a husband is possessed, in right of his wife, of an entailed estate, he may, with her concurrence, grant similar leases, which will bind the issue.

Tenant.—One that holds or possesses lands or tenements by any kind of title, either in fee, for life, years, or at will. The word in law is used with divers additions ; thus, tenant in dower, is she that possesses land by virtue of her dower ; tenant by the curtesy, he that holds for his life, by reason of a child begotten by him of his wife, being an heiress ; tenant in mortgage, that holds by means of a mortgage ; tenant by the verge in ancient demesne, who is admitted by the rod in the court of ancient demesne ; tenant by copy of court-roll, who is admitted tenant of any lands, &c., within a manor ; tenant in fee simple ; tenant in fee tail ; tenant at the will of the lord, according to the custom of the manor ; tenant at will by the common law ; tenant from year to year ; tenant by lease ; and tenant upon sufferance. So there are also joint tenants, that have equal right in lands and tenements by virtue of one title ; tenants in common, that have equal right, but hold by divers titles ; particular tenants, &c., &c.

Tender Legal.—A tender of satisfaction is allowed to be made in most actions for money demands. It need not be made by the debtor personally to the creditor personally ; it may be made through an authorised agent, and a tender to one of several joint creditors is sufficient. A tender must be absolute and unconditional, and the money must be actually produced at the time of the tender, unless that be dispensed with by the creditor. No copper coin can be tendered when the debt is sixpence or upwards. No tender of silver coin above forty shillings is legal, and Bank of England notes are a legal tender for debts above £5.

Tenure.—The manner whereby lands or tenements are holden. A tenure may be of houses, and land, or tenements ; but not of a rent, common, &c., these being incident to tenure. Under the word tenure, is included every holding of an inheritance ; but the signification of this word, which is a very extensive one, is usually restrained by coupling other words with it : this is sometimes done by words, which denote the duration of the tenant's estate ; as, if a man holds to himself and his heirs, it is called tenure in fee-simple ; if to him and his heirs male, tenancy or tenure in tail, &c. At other times, the tenure is coupled with words pointing out the instrument by which an inheritance is held : thus, if the holding is by copy of court-roll, it is called tenure by copy of court-roll. At other times, this word is coupled with words that show the principal service by which an inheritance is held ; as, where a man held by knight-service, it was called tenure by knight-service. Almost all the real property of the kingdom is, by the policy of our laws, supposed to be granted by, dependent upon and holden of, some superior lord; by and in consideration of certain services to be rendered to the lord by the tenant or possessor of this property. The thing holden is styled a tenement ; the possessors thereof, tenants ; and the manner of their possession, a tenure : thus, all the land in the kingdom is supposed to be holden directly or indirectly of the king, who is styled the lord paramount, or above all. The above maxim, and the whole of the doctrine of tenures, are founded on the feudal system, "feud," "fief," or "fee," signifying land held as a feud or military tenure, which subsisted in England by the name of knight-service ; but in process of time, many feuds were bartered for services of a certain nature, such as payment of rent, and gradually assimilated themselves to the service called *socage,* a free service very inferior, which most probably means plough-service.

Military tenures, together with all their grievances, were destroyed at the Restoration. The statute 12 Car. II. c. 24, enacted, "that the court of awards and liveries, and all wardships, liveries, *primer seisins* and *ousterlemains,* values, and forfeitures of marriage, by reason of any tenure of the king or others, be totally taken away. And that all fines for alienations, tenures by homage, knight-service, and escuage, and also aids for marrying the daughter or knighting the son, and all tenures of the king *in capite,* be likewise taken away. And that all sorts of tenures, held of the king or others, be turned into free and common socage, save only tenures in frankalmoign, copyholds, and the honorary services (without the slavish part) of grand serjeanty ; and that all tenures which shall be created by the king, his heirs or successors, in future shall be free and common socage."

Terms.—The law terms were so called because at four periods of the year the judges sit "*finis et terminus contentionum.*" They were gradually formed from the canonical constitutions of the Church, and consisted of those seasons of the year which were not occupied by the great festivals or fasts, or in which the chief business of agriculture and other rural affairs did not occur. In the early ages the whole year was devoted to hearing and deciding causes throughout Christendom, but through the interference of the Church certain holy seasons were gradually set apart from the profanation of secular business. Thus Advent and Christmas being exempted gave rise to the winter vacation; the periods of Lent and Easter to the spring vacation; Pentecost produced the third and the long vacation, occurring between Midsummer and Michaelmas, was allowed for hay-time and harvest. Sunday and other high festivals were also prohibited and became *dies non juridici.* Occasionally dispensations were granted by the Church for holding assizes and trying causes during the inhibited seasons at the request of the king to the bishops. The portions of the year not included in the ecclesiastical prohibitions formed four divisions; and from the festivals of St. Hilary, Easter Day, Trinity Sunday, and the feast of St. Michael, they were called Hilary, Easter, Trinity and Michaelmas Terms. By statute 1 Will. IV. c. 70, passed July 22, 1830, it is enacted that in the year of our Lord 1831 and afterwards,—

Hilary Term shall begin on the 11th and end on the 31st Jan.

Easter Term shall begin on the 15th of April and end on the 8th of May.

Trinity Term shall begin on the 22nd of May and end on the 12th of June.

Michaelmas Term shall begin on the 2nd and end on the 25th of November.

It is also provided by the same statute "that in case the day of the month on which any term, according to the Act of 1 Will. IV. c. 70, is to end, shall fall to be on a Sunday, then the Monday next after such day shall be deemed and taken to be the last day of the term; and that in case any of the days between the Thursday before and the Wednesday next after Easter shall fall within Easter Term, then such days shall be deemed and taken to be part of such Term, although there shall be no sittings in banco on any of such intervening days."

Test Act. — This Act is the statute 25 Car. II. c. 2, which directs all officers, civil and military, to take the oaths, and make the declaration against transubstantiation, in the Court of King's Bench or Chancery, the next Term, or at the next Quarter Sessions, or (by subsequent statutes) within six months after their admission; and also within the same time to receive the Sacrament of the Lord's Supper, according to the usage of the Church of England, in some public church, immediately after divine service or sermon, and to deliver into Court a certificate thereof, signed by the minister and churchwarden, and also to prove the same by two credible witnesses, upon forfeiture of £500 and disability to hold the said office. By 1 Geo. I. c. 13, it is enacted that no member shall vote or sit in either House of Parliament till he has in the presence of the House subscribed and repeated the declaration against transubstantiation, the invocation of Saints, and the sacrifice of the Mass. The Test Act was repealed by 9 Geo. II. c. 26, which also repealed the Corporation Act (which see).

This Day Six or Three Months. — Appointing this day six or three months for the next stage of a Bill, is one of the means adopted by the Houses of Lords and Commons to reject Bills of which they disapprove. A Bill rejected in this manner cannot be re-introduced in the same session.

Threatening Letters.—The senders of letters threatening murder are guilty of felony punishable by penal servitude for ten or three years, or by imprisonment for any term not exceeding two years ; senders of letters demanding property, &c., with menaces (without any reasonable cause), by penal servitude for life or for three years ; or by imprisonment for not more than two years ; and senders of letters threatening to accuse any one of any crime punishable by death or penal servitude in order to extort money, by penal servitude for life, or for three years, or by imprisonment for not more than two years.

Tithes are the tenth part of the increase arising from the produce of lands, payable to the rector, vicar, or perpetual curate, by endowment or prescription. They are said to be predial, mixed, and personal. Predial are such as are derived immediately from the earth by culture or tillage, as corn, grass, wood, fruit, &c. Mixed tithes arise from the product of nature, improved by the care of man, as the young of cattle, wool, milk, cheese, eggs. Personal tithes are payable in respect of the profit arising from labour, confined to fish, and corn mills, not in existence before 1315. The sovereign, rectors, and vicars, are exempt, by personal privilege, from paying tithes. Tithes are now commuted into a rent-charge, the amount of which is annually adjusted according to the average price of corn. All persons may claim an exemption, either partial or total, from tithes, by a real composition, or by custom, or by long usage. In some cases lands may obtain an exemption under the Commutation Acts from all liability either to tithe or rent-charge. For to the extent of twenty acres in the same parish, land is allowed to be given to the tithe owner as an equivalent ; and any person seized in possession of an estate in fee-simple, or fee-tail, of any tithe or rent-charge, may dispose of the same so that it shall be merged in the inheritance of the land charged.

Toleration Act, for the relief from certain penalties, of dissenters from the Church of England, except papists and persons denying the Trinity, was passed May 24, 1689, and confirmed by 10 Anne, c. 2 (1711). The clause excepting persons denying the Trinity was repealed by 53 Geo. III. c. 160, July 21, 1813, and the Roman Catholics were relieved by 10 Geo. IV. c. 7, passed April 13, 1829.

Trade and Plantations, Board of.—*See* BOARD OF.

Transportation derived its origin from banishment, which was first introduced by 39 Eliz. c. 4 (1596), and enacted that such rogues as were dangerous to the inferior people should be banished the realm. The first statute in which the word transportation is used is 13 & 14 Charles II. c. 23 (1662), by which justices were authorised to transport such rogues, vagabonds, and sturdy beggars as should be duly convicted and adjudged incorrigible, to any of the English plantations beyond the seas. It was followed by 18 Charles II. c. 3 (1666), which gave a power to the judges, at their discretion, either to execute or transport to America for life the moss-troopers of Cumberland and Northumberland. Until after the passing of 4 Geo. I. c. 2 (1717), continued by 6 Geo. I. c. 23 (1719), this mode of punishment was not brought into common operation. By these statutes the courts were allowed a discretionary power to order felons to be transported to America. The system of transportation to the American colonies lasted from 1718 to the commencement of the war in 1775. The great accumulation of convicts in 1776 led to the establishment of the system of the hulks, by 16 Geo. III. c. 43. This was followed by 19 Geo. III. c. 74 (1778), ordering the erection of penitentiaries. Transportation was resumed, and George III., by two orders in council, dated Dec. 6, 1786, fixed upon the eastern coast of Australia and the adjacent islands. The first band of convicts left England in May, 1787, and in the succeeding year founded the colony of New South Wales. Return from transportation was punishable with death, until 4 & 5 Will. IV. (1834) reduced the penalty to transportation for life. The discontinuance of transportation to Australia was announced by Lord

x

John Russell in Parliament, as determined upon by Government, Feb. 10, 1853. By 16 & 17 Vict. c. 99 (Aug. 20, 1853), penal servitude was substituted for transportation, except for fourteen years or for life. By 20 & 21 Vict. c. 3 (June 26, 1857), persons under sentence of penal servitude may be transported.

Treason.—An offence against the duty of allegiance, and the highest known crime, for it aims at the very destruction of the commonwealth itself. By 25 Ed. III. c. 2, treason is declared to be :—

1. When a man doth compass or imagine the death of the king, his queen, or of their eldest son.

2. If a man do violate the king's wife, or his eldest daughter, or the wife of the king's eldest son.

3. If a man do levy war against the king in his realm.

4. If a man be adherent to the king's enemies in his realm, giving them aid in the realm or elsewhere.

5. If a man slay the chancellor, treasurer, or the king's justices, being in their places doing their offices.

By 1 Anne c. 17, it is treason to attempt to deprive any one succeeding to the Crown, being next in succession according to the Act of Settlement. And by 6 Anne, c. 7, any person maintaining that any one has any right to the Crown otherwise than according to the Act of Settlement, or that the kings of this realm, with the authority of Parliament, are not able to make statutes and laws to bind the crown and the descent thereof, is guilty of treason.

The 3 & 4 Vict. c. 52, s. 4, provides (having reference to the contingency of any issue of her present Majesty ascending the throne while under the age of eighteen), that every person who shall aid or bring about any marriage, as well as any person so marrying, such issue under the age of eighteen, without the consent in writing of the Regent, and the assent of both

Houses of Parliament previously obtained, shall be guilty of treason. If any person within this realm or without, intend to deprive or depose the Queen from the Crown, or to levy war within this realm, in order by force to compel her to change her measures or counsels, or to intimidate either House of Parliament, or to excite an invasion of any of her Majesty's dominions, and shall express such intentions by publishing any printing or writing, or by open and advised speaking, or by any overt act, shall be guilty of felony. This was formerly a species of treason, pursuant to 36 Geo. III. c. 7, and 57 Geo. III. c. 6, which were repealed by 11 Vict. c. 12. The offence of treason must be prosecuted within three years from its commission, if committed within the realm, except in the case of a designed assassination of the sovereign. Information for open and advised speaking must be given within six days after its utterance, and a warrant for the apprehension of the offender must have been issued within ten days after and within two years from April 22, 1848. The punishment of a convicted traitor is—1st, that the offender be drawn on a hurdle to the place of execution ; 2nd, that he be hanged by the neck until he be dead ; 3rd, that his head be severed from the body ; 4th, that his body be divided into four quarters ; 5th, that his head and quarters shall be at the disposal of the Crown. The sovereign may, however, change the whole sentence into beheading. The term *high* treason was used formerly to distinguish it from petty treason, which was the killing of a master by his servant, a husband by his wife, &c. ; but as every offence which formerly amounted to petty treason is by 9 Geo. IV. c. 31, deemed murder, the term high is now obsolete, there being no necessity for the distinction.

Treasury.—The office of Lord High Treasurer was first put into commission in 1612. The Lords of the Treasury are five in number, including the First Lord and the Chancellor of the Exchequer. All these, as well as the two Parliamentary

Secretaryships, are political appointments, and are vacated on a change of Ministry. The First Lord of the Treasury has the power of controlling all the appointments made by other members of the Ministry ; he appoints archbishops and bishops, and such Crown livings as are not vested in the Lord Chancellor, are at his disposal. He is generally, but not necessarily, the Prime Minister. The Chancellor of the Exchequer now performs many of the duties in connection with the Exchequer which in former times devolved upon the Lord High Treasurer. He has the entire control of the public monies, and of all matters relating to its receipt or expenditure. The three Junior Lords of the Treasury are members of Parliament. They are expected to be in attendance on the various committees, and arrangements are made that some of them shall be in the House whenever it may sit. There are two political Secretaries—one attending to financial, and the other to parliamentary business. The permanent Under-Secretary is the official head of the department. The Treasury is the highest branch of the Executive, and exercises its supervision over all the revenue offices, and so far as receipt and expenditure are concerned, over every department of the Civil Service. Hours, 11 to 5. Whitehall.

Treasure Trove.—Money, gold, silver, &c., found hidden in the earth or other private place, the owner of which is unknown, belongs to the Crown. Concealing treasure trove is punished by fine or imprisonment.

Treating Act.—An Act passed in the present reign, enacting that any candidate at an election guilty of bribery shall forfeit £50 to any person who shall sue the same, with full costs of suit; and every voter accepting such bribery shall be incapable of voting at such election.

Trespass is a term applied to those wrongs which are committed with actual or implied force. Any injuries, or adverse contacts, committed against real property, *i. e.* land or buildings are, in the most ordinary sense of the word, "trespasses;" as entering another's house without permission, or suffering any cattle to stray upon another's field, undermining, or even piling earth against a wall, or any detrimental act, or any practice which damages in the slightest degree the property, or interferes with the owner's or occupier's right of possession. A person trespassing upon another's land can be turned off at a moment's notice; and if he enter again after notice, it is actionable. Cattle may be distrained if they do damage, and detained in the pound till the same be paid, together with the charges of impounding. Compensation to the extent of £5 for small, wilful, or malicious trespasses, occasioning actual damage, and not mere trespasses by walking over land, may be obtained by summary proceeding before a single justice. Trespasses against game are provided against by the Game Act, which authorises the owner or his agent to apprehend and detain, for even twelve hours, a trespasser who refuses to tell his true name and place of abode, and to take him before a justice; and such justice, may convict in the penalties for trespassing in pursuit of game, or doing any injury thereto. The action for trespasses against the person, goods, or land is restrained by statutes, providing that the plaintiff, whenever he recovers a verdict for less than 40s., shall have no more costs than damages, unless the judge certify, in cases of trespass to land or buildings, that the trespass was wilful, or that the freehold came in question; or in cases of trespass and assault, a beating be proved, or a tearing of clothes; in all other cases the damages must exceed 40s., or the plaintiff will not recover costs.

Triennial Parliaments were first established by 16 Charles I. c. 1 (Feb. 16, 1641). The Act was passed for the purpose of preventing the sovereign from postponing at will, and frequently indefinitely, the assembling of the Parliament. A statute of Edward III., providing that one should be held every year, or oftener if need be, had long fallen into neglect.

The chief provisions of the Triennial Act were, that a Parliament was to be *ipso facto* dissolved when it had lasted three years, and, if actually sitting at the time, on the first adjournment or prorogation ; that writs for a new Parliament were to be issued by the Chancellor or Keeper of the Great Seal within three years after the dissolution of the last ; in case of his failure to perform this duty, the peers were enjoined to meet and issue writs to the sheriffs ; in case of non-compliance with the law on the part of the peers, the duty devolved upon the sheriffs themselves ; and in case of their failure, the electors, after a certain interval, had the right of choosing their representatives; and that no Parliament was to be dissolved or adjourned, save by its own consent, in less than fifty days from the commencement of the session.   It was violated by Cromwell and the Long Parliament, and was repealed by 16 Charles II. c. 1, April 6, 1664.   Another Act of a similar character, providing that a Parliament should be held at least once every three years, and that no Parliament should last longer than three years, was assented to with great reluctance by Will. III., Dec. 22, 1694; and it was repealed, on the passing of the Septennial Act, May 7, 1716.

Trinity House (London).—This society was founded by Sir Thomas Spert, comptroller of the navy to Henry VIII., A.D. 1515, and incorporated by that king in the same year, for the promotion of commerce and navigation, by licensing and regulating pilots, and ordering and erecting beacons, lighthouses, buoys, &c.   The corporation was confirmed in the enjoyment of its privileges and possessions by letters patent of James II. (1685).   At first it seems to have consisted of seamen only, but now noblemen and gentlemen are amongst its members or elder brethren.   It is governed by a master, four wardens, eight assistants, and thirty-one elder brothers.   The Trinity House is empowered, by 17 & 18 Vict. c. 104, to appoint and license pilots for the following limits :—(1) " The London District," comprising the waters of the Thames and Medway, as high as London Bridge and Rochester Bridge respectively, and also the seas and channels leading thereto or therefrom, as far as Orfordness to the north, and Dungeness to the south ; so, nevertheless, that no pilot shall be hereafter licensed to conduct ships both above and below Gravesend. (2) "The English Channel District," comprising the seas between Dungeness and the Isle of Wight. (3) "The Trinity House Outports District," comprising any pilotage-district for the appointment of pilots, within which no particular provision is made by Act of Parliament or charter. And, in general, the employment of pilots, in the first and third of these districts, is compulsory. But the following ships, when not carrying passengers, shall be exempted from compulsory pilotage in the London District, and the Trinity House Outports Districts. (1) Ships employed in the coasting trade of the United Kingdom. (2) Ships of no more than sixty tons burthen. (3) Ships trading to Boulogne, or to any place in Europe north of Boulogne. (4) Ships from Guernsey, Jersey, Alderney, Sark, or Man, which are wholly laden with stone, the produce of those islands. (5) Ships navigating within the limits of the ports to which they belong. (6) Ships passing through the limits of any pilotage district on their voyages between two places, both situate out of such limits, and not being bound to any place within such limits nor anchoring therein.

True Bill.—The indorsement which the grand jury makes upon a bill of indictment, when having heard the evidence they are satisfied of the truth of the accusation.

Trustee, is a person who holds lands or tenements, or other property, upon the trust, or confidence that he will apply the same for the benefit of those who are entitled, according to an expressed intention, either by the parties themselves, or by the deed, will, settlement, or arrangement of another. All trusts must be expressed or declared in writing ; when the trust is not declared by a will or settlement, the deed expressing the purposes of the trust is termed "a declaration of trust." There are, however, trusts which are implied in law, and which need not be in writing, as, where a man has land or other things conveyed to him, he having purchased the same with the money of another, and for his benefit, or where the owner of property makes a voluntary conveyance to another, and declares the trust of part of it, but is silent as to the disposal of the remainder; in these cases a trust is implied, and, in technical language, results for his own benefit. The Courts of Equity only can take cognisance of trusts, whether expressed, or implied and resulting. The constitution of the courts of law are not framed for any remedy, so that the person in whom or in whose name the land or property is vested, has what is termed the legal estate, *i.e.* the law considers him the owner, as the estate is vested in him. The person for whose benefit the trust is created, is said to have the equitable estate, because his rights are morally defined and relievable in equity. Acts of Parliament have provided for the conveyance or assignment of trust-estates, where the trustees become bankrupt, insolvent, or are of unsound mind, or where they are out of the jurisdiction of the Courts of Equity; and there are scarcely any cases where the Court of Chancery cannot interpose its jurisdiction, as the property of married women, infants, and persons of unsound mind, are peculiar objects of its jurisdiction.

The office of trustee is purely honorary, and he is not entitled to any remuneration for managing the trust funds.

Trustees doing anything not in conformity with their trust, unless their discretion is enlarged, are liable for any deficiencies that may arise from such proceedings.

Trustees having all equal powers cannot act separately and independently of each other.

Fraudulent trustees are punishable by penal servitude for any term not more than seven or less than three years, or by imprisonment for not more than two years. (24 & 25 Vict. c. 96.)

Uniformity, Act of.—By 2 & 3 Edw. VI. c. 1 (Jan. 15, 1549), it was enacted that the order of divine worship contained in the book drawn up by the commissioners, "by the aid of the Holy Ghost," should be the only one used after the next Whitsuntide. Those who refused to use it, or who spoke or wrote against it, were fined for the first or second offence, and rendered subject to forfeiture of goods and imprisonment for life for the third. This statute was confirmed by 5 & 6 Edw. VI. c. 1 (1552), repealed by 1 Mary, c. 2 (1553), and restored by 1 Eliz. c. 2 (1559). It formed the basis of the Act of Uniformity, commonly so called, passed in 1662 (13 & 14 Car. II. c. 4), which contained stringent regulations with respect to the use of the Book of Common Prayer. This Act enjoined uniformity in matters of religion, and obliged all clergy to subscribe to the Thirty-nine Articles and use the same form of worship and same Book of Common Prayer; it received the royal assent May 19th, came into operation August 24, 1662, and was made perpetual as to the establishment of the church by 5 Anne, c. 5 (1706), and by the Act of Union, 5 Anne, c. 7. A similar Act was passed by the Irish Parliament (17 & 18 Car. II. c. 6) in 1665.

Union of England and Scotland.—Union, or The Union, by way of eminence, is more particularly used to express the Act 5 & 6 Anne, c. 8, by which the two separate kingdoms of England and Scotland were incorporated into one, under the title of the kingdom of Great Britain. This Union, in vain attempted by King James I., was at length effected in the year 1707, when twenty-five articles were agreed to by the Parliaments of both nations; the purport of the most considerable being as follows :—

I. That on the 1st of May, 1707, and for ever after, the kingdoms of England and Scotland shall be united into one kingdom, by the name of Great Britain.

2. The succession to the monarchy of Great Britain shall be the same as was before settled with regard to that of England.

3. The United Kingdom shall be represented by one Parliament.

4. There shall be a communication of all rights and privileges between the subjects of both kingdoms, except where it is otherwise agreed.

9. When England raises £2,000,000 by a land-tax, Scotland shall raise £48,000.

16, 17. The standards of the coin, of weights, and of measures, shall be reduced to those of England throughout the United Kingdoms.

18. The laws relating to trade, customs, and the excise, shall be the same in Scotland as in England. But all the other laws of Scotland shall remain in force ; but alterable by the Parliament of Great Britain. Yet with this caution, that laws relating to public policy are alterable at the discretion of the Parliament; laws relating to private right are not to be altered but for the evident utility of the people of Scotland.

22. Sixteen peers are to be chosen to represent the peerage of Scotland in Parliament, and forty-five members to sit in the House of Commons.

. 23. The sixteen peers of Scotland shall have all privileges of Parliament ; and all peers of Scotland shall be peers of Great Britain, and rank next after those of the same degree at the time of the Union, and shall have all privileges of peers, except sitting in the House of Lords, and voting on the trial of a peer.

These are the principal of the twenty-five articles of union, which are ratified and confirmed by statute 5 & 6 Anne, c. 8, in which statute there are also two Acts of Parliament recited ; the one of Scotland, whereby the Church of Scotland, and also the four universities of that kingdom, are established for ever, and all succeeding sovereigns are to take an oath inviolably to maintain the same ; the other of England, whereby the Acts of Uniformity of 13 Eliz., and 13 Car. II., (except as the same had been altered by Parliament at that time), and all other Acts then in force for the preservation of the Church of England, are declared perpetual; and it is stipulated, that every subsequent king and queen shall take an oath inviolably to maintain the same within England, Ireland, Wales, and the town of Berwick upon Tweed. And it is enacted, that these two Acts "shall for ever be observed as fundamental and essential conditions of the union." Upon these articles and Act 'of Union, it is to be observed, 1. That the two kingdoms are so inseparably united, that nothing can ever disunite them; except the mutual consent of both, or the successful resistance of either, upon apprehending an infringement of those points which, when they were separate and independent nations, it was mutually stipulated should be "fundamental and essential conditions of the union." 2. That whatever else may be deemed "fundamental and essential conditions," the preservation of the two churches, of England and Scotland, in the same state that they were in at the time of the Union, and the maintenance of the Acts of Uniformity which established the liturgy, are expressly declared so to be. 3. That therefore any alteration in the constitution of either of these churches, or in the liturgy of the Church of England (unless with the consent of the respective churches, collectively or representatively given), would be an infringement of these "fundamental and essential conditions," and greatly endanger the union. 4. That the municipal laws of Scotland are ordained to be still observed in that part of the island, unless altered by Parliament; and as the Parliament has not yet thought fit, except in a few particulars, to alter them, they are to remain in full force as before the Union, except in those aforesaid particulars.

Union of England and Ireland.—The legislative Union of Great Britain and Ireland was alluded to by George III. in his speech at the opening of Parliament, Jan.

22, 1800. A bill (39 & 40 Geo. III. c. 47), embodying articles of union, was introduced by Pitt, and received the royal assent July 2, 1800. The statute (40 Geo. III. c. 38) passed the Irish Parliament June 13, 1800, and the Union took effect from Jan. 1, 1801. The purport of the eight articles is as follows :—

I. Ireland and Great Britain to be united by the name of the United Kingdom of Great Britain and Ireland.

II. The succession to the United Kingdom to be the same as it stood before the Union.

III. The United Kingdom to be represented in one Parliament.

IV. Four lords spiritual of Ireland by rotation of sessions, and twenty-eight lords temporal of Ireland, elected for life by the peers of Ireland, to sit in the House of Lords. One hundred commoners to sit and vote in the House of Commons on the part of Ireland. An Irish peer not elected for the House of Lords can serve in the Commons, but *not* for an Irish constituency. No creation of an Irish peerage to take place till three Irish peerages be extinct, until their number is reduced to one hundred.

V. The Churches of England and Ireland to be united into one Protestant Episcopal Church, and the doctrine, worship, discipline, and government to be the same as established in England. The preservation of the united church to be a fundamental part of the Union.

VI. The subjects of Great Britain and Ireland to have the same rights and privileges in trade and navigation, and also in treaties with foreign powers.

VII. The interest of the national debt of each country is to be defrayed by each separately.

VIII. All laws and courts of each kingdom are to remain as

before the Union, subject, however, to alterations by the united Parliament.

The Union of England and Wales.—The finishing stroke to the independence of Wales, which had been almost abolished by the conquest of that principality by Edward I., was given by the statute 27 Hen. VIII. c. 26, which enacted:—

I. That the dominion of Wales shall be for ever united to the kingdom of England.

II. That all Welshmen born shall have the same liberties as other the king's subjects.

III. That lands in Wales shall be inheritable according to the English tenures and rules of descent.

IV. That the laws of England, *and none other*, shall be used in Wales, besides many other regulations of the police of this principality.

And the statute 34 & 35 Hen. VIII. c. 26, confirms the above, adding further regulations, and dividing Wales into twelve shires. After this act Wales still had courts within itself, independent of the process of Westminster Hall; till the statute 11 Geo. IV. & 1 Will. IV. c. 70, abolished those courts, and rendered the administration of justice in the principality uniform with that of England. By 8 & 9 Vict. c. 11, the manner of assigning sheriffs in Wales is regulated by and assimilated to that of England. The 26 & 27 Vict. c. 82, empowers the bishops of Welsh dioceses to facilitate the making provision for English services in certain parishes in Wales.

University Courts.—The Chancellor's Courts in the two Universities enjoy the sole jurisdiction, in exclusion of the Queen's Courts, over all actions and suits whatsoever, excepting where a right of freehold is concerned, and of all injuries and trespasses against the peace, mayhem and felony excepted, when a scholar or privileged person is one of the parties. By the University charter they are at liberty to try and determine these suits, either according to the common law of the land, or according to their own local customs, at their discretion. The Judge of the Chancellor's Court at Oxford is the Vice-Chancellor, who is deputy or assessor. From his sentence an appeal lies to delegates appointed by the Congregation; thence to other delegates of the House of Convocation; and if they all three concur in the same sentence, it is final, at least by the statutes of the University, according to the rule of the civil law. But if there be any discordance or variation in any of the three sentences, an appeal lies in the last resort to Judges, delegates appointed by the Crown under the Great Seal in Chancery. By 17 & 18 Vict. c. 81, s. 45, the Court of the Vice-Chancellor of Oxford is now governed by the common and statute law of the realm, and no longer by the rules of the civil law. As to Cambridge, the right of the University, or any member thereof, to claim conusance of any action or criminal proceeding wherein any person who is not a member of the University is a party, has ceased and determined.

Uses and Trusts are akin to each other; a use being in law the profit of lands and tenements, upon a trust and confidence reposed in another, that he to whose use the trust is made, shall take the profits thereof. All modern conveyances are, directly or indirectly, founded on the doctrine of uses and trusts, which has been deemed the most intricate part of our property-law. Uses and trusts, being acts of confidence reposed, are cognisable in equity, when coupled with the performance of any act tending to the benefit of the party for whose enjoyment the use or trust was created. Uses, as a term, are applied to lands of inheritance; and the party *to whose use* they are conveyed has the absolute possession. The person to whose use a conveyance is made, is termed the *cestui que* use. Uses only apply to land of inheritance: the trust, being a creature of equity, only attaches on the profits or personalty. Uses and trusts do not practically interfere with the purchaser's possession of land: they are only used when estates are settled, or it is requisite to vest the property in third persons, without interfering with the temporary possession, which may be vested in A. in trust for B. for life, remainder to C. for life, remainder to D. and his heirs, and the like of trusts.   Persons, also, whose estates are in trust, can sell their estates independent of their trustees, though it is safer to obtain their concurrence, as they may have had notice of claims affecting the *cestui que trust* property, and, of course, would be considered as trustees for those claimants in equity.

The reader is referred to the second volume of Blackstone's Commentaries, c. xx., and to Wharton's Law Lexicon, article Uses, for more information on this head.

Usury.—The offence of taking a greater interest than £5 per cent. per annum, which is punishable by a forfeiture of treble the money borrowed, one half to the prosecutor, the other half to the Crown.   By an old statute, the repurchase of goods (with knowledge of their being the same) at a lesser price, of the party originally selling the same, subjects the party to the same penalty.   It seems any transaction, whereby to secure by indirect means the repayment of a loan with more than lawful interest, is usurious, and therefore not good in law. And, in some particular instances, the actual advance of *money* is not necessary to constitute usury, for *goods* may be delivered. The question of usury, or whether a contract is a colour and pretence for an usurious loan, or is a fair and honest transaction, must, under all its circumstances, be determined by a jury.   Usurious bargains, or, rather, loans *morally* usurious, are often protected by lending the money upon contingency, as annuities, or making the repayment to depend upon certain lives being in existence at a particular time; but these last can be set aside upon terms, if outrageously oppressive.   By 13 Geo. III. c. 63, the highest rate of legal interest to be taken on any contract by any British subject in the East Indies is £12 per cent. The 17 & 18 Vict. c. 90, repeals all existing laws against usury.

Vaccination.—Dr. Edward Jenner's attention was first directed to this subject A.D. 1768, and he tried it on a boy with matter procured from the hand of a dairymaid who had contracted cow-pox, May 14, 1796. The boy was inoculated with small-pox matter by way of experiment, July 1, 1796, and no disease followed. An act (3 & 4 Vict. c. 29) to extend its practice was passed July 23, 1840; and another (4 & 5 Vict. c. 24) provided for its gratuitous performance to the poor, June 21, 1841. An act to extend and enforce the practice of Vaccination (16 & 17 Vict. c. 100) was passed Aug. 20, 1853, which has been amended by 21 Vict. c. 25, and 24 & 25 Vict. c. 59.

Vagrants, or Vagabonds.—This class of wanderers is referred to in the "Statute of Labourers" (23 Edw. III. c. 1), passed A.D. 1349. Numerous penal enactments were made to prevent the increase of vagrancy. By 1 & 2 Edw. VI. c. 3 (1547), any person who had offered them work which they refused was authorised to brand them on the breast with a V, hold them in slavery for two years, feed them during that period on bread and water, and hire them out to others. Inoperative from its severity, this Act was repealed in 1549. The privy council having issued circular letters to the sheriffs of counties to apprehend all "vagabonds and sturdy beggars, commonly called Egyptians," 13,000 were taken up in 1569. All previous laws on the subject were remodelled by 17 Geo. II. c. 5 (1744), which distributed them into the three classes of—idle and disorderly persons, rogues and vagabonds, and incorrigible rogues. The law is at present regulated by 5 Geo. IV. c. 83 (1824), amended by 1 & 2 Vict. c. 38 (July 27, 1838).

Verdict.—The determination of a jury declared to a judge. The verdict is either general or special. If there be several issues, the verdict may be distributed, some issues being found for the plaintiff and others for the defendant. A verdict must comprehend the whole issues submitted to a jury in the particular cause. A special verdict must state the facts proved at the trial, and not merely the evidence given to prove those facts, otherwise it will be insufficient and the Court will award a trial *de novo*.

Verdicts in criminal cases may be either general as guilty or not guilty ; or special, setting forth all the circumstances, and praying the judgment of the Court, whether upon the facts stated, there exists a crime in law.

Verge.—The compass of the Queen's Court, which bounds the jurisdiction of the Lord Steward of the Household : it appears to have been about twelve miles.

Vestries are meetings in the " vestry," which is a place or room adjoining to a church, where the vestments of the minister are kept. The minister, churchwardens, and chief men of a parish, do generally constitute a vestry, and they appoint a clerk, styled a " vestry clerk," who draws up and enters their acts in a book of which he generally has the custody. The office of a vestry clerk is not fixed, but temporary, and at will. Vestries for church matters are to be regularly called by the " churchwardens, with the consent of the minister : " for the statute law has not altered the general authority under which, or the persons by whom, vestries are to be called. The persons who are ordinarily entitled to be admitted to a vestry generally are, parishioners paying scot and lot, and all persons occupying land in the parish, although " foreigners " or out-dwellers. And the rector, vicar, or curate also has a right to be admitted into the vestry, and to vote, although not assessed to the church-rates, and the minister has a right to preside over the meeting, whether rector, vicar, or perpetual curate, and, indeed, the minister is entitled to preside. The majority of the vestrymen present bind the absent parishioners in the matters which properly and legally are cognizable by a vestry, which are the investigation into, and restraining the expenditure of the parish funds, and the enlarging or alteration of the churches or chapels within the parish. The appointment of many of the parish

Y

officers rests also with the vestry, and certainly in all weighty matters the vestry has a superintending and controlling authority. A custom has obtained in large and populous parishes of yearly choosing a select number of the chief parishioners to represent and manage the concerns of the parish for that year. They are called a select vestry.

Vice Admiralty Courts. — Tribunals established in Her Majesty's possessions beyond the seas, with jurisdiction over maritime causes including those relating to prize. Their jurisdiction is amended and clearly set forth by the " Vice Admiralty Courts Act," 26 Vict. c. 24.

Vice Chamberlain.—A great officer, next under the Lord Chamberlain, who, in his absence, has the control of all officers appertaining to that part of the royal household which is called the chamber above stairs.

Vice-Chancellors in Equity. — There· are three : the Vice-Chancellor of England and two juniors. Each of these sits separately from the Lord Chancellor and Lords Justices, to whom an appeal lies from their decisions.

Viscount (*Vice Comes*), was anciently an officer under an earl, to whom, during his attendance at Court, he acted as deputy to look after the affairs of the county. But the name was afterwards made use of as an arbitrary title of honour, without any shadow of office pertaining to it, by Henry VI. A viscount is created by patent as an earl is ; his title is Right Honourable, and he ranks between an earl and a baron.

Volunteer Act.—An Act passed in 1863 (26 & 27 Vict. c. 65), which repealed the statutes on the subjects previously in force. It is divided into seven parts :—1. The organisation of the volunteer force. 2. Actual military service. 3. Discipline. 4. Rules and property of corps. 5. Acquisition of land for ranges. 6. Exemptions ; and .7., Miscellaneous provisions. Royal Naval Volunteers, see 22 & 23 Vict. c. 40 ; and 24 & 25 Vict. c. 129.

Vulgar Errors. — Erroneous notions. The following are a few of the most prominent, in reference to legal matters :—

1. That a funeral procession passing over private grounds creates a public right of way.

2. That it is lawful to arrest and detain a dead body.

3. That first cousins may intermarry, and that second cousins may not : whereas they may both marry with each other.

4. That a butcher or surgeon cannot be sworn as a juryman on a coroner's inquisition.

5. That all persons born at sea, claim a right of settlement in Stepney parish.

6. That a lease for more than ninety-nine years constitutes a freehold.

7. That a husband is punishable for his wife's criminal acts.

8. That to disinherit a child the sum of one shilling should be bequeathed.

9. That it is penal to open a coal mine, or to kill a crow within five miles of London.

10. That the sovereign signs the death warrant for the execution of a criminal.

11. That a woman by marrying a man under the gallows will save him from execution.

12. That it costs only 1s. 1½d. to be hanged.

13. That old statutes have prohibited the planting of vineyards ; or the use of sawing mills, &c., &c.

Wales, Union of. *See* UNION OF.

War Office.—The present organisation of the War Office dates only from 1854-5, when the extensive Ordnance departments, the Commissariat, and the Secretary at War were abolished, and the duties transferred to the Secretary of State for War. By this consolidation of offices an establishment was formed having the administration of all war matters and the entire supervision of the army at home and abroad. The Secretary of State for War is assisted in the discharge of his official duties by two Under-Secretaries of State and a large staff of military and civil officials. Hours, 10 to 4. Pall-mall.

Wagers.—It is well established at common law that a wager is a legal contract, which the courts are bound to enforce, although it be in respect of a matter which is trifling, or in which the parties have no interest; but if it be on a subject which is illegal, or which offends against public policy, it is void. And wagers which tend to affect the feelings and interests of third parties, or lead to indecent exposures and examinations, or are, in any manner, *contra bonos mores*, are void. But by 8 & 9 Vict. c. 109, wagers are considered void.

Ward.—The relation of guardian and ward is very similar to that of parent and child. When the care of infants is vested in the Chancellor, he will compel, or rather assist, a guardian in compelling a ward to obey the reasonable desires of a guardian, in relation to education and advancement in life. A guardian can have a writ of *habeas corpus* to recover possession of his ward, if detained without the ward's consent, or he may proceed, by petition to the Chancellor, to regain the custody of the infant. To abduct a ward from the custody of his guardian is a misdemeanor. With regard to female wards, if they be placed under the control of the Court of Chancery, and almost any property will give the Court jurisdiction, a very jealous power is exercised, it being deemed a contempt of that Court to marry one of its wards without consent, wittingly or unwittingly. Where a marriage is contemplated between a gentleman and a ward of Court, proposals are laid (by leave previously obtained of the Court) before a Commissioner in Chancery, who reports upon the fitness of the marriage, and a settlement is prepared accordingly; or, in consideration of the intended husband making a settlement, the ward's property may be paid over to them both on marriage, or otherwise. Guardians misconducting themselves may be removed.

Wardmote.—A court held in every ward in London. The wardmote inquest has power to inquire into the state of the efficiency of the police ; to provide against fire ; to put down gaming-houses ; to punish beggars and vagrants ; to see that the weights and measures are lawful, &c.

Wards and Liveries, Court of.—A court erected by 32 Hen. VIII. c. 46, and abolished by 12 Car. II. c. 24.

Warrants of Attorney and Cognovits.—These are writings, the effect of which is to enable another party to obtain a judgment in a civil action against the person subscribing them. A warrant of attorney is an authority under seal to certain attorneys, or, indeed, any attorney, to appear for the party subscribing the same, in a named court, in an action of debt for a specific sum, which is of sufficient amount to cover a principal sum, interest, and all expenses, as due upon an account stated, or for money borrowed ; and, thereupon, to confess judgment, or otherwise to suffer a judgment in any manner to pass against the party, in order that execution for the said sum and all other expenses may issue against him. This is often used as a security where no action is pending, and a most conclusive one it is, for it gives the holder of it (who must be the person named therein, at whose suit the proceedings are to take place, or his executors or assigns) absolute authority to levy an execution upon the defendant, or to take his person. Judgments may be entered up upon this instrument at any time within twenty years, if the subscribing party be alive ; but, after ten years old, the courts require that notice may be given the party, so that he may be able to show cause against its being put in force.

Where a female marries after having given a warrant of attorney, judgment may be entered up against her and her husband. Persons in custody (not taken in execution), who execute this security as a consideration for their being liberated, must have the presence of an attorney, who is bound to explain the nature of this security : if this requisite is not complied with, the instrument can be set aside. By 1 & 2 Vict. c. 110, it is enacted that from and after the 1st of October, 1838, no warrant of attorney to confess judgment in any personal action or *cognovit actionem*, given by any person, shall be of any force, unless there shall be present some attorney of one of the superior courts on behalf of such person, expressly named by him and attending at his request, to inform him of the nature and effect of such warrant or cognovit before the same is executed, which attorney shall subscribe his name as a witness to the due execution thereof, and thereby declare himself to be attorney for the person executing the same, and state that he subscribes as such attorney.

Warrants of attorney and cognovits are legal instruments, of which the courts will take notice, upon a summary application by motion in term time, if they are wrongfully or wickedly used, or if the consideration was illegal or grossly usurious; but this summary jurisdiction applies chiefly to warrants of attorney, which are given usually independent of any action, whereas cognovits are a proceeding in an action; yet, if an action is commenced for the sole purpose of a cognovit being given in order to enforce an illegal consideration or usurious demand, the same reason will apply, and the court interfere accordingly.

Warranty.—The seller of goods is not liable to the purchaser, if the purchaser be disturbed by adverse claimants, or the quality is deficient, except there is an express warranty or promise of indemnity, or there has been fraud or wilful misrepresentation, or, what is the same thing, concealment.

The buyer paying a liberal price for the articles does not imply a warranty. This contract should be expressed; and where the magnitude of the transaction would ordinarily induce the caution, it should be reduced into writing.

A warranty must ordinarily be special, and not generally, as to the goodness of the thing sold; it should be made at or before the actual sale, and not after it.

It is not necessary to return the goods previously to an action being commenced for damages; for the buyer may recover the difference between the sum he gave and that produced by a re-sale, or the difference between the real value (if he keep them) and the sum he paid. It is safer, however, to offer to return the goods; and in cases where the terms of the warranty are to "take back the goods, and return the money," such offer to return must be made before action brought, and within a reasonable time after a discovery of the misrepresentation. If the seller refuse to take back the goods, they remain at his own risk, and the buyer, notwithstanding, may proceed to recover the whole sum.

Ways.—There are four kinds of way:—1, a footway; 2, a horseway, which includes a footway; 3, a carriage way, which includes both horseway and footway; 4, a driftway. Although a carriageway comprehends a horseway, yet it does not necessarily include a driftway; it is said, however, that evidence of a carriageway is strong presumptive evidence of the grant of a driftway. A right of way may be either public or private; ways common to all the queen's subjects are called highways. A way leading to a market town, and common for all travellers, and communicating with any great road, is a highway; but if it lead only to a church, or to a house, or village, or to the fields, it is a private way; whether it be a public or private way, it is a matter of fact, and depends much on common reputation. The public may have a right to a high road as a common street, although there be no thoroughfare.

It may be taken as a general rule, that where the public have for twenty years, or private parties for thirty years or more, used the way without interruption, in the case of the public, a dedication, and to the private party or class of individuals, a licence or permission, will be presumed, and after sixty years' uninterrupted enjoyment or use by both, nothing can avail in favour of the owner of the land.

Ways and Means, Committee of.—This committee, which is always one of the whole House, inquires into the funds by which the expenditure of the nation is to be sustained. Loans, duties, taxes, tolls, and every kind of means for raising revenue are submitted to a committee of Ways and Means. The propositions of Government on these subjects are reduced to the form of resolutions, and such as are agreed to reported to the House. Those which may be there adopted are embodied into bills, and in due course become law. The Lords may reject but cannot modify, nor can they insert pecuniary penalties in any bill whatever.

Weights.—A national standard of weight was first established in England A.D. 1197, and a uniformity of weight throughout the kingdom was ordered by 9 Hen. III. c. 25 (1225). By 51 Hen. III. st. 1, c. 3 (1266), an English penny, weighing thirty-two wheat corns from the midst of the ear, was made the standard weight. The weight of the pound was regulated by 31 Edw. I. c. 1 (1303), and a uniform weight throughout the realm was ordered by 27 Edw. III. st. 2, c. 10 (1353). By 8 Hen. VI. c. 5 (1429), every city was ordered to have a common balance and weights, for the free use of the inhabitants. Standard weights of brass were ordered to be made and sent to every city and borough by 7 Hen. VII. c. 4 (1490), which was extended and confirmed by 11 Hen. VII. c. 4 (1494). Avoirdupois weight is first mentioned by 24 Hen. VIII. c. 3 (1532), where it is ordered to be used in the sale of butchers' meat. Uniformity of weights and measures was again enjoined by 16 Charles I. c. 19 (1648). The House of Commons appointed committees in 1758, 1759, and 1790, to examine the best means of securing an accurate standard of weights and measures. By 35 Geo III. c. 102 (June 22, 1795), the justices at quarter sessions were empowered to appoint examiners of weights and scales, and in 1814 parliament appointed another committee to consider the question of standard. The prince regent instituted a commission for the same purpose in 1819, which presented reports in 1819, 1820, and 1821, and procured the Act 5 Geo. IV. c. 74 (June 17, 1824), for establishing uniformity of weights and measures. This was amended by 4 & 5 Will. IV. c. 49 (Aug. 13, 1834), and both Acts were repealed by 5 & 6 Will. IV. c. 63 (Sept. 9, 1835). Troy weight is ordered to be used in sales of bullion and precious stones by 16 & 17 Vict. c. 29 (June 14, 1853). Further provisions for legalizing and preserving the standard were made by 18 & 19 Vict. c. 72, 22 & 23 Vict. c. 56, 23 & 24 Vict. c. 146, and 24 & 25 Vict. cc. 75 and 79.

Will.—The legal declaration of a man's intentions, which he wills to be performed after his death. The law with respect to wills is now regulated by 7 Will. IV. and 1 Vict. c. 26, commonly called the Wills Act.

The *first* section enacts, that the word "will" shall extend to a testament, and to a codicil, and to any other testamentary disposition, and also defines the meaning of the words "real estate" and "personal estate" as used in the Act.

The *second* section repeals various previous Acts relating to wills.

The *third* section enacts that it shall be lawful for every person to bequeath, or dispose of real estate, and all personal estate which he shall be entitled to at the time of his death, and the power given shall extend to all real estate of the nature of customary freehold or tenant-right, or customary or copyhold; also all estates *pur autre vie*, all contingent interests, and all rights of entry and property acquired even *subsequently* to the execution of his will.

The *fourth* section provides for the payment of the stamp duties, fines and fees.

The *fifth* section enacts, that when any real estate of the nature of customary freehold or tenant-right, or customary or copyhold, shall be disposed of by will, so much of the will as shall contain such disposition shall be entered on the court-rolls of the manor or reputed manor of which it is holden; and the lord shall be entitled to the same fine, heriot, dues, duties and services from the devisee as would have been due from the customary heir, in case of the descent of the same real estate.

The *sixth* section enacts, that if no disposition by will be made of any estate *pur autre vie* of a freehold nature, the same shall be chargeable in the hands of the heir, if it come to him by reason of special occupancy, as assets by descent, as in the case of freehold land in fee-simple; and in the case of there being no special occupant of any estate *pur autre vie*, whether freehold or customary freehold, tenant-right, customary or copy-hold, or of any other tenure, and whether a corporeal or incorporeal here-ditament, it shall go to the executor or administrator of the party that had the estate thereof by virtue of the grant, and if it come to the executor or administrator either by reason of a special occupancy, or by virtue of this Act, it shall be assets in his hands, and shall be applied and distributed in the same manner as the personal estate of the testator or intestate.

The *seventh* section enacts, that no will made by any person under the age of twenty-one years shall be valid. At common law, idiots, lunatics, (except during lucid intervals), persons imbecile from disease, old age, or drunkenness, are incapable of making a will. One who is born deaf and dumb is presumed by the law to be an idiot; but such presumption may be rebutted; and if it can be proved that he understands the nature of the act, and desires to make a will, he may declare his will by signs and tokens. In the case of a blind testator, it is necessary to prove his knowledge and approval of the contents of the will he has executed. Wills made under mistake, or obtained by fraud, or by undue influence, are inoperative. Traitors and felons are incapable of making testaments from the time of their conviction, except as to trust property. A *felo de se* cannot make a will of personalty, although he may devise lands. Out-laws are incapable of making wills of personalty so long as the outlawry continues; but he who is outlawed in a personal action may devise his lands. An alien friend may make a will of personalty, but not of realty. An alien enemy, unless he has obtained the Sovereign's license to reside in this country, is incapable of making any will.

By section *eight* no will made by any married woman shall be valid, *except* such a will as might have been made by a married woman before the passing of this Act.

A married woman, as a general rule, is incapable of devising lands and of making a testament of personalty without her husband's consent. The husband may, however, by waiving his right to be his wife's administrator, empower her to make a will of personalty, but he may revoke his assent at any time before probate, and it is therefore necessary to prove his assent when probate is prayed. His assent only gives validity to the wife's will if he survives her.

To this general rule there are some exceptions. A married woman may, by special custom, devise her copyholds. She may also make a will in pursuance of an ante-nuptial agreement, or of a post-nuptial agreement for consideration, or by virtue of a power; and she may dispose of per-sonalty actually given and settled, or agreed to be given and settled to her separate use, whether it be in possession or in reversion, and this rule extends to savings out of her personal property. In these cases probate can be obtained without the husband's assent, limited to the property of which the testatrix had power to dispose.

A wife who has obtained a protection order for her property, on the ground of her husband's desertion, or who has been judicially separated from her husband, may dispose of her property in all respects as if she were a *feme sole*.

A married woman, who is an executrix, may make a will for the mere purpose of devolving her representative character on another, even without her husband's assent. The Act will probably not be held to dispense with the surrender to the use of the will of a married woman, as to lands which she may devise by special custom, inasmuch as a surrender implied an examination of the married woman by the steward, touching her free will and intention. If the husband have abjured the realm, or been banished, the wife's disability ceases both as to real and personal estate.

The *fourteenth* section enacts, that if any person, who shall attest the execution of a will, shall, at the time of the execution, or at any time afterwards, be incompetent to be admitted a witness to prove the execution thereof, such will shall not on that account be invalid.

The *fifteenth* section enacts, that if any person shall attest the execution of any will, to whom or to whose wife or husband any beneficial devise, legacy, estate, interest, gift, or appointment, of or affecting any real or personal estate (other than and except charges and directions for the payment of any debt or debts) shall be thereby given or made, such devise, &c., shall, so far only as concerns such person attesting the execution of such will, or the wife or husband of such person, or any person claiming under such person or wife or husband, be utterly null and void, and such person, so attesting, shall be admitted as a witness to prove the execution of such will, or to prove the validity or invalidity thereof, notwithstanding such devise, &c.

The *sixteenth* section enacts, that in case by any will any real or personal estate shall be charged with any debt or debts, and any creditor, or the wife or husband of any creditor whose debt is so charged, shall attest the execution of such will, such creditor shall be admitted a witness to prove the execution of such will, or to prove the validity or invalidity thereof.

The *seventeenth* section enacts, that no person shall, on account of his being an executor of a will, be incompetent to be admitted a witness to prove the execution of such will, or a witness to prove the validity or invalidity thereof.

The *ninth* section enacts, "that no will shall be valid unless it shall be in writing and executed in manner hereinafter mentioned; (that is to say) it shall be signed at the foot or end thereof by the testator or by some other person in his presence and by his direction, and such signature shall be made or acknowledged by the testator in the presence of two or more witnesses present at the same time, and such witnesses shall attest and shall subscribe the will in the presence of the testator; but no form of attestation shall be necessary." Some doubts having arisen as to the meaning of the words "foot or end thereof" in this sect. the 15 Vict. c. 24, was passed which enacts, "that every will shall, so far only as regards the position of the signature of the testator or of the person signing for him as aforesaid, be deemed to be valid within the said enactment as explained by this Act, if the signature shall be so placed at or after, or following, or under, or beside, or opposite to the end of the will, that it shall be apparent on the face of the will that the testator intended to give effect by such his signature to the writing signed as his will, and that no such will shall be affected by the circumstance that the signature shall not follow or be immediately after the foot or end of the will, or by the circumstance that a blank space shall intervene between the concluding word of the will and the signature, or by the circumstance that the signature shall be placed among the words of the testimonium clause, or of the clause of attestation, or shall follow or be after or under the clause of attestation, either with or without a blank space intervening, or shall follow or be after or under or beside the names or one of the names of the subscribing witnesses, or by the circumstance that the signature shall be on a side or page or other portion of the paper or papers containing the will whereon no clause or paragraph or disposing part of the will shall be written above the signature, or by the circumstance that there shall appear to be sufficient space on or at the bottom of the preceding side or page or other portion of the same paper on which the will is written to contain the signature ; and the enumeration of the above circumstances shall not restrict the generality of the above enactment, but no signature under the said Act or this Act shall be operative to give effect to any disposition or direction which is underneath or which follows it, nor shall it give effect to any disposition or direction inserted after the signature shall be made."

The *eleventh* section excepts from the rule that all wills must be in writing, wills of personal estate made by soldiers in actual military service, or seamen at sea. This exception includes military and naval officers of all ranks.

With regard to the revocation of wills, it is enacted by the *eighteenth* section "that every will made by a man or woman shall be revoked by his or her marriage, except a will made in exercise of a power of appointment, when the real or personal estate thereby appointed would not, in default of such appointment, pass to his or her heir, customary heir, executor, or administrator, or the person entitled as his or her next of kin under the Statute of Distributions ;" by the *nineteenth* section, "that no will shall be revoked by any presumption of an intention on the ground of an alteration in circumstances ;" by the *twentieth* section, "that no will or codicil or any part thereof, shall be revoked otherwise than as aforesaid, or by another will or codicil executed in manner hereinbefore required, or by some writing declaring an intention to revoke the same, and executed in the manner in which a will is hereinbefore required to be executed, or by the burning, tearing, or otherwise destroying the same by the testator, or by some person in his presence and by his direction, with the intention of revoking the same ;" and by the *twenty-third* section, "that no conveyance or other act made or done subsequently to the execution of a will of or relating to any real or personal estate therein comprised, except an act by which such will shall be revoked as aforesaid, shall prevent the operation of the will with respect to such estate or interest in such real or personal estate as the testator shall have power to dispose of by will at the time of his death."

The *twenty-first* section relates to obliterations, interlineations, and other alterations in wills, and enacts, "that no obliteration, interlineation, or other alteration made in any will after the execution thereof shall be valid or have any effect except so far as the words or effect of the will before such alteration shall not be apparent, unless such alteration shall be executed in like manner as hereinbefore is required for the execution of the will, but the will with such alteration as part thereof shall be deemed to be duly executed if the signature of the testator and the subscription of the witnesses be made in the margin or on some other part of the will opposite or near to such alteration, or at the foot or end of or opposite to a memorandum referring to such alteration, and written at the end or some other part of the will."

The *thirteenth* section enacts, "that every will executed in manner hereinbefore required shall be valid without any other publication thereof."

With regard to the revival of a revoked will, the *twenty-second* section enacts, that no will, or codicil, or any part thereof, which shall be in any manner revoked shall be revived otherwise than by the re-execution thereof, or by a codicil executed in manner hereinbefore required, and showing an intention to revive the same ; and when any will or codicil which shall be partly revoked, and afterwards wholly revoked, shall be revived, such revival shall not extend to so much thereof as shall have been revoked before the revocation of the whole thereof, unless an intention to the contrary shall be shown."

As to the time from which a will speaks, the *twenty-fourth* section enacts, "that every will shall be construed, with reference to the real estate and personal estate comprised in it, to speak and take effect as if it had been executed immediately before the death of the testator, unless a contrary intention shall appear by the will."

As to the construction of a general devise of lands, the *twenty-sixth* section enacts, "that a devise of the land of the testator, or of the land of the testator in any place, or in the occupation of any person mentioned in his will, or otherwise described in a general manner, and any other general devise which would describe a customary, copyhold, or leasehold estate if the testator had no freehold estate which could be described by it, shall be construed to include the customary copyhold and leasehold estates of the testator, or his customary copyhold and leasehold estates, or any of them, to which such description shall extend, as the case may be, as well as freehold estates, unless a contrary intention shall appear by the will."

As to the expressions necessary to execute a general power, the *twenty-seventh* section enacts, that a devise or bequest in general terms, of real or personal property, shall be construed to include any property, coming within the description, which the testator may have power to appoint in any manner he may think proper, unless a contrary intention shall appear.

The *twenty-ninth* section enacts, "that in any devise or bequest of real or personal estate, the words "die without issue," or "die without leaving issue," or "have no issue," or any other words which may import either a want or failure of issue of any person in his lifetime or at the time of his death, or an indefinite failure of his issue, shall be construed to mean a want or failure of issue in the lifetime or at the time of the death of such person, and not an indefinite failure of his issue, unless a contrary intention shall appear by the will, by reason of such person having a prior estate-tail, or of a preceding gift, being, without any implication arising from such words, a limitation of an estate-tail to such person, or issue, or otherwise; provided, that this Act shall not extend to cases where such words as aforesaid import if no issue described in a preceding gift shall be born, or if there shall be no issue who shall live to attain the age, or otherwise answer the description required for obtaining a vested estate, by a preceding gift to such issue."

As to the estate of trustees under a general devise the *thirtieth* section enacts, that "where any real estate (other than or not being a presentation to a church) shall be devised to any trustee or executor, such devise shall be construed to pass the fee-simple or other the whole estate or interest which the testator had power to dispose of by will in such real estate, unless a definite term of years, absolute or determinable, or an estate of freehold, shall thereby be given to him expressly or by implication."

The *thirty-first* section enacts, that "where any real estate shall be devised to a trustee, without any express limitation of the estate to be taken by such trustee, and the beneficial interest in such real estate, or in the surplus rents and profits thereof, shall not be given to any person for life, or such beneficial interest shall be given to any person for life, but the purposes of the trust may continue beyond the life of such person, such devise shall be construed to vest in such trustee the fee-simple, or other the whole legal estate which the testator had power to dispose of by will in such real estate, and not an estate determinable when the purposes of the trust shall be satisfied."

The *thirty-fourth* section enacts, "that this Act shall not extend to any will made *before* 1st January, 1838, and that every will re-executed or republished, or revived by any codicil, shall for the purposes of this Act, be deemed to have been made at the time at which the same shall be so re-executed, republished, or revived; and that this Act shall not extend to any estate *pur autre vie* of any person who shall die *before* 1st January, 1838."

The *thirty-fifth* section enacts, that this Act shall not extend to Scotland.*

---

* Wharton's "Law Lexicon," article "Will condensed."

Witness.—One who gives evidence in a cause ; and, being an indifferent party, is sworn to "speak the truth, the whole truth, and nothing but the truth." The process for compelling the attendance of witnesses before courts of law, examiners in chancery, or the exchequer, or the criminal courts, is a writ of *subpœna*, commanding the witness that, *under a penalty*, he appear and testify in a certain cause, naming it, on the part of the plaintiff or defendant. Refusal or neglect, after a sufficient sum tendered for expenses, subjects the party to an attachment for contempt, or £100 penalty, and damages to the party grieved. Witnesses are entitled to their expenses going, staying, and returning ; and if these are not tendered with the subpœna, they may refuse to give evidence ; but in and near London, it is not usual to give witnesses more than 1s. with the subpœna. Medical men and attornies, and those whose time is part or means of their subsistence, are also entitled to daily remuneration and refreshments while attending the court. In criminal cases, attachment is the only means of punishing a witness who refuses to attend ; indeed, attachment in civil cases is the more efficacious process, as an action for damages is attended with considerable difficulties. The witness being in court, is sworn according to the forms prescribed by his religious persuasion ; the Christian on the New Testament, the Jew on the Pentateuch, the Mahomedan on the Koran, the Hindoo by a cup of water, and other heathens in such a manner as will, in their minds, create a moral obligation to tell the truth ; but those who have no idea of a God or a future state, are excluded from giving testimony. Persons convicted of infamous crimes, perjury, barratry, bribing a witness, subornation of perjury, and persons convicted of treason or felony, are incompetent to give evidence.

Woods, Forests, and Land Revenues, Office of.—The Commissioners of Woods and Forests, acting under the general authority of the Treasury, have the entire management of the royal forests and woodlands, and the manors and lands of the Crown in Great Britain and Ireland. All sales, purchases, and exchanges of Crown or public property, are made through this department, subject to the sanction of the Treasury. The present Commission dates from 1810, when the Surveyor-General of the King's Woods, Forests, Parks, &c., were amalgamated with the Surveyor-General of the Land Revenues of the Crown. In 1816 the duties of the Receivers of the Crown Rents were transferred to the New Commission. In 1821 the Commissioners were empowered to grant all leases of Crown lands ; and in the same year the office of Surveyor of Works and Public Buildings was united to the Woods and Forests Commission, and remained a branch of that department until the year 1851, when it was again made a distinct office. Hours 10 to 4. Whitehall-place.

Works, Board of.—This office controls all expenditure connected with the maintenance or repair of the Royal Palaces and the erection and furnishing of the chief public buildings and offices. It regulates all the great metropolitan improvements and submits to the Treasury all estimates of the cost of public works. The Commissioner of Works is assisted in the discharge of his duties by a staff of secretaries, surveyors, clerks, &c. Whitehall Place.

THE END.

BRADBURY, EVANS, AND CO., PRINTERS, WHITEFRIARS.

BY THE SAME AUTHOR.

SECOND EDITION.

A

REFERENCE BOOK OF ENGLISH HISTORY,

CONTAINING

TABLES OF CHRONOLOGY AND GENEALOGY, A DICTIONARY OF
BATTLES, OUTLINES OF BIOGRAPHY, AND

A DIGEST OF THE ENGLISH CONSTITUTION.

OPINIONS OF THE PRESS.

"This Book of Reference will undoubtedly occupy a prominent place in our educational literature......To candidates for the various competitive examinations, this Reference Book will prove invaluable."—*Standard.*

"It is limited to our own country, and the dates and other information embodied in a tabular form make it a very useful companion to the literary man and the teacher......We have reason to know that its accuracy has been well tested, and we can strongly recommend it to our readers."—*Record.*

...... "Mr. Ewald's book will prove very useful......The whole tribe of common-place examiners will be somewhat puzzled to find questions in English history upon which this little book has not touched......Mr. Ewald's book is better than many which have gone before."—*Reader.*

...... "Mr. Ewald has well fulfilled the promise of his title-page, and has provided for those candidates who take in the subject of English History an excellent book of reference. The arrangement is methodical and consistent; the Tables of Chronology and Genealogy are carefully and clearly set forth; and the Dictionary of Battles and Sieges, being in alphabetical order, will be found eminently useful."—*London Quarterly Review.*

"In the few instances we have consulted this book of reference we have found Mr. Ewald most correct in his dates and information......For the various competitive examinations it will prove invaluable."—*Morning Herald.*

"We can confidently recommend this work as a companion for readers of history and biography, or as a book of reference for general use, in which facts and dates that may have slipped from the memory can be readily ascertained."—*Press.*

"It is a singularly comprehensive, elaborate, and useful work. The Table of Chronology will be of great service to the student, setting forth as it does a brief summary of the various important events which have influenced the current of English history from the invasion of Julius Cæsar to the present time. The span is immense, and of necessity the web of the narrative must be very crowded; still within the compass a great deal is done."—*British Standard.*

...... "Prepared with great care from the best sources, and upon a good plan......Such a book should be serviceable to students, writers, and talkers."—*Illustrated London News.*

"Mr. Ewald deserves the thanks of all students of history for his very valuable book of reference."—*Public Opinion.*

F. WARNE & CO., BEDFORD STREET, COVENT GARDEN.

Lightning Source UK Ltd.
Milton Keynes UK
UKHW011308070119
335137UK00016B/1046/P